IN SEARCH OF
THE CRAIC

IN SEARCH OF
THE CRAIC

One Man's Pub Crawl Through Irish Music

Colin Irwin

André Deutsch

First published in Great Britain in 2003
This paperback edition published in 2004 by

André Deutsch
an imprint of the
Carlton Publishing Group
20 Mortimer Street
London W1T 3JW

A catalogue record for this book is available from the British Library

ISBN 0 233 00095 X

The publishers would like to thank the following sources for their kind
permission to reproduce the pictures in this book:

p1: Christy Moore by Steve Double/S.I.N./Corbis;
Shane MacGowan by Kim Tonelli/S.I.N./Corbis
p2: Planxty by Tara Music Company Ltd; Sinead O'Connor by Neal
Preston/Corbis Outline; The Chieftains by Keith Morris/Redferns
p3: Fungie by David Cairn/Rex Features
p4: Clannad by Tara Music Company; Mary Coughlan by Hayley
Madden/Redferns; Enya courtesy of Corbis SYGMA
p5: Frankie Gavin by greenfiddleagency.com;
The Dubliners by Dezo Hoffman/ Rex Features.
The remaining photographs are from the Author's private collection.

Every effort has been made to acknowledge correctly and contact the
source and/or copyright holder of each picture, and Carlton Books
Limited apologies for any unintentional errors or omissions which will
be corrected in future editions of this book.

Typeset by E-Type, Liverpool
Printed and bound in Great Britain by Mackays

CONTENTS

Dedicated to my cousin Andy Oscroft,
a hip hop fan.

ACKNOWLEDGEMENTS

Thanks to …

Val for the idea, the title and unwavering support and inspiration throughout this and many other odysseys.

Ian Gittins, man of a thousand anecdotes, for endless advice, encouragement, pints and copy editing.

Kevin, Christy, Donald, and my mum and dad for numerous contributions to the journey.

Alan O'Leary, my Irish music muse.

John Douglas Spencer Wheeler, my original guru.

The late Wally Whyton, Dolores Keane's biggest fan and my mentor for a decade.

Christopher Cathles for keeping those 'Singing Families Of Ireland' tapes.

Matt Molloy, Tommy Peoples, Siobhan Peoples, Eoin Duignan, Eilis Kennedy, Frankie Gavin, Peter Pandula, Dervish, Donnchadh Gough, Sinead O'Connor, Mary Coughlan, Christy Moore, Altan, Leo Brennan, Jim O'The Mill, Ian Anderson, Dolores, Sarah and Rita Keane, John and Imelda Tierney, Reg Hall, Joan McDermott, Harry Bradshaw, Mick Dalton, Tom Sherlock, Karen Ryan, Martin Hayes, The Dubliners, Liam Clancy, Seamus Tansey, Ol' McDermott and all the others who contributed, whether they knew it or not.

The Irish Traditional Music Archive, Dublin; Na Piobairi Uilleann, Dublin; Coleman Centre, Gurteen, Co. Sligo; Return To Camden Festival, London; Roundstone Musical Instruments, Roundstone, Co. Galway.

All the great B&Bs in Ireland (but not the crappy one in Lisdoonvarna); the bookies who took my money; all those bars where the session defeats the juke box. And, from Planxty to Shane MacGowan, all the musicians who provided the soundtrack for the journey and the writing, especially the unsung ones.

Mr Jameson and Mr Bushmill, who helped me make it through the night.

Oh, and the St Kitts Tourist Authority.

INTRODUCTION

Just What The World Needs: Another Bloody Book About Ireland

There's a man on stage with a feather in his hair, a bow and arrow slung round his neck and red warpaint on his face singing 'Your Cheating Heart' by Hank Williams. He's in a band called The Indians. There's a heaving mass of whooping Irish people of all ages, shapes, sizes and bad haircuts who are collectively drunker than anyone I've ever seen in my life. There's Guinness streaming across the floor at such a rate they seem to have cut out the middle man and are pumping it right off the Liffey.

And there's a girl in the corner staring hard at me as if I've just landed from Planet Zog. 'Hey you,' she hollers in a bloodcurdling voice that cuts right through the howls of the dancers, and the roar of The Indians scalping Hank Williams. 'Hey you! You come over here!' I look around, assuming Phil Lynott or Val Doonican or some such icon of the era has materialised behind me. She gesticulates ever more urgently. 'Get yer ass over here!' Slaloming along the floor on the black river, I land in a heap at her feet. She and her group of mates laugh, compounding the humiliation by persuading all-comers to come and gawp. 'You deliver the milk, don'tcha?' yelps the girl triumphantly. I look at her in increasing wide-eyed wonder. 'You're our milkie.' Sorry? 'Sean, isn't it?' No, my name is ... She's not listening. 'Hey, this is Sean, our milkman!' They queue up to shake my hand and buy me drinks. Milkmen are very popular in Ireland.

I continue to protest. I've never been to Dublin. Never ever been to Ireland before. I'm here on a writing mission for *Melody Maker*, which used to be a music paper. The Editor, you see, had had a brilliant idea. 'There's this weird scene in Ireland,' he'd said gleefully, a week earlier. I'd looked at him blankly. 'See, there's all these groups over there ... you know, *Irish* groups ...' No!!! Irish groups? In *Ireland*? Pull the other one! He'd sensed my scepticism. 'Yes ... Irish groups but they're playing ...' Dramatic pause. 'They're playing *country & western music!*'

The Editor had stepped back to appreciate fully my gasps of astonishment and wonder. Undeterred by my somewhat quizzical reaction, he'd ploughed on … 'And people actually LIKE them! Isn't that great?' *Is* it? 'Yeah, these bands … they have funny names and they, er *dress up*.' They dress up? 'Yes. Like as cowboys, and Indians, and funny things like that.' I'd hesitated to mention that the night before I'd seen an overweight Gary Glitter grotesquely squeezed into turkey foil and a mad wig hamming it up like an amateur dramatic society production of *Oklahoma,* and singing glorified nursery rhymes in front of a seething mass of squealing teenage girls. How mad was *that*?

In fact, a journalistic apprenticeship writing up magistrates' courts, local council meetings and village fetes hadn't prepared me for the impossibly absurd paradoxes that rule the pop music industry – or the people who commentate on it. I was still having trouble coming to terms with an environment where people leaving their homes to go and watch country & western bands – whether they dressed up as cowboys, Indians or Edwardian washerwomen – was apparently considered barmy enough to warrant a plane ticket to Dublin. Chortling heartily, my Editor clearly didn't agree. 'Oh, we'll have great fun with this. I mean, it's country music, which is *American* music, right? And country music is *awful*, right? And these bands are *Irish*, right? This is such a *great* feature.' I was down on my hands and knees searching for his marbles when he delivered the *coup de grâce.* He leaned over conspiratorially. 'The thing is, I've got the headline already.' You have? A smug pause … and then the triumphant delivery: 'SHAM ROCK!'

So, on the basis of a terrible pun, I'd been despatched to Dublin to write a patronising feature about the folly of the Irish going out to see bands who dress up as cowboys and Indians and play bad country & western songs. That's why I'm getting wrecked in some Guinness-puddled ballroom with a group of new best mates convinced that I'm Sean the milkman. 'That's a strange accent you have there,' says the chief beneficiary of my pint a day, whose name is Roisin. 'If I didn't know you better, Sean, I'd say you had an English accent.' Yes, yes, yes, I *do* have an English accent, Roisin. 'It's very good that, Sean,' says Roisin. 'It sounds just like a *real* English accent. Now where will you have learned to do an accent like that?' Er, *England*? 'Oh Sean, you are a scream, y'really are!'

At this point, a gorilla in the mist lurches over and prods me with a wayward finger. 'Oi, I want a word with you.' There's menace in his eyes – all four of them – and my heart sinks. Is this Roisin's jealous boyfriend getting the wrong end of the stick? A militant republican intent on wreaking instant vengeance for centuries of English wrongs? Or just a tanked-up local hoolie looking for some sport with the stranger in town? No. The ape sways, and waves a finger accusingly. 'Yew, yer bastid …' Who me? 'Yer you! You only delivered one pint on Friday. Me ma always has two pints. You wait till me ma gets hold of you …'

I am to spend the next few days trawling through Ireland in search of the icons of the showband circuit: my old mates The Indians, of course; The Cadets (who wear naval uniforms!); Patricia & The Crackaways (a girl from a knitwear catalogue backed by a Buddy Holly lookalike contest); the Detroit Showband (bow ties and sky-blue jackets); Ray Lynam & Philomena Begley, later immortalised by Shane MacGowan in The Pogues' *A Pair Of Brown Eyes*; and the biggest of the lot – literally – Big Tom & The Mainliners. Everybody I spoke to said, 'Oh you gotta meet Big Tom!' or 'Have ye met Big Tom yet? He's the king!' Sadly, I never get to meet Big Tom. 'Ah … Big Tom,' says an agent/manager type person. 'He's taking a break right now, he's out in the country … you got to meet him … but not right now.'

Far more importantly, though, I get to see a lot of hilariously dreadful music and fall irrevocably in love with that irresistible mix of outrageous charm, effortless articulacy, irreverent humour, steadfast spirit and barely contained madness that typifies the Irish character. I get to talk to lots of agents, managers and people who have milk delivered who see nothing untoward about bands travelling around Ireland playing country music in the fabled ballrooms (and, in time, neither do I). It seems no time before I'm being entertained with an unspeakable mixture of Guinness and crème de menthe by the manager of a showband whose gimmick is … they don't have a gimmick, and dress not in pantomime costumes but as *themselves*.

'It's a radical move but y'know, the fans love it … they *love* it!' says Yer Man their manager, who clearly didn't merely kiss the blarney stone, but sucked out its larynx and swallowed it whole. He tells me the story of the ballrooms of romance scattered around the west of Ireland, where the showbands have taken residence commanding big fees, and the rural communities gather in search of husbands and wives. He sees nothing untoward in this quirk of country life or the bands – their wardrobes or their preferred style of music – who are its catalyst.

Then Yer Man excuses himself to line up another queue of Guinness and crème de menthes from the bar and a sinister voice suddenly appears in my ear. 'You're barking up the wrong tree, y'know …' he says solemnly. I *am*? 'Yes. This isn't what you should be writing about at all. You need to hear some *real* Irish music.' And where, pray, do I hear this real Irish music? 'Come with me ...'

The stranger gave me directions and the journey I embarked on has lasted over twenty-five years and shows no signs of abating. It's encompassed bars at the back of beyond in Clare and Kerry, festivals from Ballisodare to Lisdoonvarna, sessions across Cork and Connemara, nights that never end in Dublin and Donegal. It has involved Venezuelan ambassadors, strange girls in my bed in Sligo, and eccentric encounters with assorted rock legends in Dublin. It has involved Roses Of Tralee, Eurovision Song Contests, the birth of *Riverdance*, some nights that I frankly have little memory of ... and a great deal of time spent in the company of some of the most exhilarating musicians – often also the most colourful characters – on planet Earth. Planxty, Horslips, The Bothy Band, De Dannan, The Chieftains, Christy Moore, Sinead O'Connor, Dervish, Moving Hearts, Dolores Keane, Clannad, Altan, Paul Brady, Tommy Peoples ...

Sadly, The Indians are no longer around, but Irish traditional music has developed and flourished in unimaginable ways. From Muhammad Ali on, there aren't many living Americans who don't claim Irish ancestry, and barely a city from Tokyo to Toronto that doesn't boast an Irish theme bar. A new hotel seems to go up in Dublin every week, and they reckon Ireland has Europe's fastest growing economy. After many bitter centuries of enduring the endless tragedy of watching its sons and daughters forced to leave its shores, Ireland – for the first time in its history – is embracing immigrants. It's a sexy time to be Irish right now. But a confusing one, too, when your nation's cultural heritage is defined by clichéd Plastic Paddies and theme bars, or by The Corrs, or the latest Guinness ad, or Michael Flatley wiggling his arse.

They all talk about *the craic*, that indefinable definition of Ireland's collective passion and capacity for a good time. Whatever else you say about the Irish, they know how to enjoy themselves and they do entertainment like nobody else. Scholars pooh-pooh the term *the craic* as a Johnny-come-lately phrase that historically has no real reference in the country's culture ... but try telling *that* to the Irish Tourist Board.

So, this is my story of one recent trip around Ireland. It lasts just a few weeks, but there again, it's been ongoing for twenty-five years. And for those who are its primary heroes, it's a journey that's taken hundreds of years. It involves endless bars, copious amounts of music, drinking and talking bollocks (as do most of my visits to Ireland). But this time there is intent as well: to unveil the myth of *the craic* and those great characters, past and present, who've served to create it. To see what effect soaraway economic growth is having on the country's basic values and renowned hospitality. To find the legendary Tommy Peoples, the incredible fiddle player who seemed to disappear when I first started coming to Ireland. And to calculate how many times I'd hear 'Fields Of Athenry' sung by pub singers in one night.

There's nothing academic here, then. There are many people far better qualified to give you the history of Irish music – and some of them have. But traditional music *is* a consuming passion and, let's face it, it would be impertinent to write a book about Ireland without mentioning some of its unsung musical heroes like Michael Coleman, Johnny Doran, Seamus Ennis, Turlough O'Carolan, Sean O'Riada, Micho Russell and Margaret Barry. Oh, and Tommy Peoples. But we'll see if we can't get Bono, Mick Jagger, Sinead O'Connor and Elvis in here too. And did I mention that Muhammad Ali is an Irishman?

Okay, hands up, I admit it. This is a glorious, glorified pub crawl. It's a dirty job, but someone's got to do it …

Chapter one

WEXFORD: HORSEFLESH, MARGARET BARRY & POLE DANCING

I know a bloke who met a bloke who knew another bloke whose sister's boyfriend's cousin went on his holidays to Ireland. One night he found himself in a pub in Tipperary. As you do. He quickly found himself in warm, engaging banter with the regulars, putting the world to rights, telling the story of his life. With a few embellishments obviously. As you do. Then one of them points to an ol' fella quietly minding his own business, nursing a frothy one at the bar. 'You see Feargal over there, do ya?' Yep, he does. 'Feargal does the races.'

Our chum looks across at the wizened figure across the way. He's impressed, if quizzical. Feargal's clearly too old, and too frail, to be a trainer or a jockey. A bookie, perhaps? 'Yeah, he's great, is Feargal ...' They both gaze admiringly at Feargal for a few seconds. Then the local seizes the moment. 'Hey Feargal,' he shouts. 'Do the races!' The old chap at the bar frowns and looks pained. 'Not tonight, Michael,' he says in a low voice. 'He's playing hard to get,' confides the self-appointed entertainments officer in a stage whisper, and then again addresses the bar, 'Come on now, Feargal, yer man here has come over all the way from England, you can't let him drink all night and not do the races, now can you, Feargal?'

Feargal scowls, but the locals detect signs that he's wavering and begin to barrack encouragement. Quickly, the whole bar is at it, ganging up on the reluctant Feargal in animated unison. A gentle rumble of 'Come on Feargal' swiftly escalates into an all-conquering chant of 'RAY-SEZ! RAY-SEZ! RAY-SEZ!'

Feargal sighs, and bows to the inevitable. He removes his cap, revealing a Bobby Charlton sweep of straggly silver hair, and the bar is suddenly consumed in silence and concentration. Feargal turns away from them, and focuses. His whole demeanour dramatically, almost magically, transforms. The old man supping quietly at the bar is suddenly altered into an alert, vigorous figure, his body taut, his mind sharp, his eyes closed.

Feargal adopts the upright stance of a boxer awaiting the first bell, a hand cups around an imaginary microphone and in brisk, urgent, concise tones, he begins to speak: 'This is the big one ... eight magnificent animals lining up at The Curragh for this mile handicap ... first into the stalls goes that beautiful colt Celtic Dream ... he looks grand ... next in is the favourite Jack Judge's Bet – I just wonder if he's recovered from that nasty fall at Tramore the other day. I can see the veteran Tommy P in blinkers there, and wouldn't the crowd here just love to see him roll back the years! Then comes the grey Athenry Field, another old favourite Blazing Saddles going in now ... I can see English Drinker being pushed in, he's the mystery horse in the race. There's Pride Of Tip sweating a bit ... and they're having a bit of trouble there with the Sheikh's horse, Moneybags The Third ... oh my, he's very agitated and ... oh what's happened how ... he's thrown his jockey off! I wonder if they'll get Moneybags The Third started in the race at all ...'

He pauses and behind his back the regulars are whispering urgently as they pass notes to the barman, who scribbles furiously on a pad as money changes hands at a frantic pace. The antics of Moneybags The Third have clearly thrown the market into confusion. It's one of Feargal's favourite ploys, apparently. If it's the Sheikh's horse it's got to be good, but then ... it throws its jockey at the start! Bluff? Double bluff? 'Ten on Moneybags,' says a big feller in a trilby, but there's a pile of change going on Athenry Field, 'cos everyone's a sucker for a grey. The babble of conversation mounts ... Pride Of Tip is the emotional choice, but didn't he say Celtic Dream looks a million dollars? And what about Jack Judge's Bet? He's the favourite and the bookies don't often get it wrong, but what about that fall at Tramore last time out? Anyone for English Drinker? Nah ...

The commanding voice of Feargal stops their chatter in its tracks. 'Moneybags has been remounted and yes, he's going into the stalls,' says Feargal. A small, smug smile and a nod of satisfaction from the man in the trilby, while supporters of the grey Athenry Field curse silently. 'And they're off!' There's a spontaneous burst of applause from the crowd.

'Celtic Dream is the first to show, but Blazing Saddles is breathing down his neck, Jack Judge's Bet is coming up fast on the rails ... one of the horses got a terrible start and is miles behind ... can't see who it is ... I think it's Tommy P, no, it's Moneybags The Third, he's at least ten legs off the pace and I can't see him making up that ground ...'

A few furtive glances are aimed at the man in a trilby, who scratches his nose and stares impassively back at all and sundry.

'Celtic Dream is running magnificently, he's about two lengths clear of Jack Judge's Bet and Blazing Saddles ...' Roars of excitement and encouragement betray those who've staked their houses on Celtic Dream, followed by a volley of 'Ssshhhh' from the others straining to hear news of their trailing steed's advancement up the field. 'Celtic Dream is ROMPING away with it,' Feargal is saying. 'Four furlongs to go and he must be at least eight lengths clear and he's still going strong. It'll be hard for anyone to catch him now in this form ...'

There's a man on the table, with his shirt off, waving it above his head shouting 'Come on, Celtic Dream, you BEAUTY!' Feargal's voice speeds up. 'Celtic Dream is now ten lengths clear. Jack Judge's Bet already looks tired, Tommy P moves into second place, Athenry Field is going well, moving up the field. Moneybags still brings up the rear but he's making ground up fast on the next horse, Pride Of Tip'. The man in the trilby sinks back into his seat, feigning indifference.

'Two furlongs from home and surely no one can catch Celtic Dream now. Athenry Field snatches second place from Tommy P, the jockey gives English Drinker a tap with his whip and ... and ... oh my, this is incredible, what a sensation!' The entire bar stops drinking mid-gulp, grins freeze on faces, even the American backpacker who's only come in to use the toilet screeches to a halt. 'I don't BELIEVE it!' roars Feargal, like a coronary-afflicted Victor Meldrew. 'Celtic Dream has STOPPED!'

The whole pub stares, open-mouthed, at Feargal. Stopped? *Stopped?!* Waddya mean, *stopped*? There's shock and outrage from the Celtic Dream supporters, incredulity from everyone else, even the suspicion of a chuckle from Trilby Man. Unfazed, Feargal's away again. 'It's just like Devon Loch in the 1955 Grand National. He's looked at the crowd, swerved and stopped. He's just standing there looking at the crowd with the jockey still on his back and the other horses are now all piling past him.'

A million questions are thrown at Feargal but he's not listening, he's off again. 'The grey Athenry Field has hit the front but it's tight ... it's very tight. Tommy P and English Drinker and Jack Judge's Bet are right there. They've got a furlong to run and it's neck and neck! The grey has got his nose in front but English Drinker is battling back, matching him stride for stride. Tommy P is under pressure ... Jack Judge fades ... it's between Athenry Field and English Drinker. There's nothing between them ... it's too close to call ...'

There's carnage in the bar. Celtic Dream supporters are crying in their beer, Athenry supporters have turned greyer than the imaginary horse carrying their hopes and quite frankly nobody gives a toss about English Drinker (least of all the English drinker – he's a Blazing Saddles fan). 'Athenry Field … English Drinker … it's neck and neck!,' booms Feargal, his voice beginning to get hoarse. 'But there's another horse going like the wind on the outside … it's … Moneybags The Third! He's catching them … oh what a finish … a hundred yards to the line … it's Athenry Field, no, it's English Drinker, no, it's … Moneybags … no it's … a photo finish!'

There's a babble of protest from the throng. Feargal hasn't pulled *this* trick before. The big feller in the trilby saunters to the bar and nonchalantly orders a pint. 'What are y'having, Feargal?' he courteously enquires. A second pint is poured, and Feargal's solemn voice once again fills the room.

'The result of the photo finish: the winner, by a short head, is Moneybags The Third. Second is English Drinker, by a neck from Athenry Field …' The man in the trilby collects the pot of money, while Feargal reaches for his fresh pint and discusses his commentary with the unlucky punters, who seem to bear no malice about the strange and dramatic events of the race.

'I was sure the grey was gonna do it,' says one. 'Aye, he made a fine race of it,' nods Feargal sagely, warming to the post-race analysis. 'And I thought we'd have a bit of craic with English Drinker for the English feller in here tonight, but the Sheikh's horses … they are *so* strong. It's the winter training in Dubai, y'see … makes all the difference. That Moneybags is a good horse all right … temperamental but good …' A guy who'd lost his shirt on Pride Of Tip marches menacingly up to Feargal. 'I want a word with you, Feargal!' 'What's the problem, Michael?' 'Your commentary, Feargal, you made a big mistake there, you did, a big mistake.' 'Why's that then, Michael?' 'You said Devon Loch stopped in the 1955 Grand National … it was 1956.'

The man in the trilby hat quietly departs the scene of the crime …

Well, that's how the sister's boyfriend's cousin of the bloke who met a bloke who met the bloke I know told it, anyway. So it's a true story. And even if it's not a true story, it *could* be. And by God, it *should* be.

That's the point about Ireland, and what I love about the place: such things *do* happen. Irish bars should have a sign above the door, proclaiming 'Abandon Your Traditional English Reserve All Ye Who Enter Here'. You don't go into a bar in Ireland for half of mild, a quiet night and a ticklish crossword. Once you cross that threshold and approach the bar, you relinquish all rights to your own privacy. Graphic personal histories are freely offered … and expected back with interest in return. Resistance is ill-advised and futile, and once you understand that, you'll be fine.

The other key is that the Irish get the basics of life right – music, drink and racing. I mean, what else is there, really? They're big on literature too, of course. The Irish read more than any other country in Europe, Sinead O'Connor tells me much later in the journey (I figure it's always a good idea to get the name-dropping in early). What do they read, Sinead? 'They read about their own history,' she says, launching into a long and involved analysis of the Irish penchant for, well, self-analysis. So, music, drinking, racing and literature, then. Okay, they're pretty big on religion, too, but best not go there, eh?

It's the priority given to these key features of a civilized life that keeps dragging me back to Ireland. The land has changed in so many ways in the quarter-century I have been visiting, yet its essential heartbeat hasn't shifted one iota. At least that's what I keep telling people. Musicdrinkingracing, musicdrinkingracing, musicdrinkingracing … I repeat like a mantra, until suddenly I start to wonder: Is it still true?

Irish culture has impregnated all manner of nations in all manner of ways in recent years. *Riverdance*, blah blah; Michael Flatley, bless him; *Ballykissangel*, giggle; *Father Ted*, chortle; Daniel O'Donnell, guffaw! Lawdy Miss Claudy, you even get Irish theme bars in China now, and perceptions of the Irish character have infiltrated the global consciousness to the point where it's hard to see exactly where reality ends and cliché begins. Heaven help us, there's so much crap released under the deceitful banner of Celtic music that you've half a mind to set fire to it, jump in a time machine and go back to the days when, for most people, Irish music comprised the fey parlour songs of John McCormack, Delia Murphy and Dan Donovan.

The marketing face of Ireland is not just about leprechauns, shamrocks and pints of Guinness any more: it's the whole national character that they're selling now. Musicdrinkingracing, indeed. So this is my equivalent of REM's fear of losing their religion. I've come on a specific quest for the emotional heartbeat, and the musical soul, of Ireland. My intensive pre-tour research suggests this may well involve a good deal of music, a fair few pints and a bit of racing, too.

It's mad, raucous, noisy, drunken, thrilling … and that's just the ferry over there. See, this is another thing. If you're going to do Ireland *properly*, you don't go on an aeroplane. If God had meant you to fly to Ireland, He'd have put an airport at Knock. Oh, right. He did.

Knock is a tiny, quiet little community in Mayo, in the west of Ireland. Well, it *was* quiet until the Virgin Mary decided to pay a visit to the local parish church in 1879. Since then, they've had the Pope, Mother Theresa and every Catholic in the western hemisphere making pilgrimages to this miraculous spot, adding further holy fame to a town groaning under the weight of Our Lady memorabilia, B&Bs and rosary gift shops. A certain Father Horan bent a few important ears and, Hey Presto! Knock had its own airport!

'From Fatima to Bethlehem, from Lourdes to Kiltimagh/There's never been a miracle like the airport up in Knock,' sings Christy Moore on his wonderfully caustic 'Knock Song'. At least Christy got a good song out of it. For others, (Okay, for *me*), Knock Airport is a hated symbol of the easy access which erodes values and threatens our hopelessly romantic vision of the unspoilt beauty and unquenchable character we cherish so much about the west of Ireland. And don't even start me off on Shannon Airport. Or indeed Donegal Airport, which proudly amended its name to Donegal *International* Airport on the basis that a plane once flew there from Glasgow.

So the boat it is, then. That mad, frantic dash for Holyhead (or indeed Pembroke or Fishguard or Stranraer), when you realise you need a miracle of Knock proportions to get to the ferry on time after being stuck behind the biggest lorry in the world for 30 miles. The ransacking of suitcases, when you can't find your ticket. The honking of cars all around, following a desperate sprint to the loo at the dock's terminal just as they start loading cars on to the boat means you are holding up the complete passenger system.

Then, once on the boat, there's that crazed rush for a seat. Which deck are those nice Pullman seats on again? There's a half-acceptable bench available on the lower deck – primitive, but it could do the job – but you're sure those nice Pullmans are just one flight up. They're not. And by the time you've got back down again, there's a party of schoolchildren from Crewe in place howling at the Moon.

Several tours of the boat later – head pounding from the din of the slot machines, the flashing lights and disco in the kids' area, the lads noisily drinking the bar dry and wanting to be your new best friend – you join the Oz backpackers asleep on the floor. By the time you dock at Rosslare, you've been trampled by a combination of Giant Haystacks, Rik Waller and Luciano Pavarotti, had beer spilled over you by the entire front line of the London Irish rugby squad, and been used as a goalpost by an army of squawking kids who think they're David Beckham (and certainly sound like him). I love that Rosslare ferry.

Once, travelling *en famille* years ago, inclement weather delayed the afternoon crossing by several hours. We finally docked at Rosslare around 8pm, in thick mist and driving rain, to start the long drive to a pre-booked cottage in Kerry. By the time we got to Cork, our spirits – as well as sense of direction – were flagging. We had been due to pick up the keys for the cottage at a pub in Glenbeigh by 9pm, so stopped at a garage to call the pub to warn that our arrival would be considerably later and, as the pub would be shut by the time we arrived, could they leave the keys for our cottage under the garden elf or something?

There was something distinctly odd about the chap in the garage. He seemed to be speaking Esperanto for one thing. 'Do you have a phone I could use, please?' seemed a fairly straightforward question, which didn't really warrant the confused frown and the unintelligible gabble I got in return. 'This was in Cork, you say?' said an Irish friend from Dublin when I told the story later. 'Ah sure, they're all mad in Cork. Even the Irish don't understand what they're talking about in Cork.'

Eventually, the geezer in the garage rather furtively beckoned me to follow him behind the counter into a back room that looked as if it had been used in a training video for the Irish Institute Of Advanced Ransacking. Careful to step over a sleeping cat, a box of crockery and a broken petrol pump, he opened the door to what looked like a broom cupboard and pushed me in. Well, it didn't *look* like a broom cupboard, it *was* a broom cupboard. A broom hit me on the head to prove it. He slammed the door behind me, leaving me in total darkness assuming he was the mad petrol killer of Cork who got his jollies locking tourists into broom cupboards, letting them mature overnight and eating them for breakfast.

In the blackness I felt around, putting my hand on something suspiciously sticky before locating a phone on the wall. By now my eyes had adjusted to the darkness, and I made out the shape of a telephone on the wall that Alexander Graham Bell himself would have rejected as being laughably primitive, one of those ancient Press Button A, B and C jobs. I lifted the phone and was amazed to hear a dialling tone. I put the money in, dialled the number of the pub in Kerry and pressed every button in sight. It gobbled up the money but provided not so much as a haughty telephonist in return. Every bit of loose change in my pocket went into that phone and Buttons A, B and C got the mother of all work-outs, but there was no pub, no Kerry, no human life at all.

Giving up, I waited for the mad petrol killer to claim me for his breakfast. I hammered on the door, yelling for help, in the pious hope that at least I might be able to alert some other passing innocent that devilment was afoot in this cupboard and they'd at least be able to avoid my fate. Presently the door creaked open and the killer himself stood staring at me. 'I ... er ... the phone ... um ... I can't seem to ... I mean, I've dialled and put money in and ... well, I can't seem to get through ...' He looked at me with ill-disguised scorn. 'Where are you trying to telephone, anyway?' 'Where? A pub. A pub in Glenbeigh. In Kerry.'

I swear the man stared at me for a full minute, and then something terrifying happened. His face appeared to disintegrate, his mouth opened revealing an alarming toothless void, and an eerie howl began to emerge from the pit of his stomach. I was aghast. And then it suddenly hit me. He was *laughing*. 'Kerry? *Kerry*?!? You should have said. This is a Cork telephone. You won't be able to telephone Kerry on this telephone. This telephone doesn't reach to Kerry, y'see. You can telephone Cork but you cannot telephone Kerry. Not on this telephone, d'ya see now?' I quickly fled, dived straight into the car, hit the accelerator hard and didn't say a word to my good lady Mrs Colin about the encounter until we were several miles clear and there were no signs of pursuit from the petrol killer or one of the exhibits in the broom cupboard.

It felt good to be back on the highway. Mind you, it would have felt even better had we been travelling in the right direction – we only noticed our mistake a couple of hours or so later as we started to close in on Rosslare again. Mrs Colin and our two small sons in the back of the car weren't wildly impressed, and there was the odd moment, I shamelessly confess, when it seemed easier to carry right on back to the docks rather than again attempt the seemingly impossible task of finding Kerry. We may even have been early enough to get a Pullman seat.

Instead, we turned the car right around and headed back to Cork, breaking the land speed record for VW Beetles as we passed the garage patrolled by the petrol shop murderer. There followed a long and tortuous hard day's night driving for hours without road signs, streetlights, towns or the remotest suspicion other human life existed. It felt like being in one of those movies where aliens have wiped out the entire human race, except for one family who are left desperately seeking other survivors. The puncture was the icing on the cake – not, of course, that we realised it was a puncture at the time. We spent an hour complaining about the state of Irish roads as the tyre shredded and we shuddered along on the wheel rim for miles.

It was 3.45am by the time we rolled into Glenbeigh. It was 4.30am by the time we found the pub where we were supposed to be collecting the key to our cottage. 'We'll just have to sleep in the car outside the pub until they open up in the morning,' said Mrs Colin sagely. I braved the storm for a closer look at the pub just to see if they'd left a note for us on the doorstep containing the key to our cottage. Approaching the front door I noticed a light round the back and a door ajar. I pushed it and entered, following the light. There was a low sound of voices. And music. I opened another door and the sound of music grew louder: fiddles and accordions. I stood outside the door for a moment, listening, and then opened it. I stood bedraggled in the doorway, to face the sight of a wedding ceili in full flight.

The music stopped, and the guests looked at me in wonder. 'Come in, come in ...' said a grinning man with an impossibly red nose, a tie round the back of his head and twisted braces holding up a pair of trousers that looked like they'd had a nasty encounter with a privet hedge. He looked at me dripping sopping hair all over his carpet, said, 'Look at you, wee feller, you don't even have a drink,' and thrust a glass of champagne into my hand. 'Come over here, have you met Mary? She's the bride, y'know.' Yes, I said, the white dress was a bit of a giveaway. I offer her my congratulations. 'Aw thanks,' she says, hugging and kissing me like a long-lost cousin. 'Where's the lucky bridegroom, Mary?' 'Oh *him*,' she says scornfully, 'he passed out hours ago. But never mind that, will you not have a dance with me?' 'Well, I don't, I mean ...' 'Ah sure you will, it's me wedding day, after all ...'

So, drenched and downing champagne, I danced a rather demented waltz-cum-jig with a young bride I'd never met before in a place I'd never been before at 4.30 in the morning. And you know the weirdest thing of all? It all seemed so perfectly natural. 'Who are you, anyway?' asked the bride's dad, matter-of-factly, after I'd finished twirling his daughter and was pouring another glass of champagne. That reminded me why I was there, and launched into a long explanation of the horrific journey to our holiday cottage. 'I didn't think anybody would still be up,' I said. 'What time is it anyway?' asked the father of the bride. 'Half past four in the morning.' 'Jeez,' he said, shaking his head. 'What sort of time is that to be turning up for a wedding?'

He produced a key to our cottage, and embarked on a long, rambling and wholly incomprehensible description of how to get there. Somehow, he sensed he wasn't in the presence of Vasco de Gama. 'Ah don't worry, I'll take you there. It's not far. And my daughter got married today.' We went outside, he got into an old Jeep, indicating I should follow in the Beetle, and shot off into the darkness as if the hounds of hell were on his tail. There followed a terrifying chase, as I desperately tried to hang on to his back lights as he swerved and skidded around a narrow road so bumpy it felt like we had four punctures. The steeper, narrower and cruder the road became, the faster the bride's father drove, his wheels spinning as he took corners at 70mph and, to the accompaniment of squealing kids and sharp intakes of breath from Mrs Colin, I diced with death in an attempt to keep up. It crossed my mind that he may have had a drink.

Scattering sheep and cows at every turn, he eventually screeched to a halt outside a remote, isolated tumbledown cottage, threw the keys at me, shouted, 'See you tomorrow. I'm just going for a wee drink,' and was away again in a hail of dust. Incredibly, the keys fitted the cottage and we were all asleep in seconds.

Next day, we looked out of the window, and gasped. Somebody had dumped us on top of a picture postcard. The sky was blue, the sun was shining, angry waves battered against steep cliffs and, as far as the eye could see, there were miles and miles of beautiful golden sands. We were so remote and so high that we wondered momentarily how on earth we had got up here. Then our eyes settled on the one narrow, partially unmade lane leading to our cottage. Sheer drops either side, 90-degree bends, cows everywhere. And I swear I saw one of the little people winking at me from the side of the road.

But that was then, and this is now, and the portents are good. We make the ferry with … ooh, *seconds* to spare … and the crossing is smooth. I'm just nodding off contentedly in a quiet corner seat when the Duke Ellington Orchestra suddenly explode into action. There's nowt wrong with the Duke, of course, 'cept he's long dead, and this band seems to be hitting some wrong notes. They seem to be sacrificing quality for volume. Still, it's – what? – a 20-piece jazz orchestra on an Irish ferry, so they deserve investigating.

I follow the strains of 'The A-Train' into the bar next door, anticipating the joint jumping to Dixieland's finest. Five old ladies are sitting at a table staring hollow-faced at one man dressed in a sparkling blue waistcoat, playing saxophone over some serious backing tapes. 'YEAHH!' he's yelping at the end of it. 'I want everyone on the floor dancing to the next one … come on … you all know it, let your hair down … it's a little number called "Rock Around The Clock". Here we go now …' And there he is swivelling porky hips, yelping 'One o'clock, two o'clock, three o'clock rock' while the five old ladies gaze glumly at him.

There are to be no epic drives from Rosslare to Kerry this time. This time we'll head north slowly. There's no timetable and no agenda beyond the sacred creed of musicdrinkingracing. To avoid the horrors of the previous journey, we decide to stop at Wexford town, the first serious place where it's possible to lick your wounds after the dogfight off the boat at Rosslare without being engulfed by seagulls.

In truth Wexford is not an ideal starting point for any journey into the soul of Irish culture. It's a psychological thing, but I've never really thought of it as being a *real* part of Ireland due to those apron strings – or boot laces – that allow you to hear British radio stations so loud and clear. You know how it is, you're listening to the build-up to the day's footie games on the car radio as you pile into Pembroke Dock for embarkation, and by the time you've made it across to the other side of the water and are following the signs to Wexford you are listening to the match reports on the same station. Which is good, of course, when you're desperate to hear the results, but surely Ireland is about radio stations where you listen to local death notices and appeals about lost dogs, not hearing how Man United got on against Arsenal? It's a theory that gets blown out of the water a couple of weeks later, driving round the hilly back roads of East Clare in pounding rain listening to the Merseyside derby, but we'll conveniently draw a veil over that for the minute.

I only ever stopped in Wexford once before – for fish and chips on a Saturday night – and was mightily impressed by the rate at which guys in denim jackets were being flung out of the front doors of shady bars while bands who thought they were the Pogues were creating some agreeably hideous din within. Gosh, I thought, this looks like my kind of place, I must return some day. Twelve years later (it took that long to find a denim jacket) I'm back to find a bar that might want to fling me out on the street.

Driving into town we pass a big sign saying WEXFORD – HOST TOWN TO POLAND. There is some indecipherable small print beneath it about some sort of special Olympics, but the sign immediately causes consternation. Wexford is the host town to Poland? What, *all* of it? What happened between Pembroke and Rosslare? Had the Germans invaded again? Or maybe the Russians? Visions of the entire population of Poland being evacuated and parachuted into Wexford swim before my eyes. Maybe on a Saturday night here we might be better off looking not for music, but for Pole dancing.

Narrow of street and consumed by traffic, Wexford isn't in truth the sexiest town in the western world (give or take a bit of Pole dancing, obviously). Invented by Vikings, its name is derived from the Norse for 'inlet of the mudflats', which doesn't suggest a wild night on the tiles, frankly. Oliver Cromwell beat the crap out of it in 1649, and the town still looks shell-shocked. I can't imagine what Jack Kennedy thought when he came here to visit the land of his ancestors, shortly before his assassination. But as dusk falls things begin to look up. The dowdy middle-aged landlady who'd greeted us at the B&B a couple of hours earlier rather dramatically re-emerges in brazen temptress regalia, all daringly short skirt and heaving bosoms. 'I'm off for a night on the town … with my daughter,' she says with a wink. 'Have fun.' Yeah, okay, we will, but probably not as much as you'll be having …

The next couple of hours are spent wandering round Wexford wondering where the landlady could possibly have gone dressed like *that*. Still, some fascinating facts are gleaned on the way. I bet you didn't know the Bull Ring in the centre of town is so named because it was once the venue for bull-baiting. Or that Henry II came to Selskar Abbey here after that nasty business with Thomas à Beckett. Or that the statue in the centre of town commemorates John Barry, who founded the American Navy (presumably before he wrote all those *James Bond* themes). Or that Wexford is twinned with Coueron in France. No, thought not. Somebody tried to convince me that *Ballykissangel* was filmed nearby, but they were drinking a Bacardi Breezer at the time so the evidence is obviously suspect.

Cromwell, Kennedy and pouting landladies apart, Wexford could be any town in the north of England on a Saturday night. Shaven-headed bouncers dressed in ill-fitting dark suits and bow ties man the doors of the pubs, looking like they've come straight from some boxing awards dinner. That's always confusing. If you're there to deal with drunken hoolies up for a bit of sport on a Saturday night, why put on your best suit? It'll only get ruined.

Instinctively I quicken my step as I pass, lest they suddenly develop a strange premonition of me transforming into a crazed bar-wrecker and decide to swoop first and ask questions later. Then the penny drops. They're not really pub bouncers at all, they're KGB agents on the look-out for Polish refugees! Bastards. I resolve to go up to one of them and tell them to leave the poor Poles in peace ... but I don't speak Russian.

In fairness, nobody had suggested this corner of the south east was ever a hotbed of Irish music and, wandering aimlessly past a selection of those rather soulless modern pubs where a young clientele drinks Alcopops all night, we rue the decision not to head for Enniscorthy, venue of the blue riband of all traditional Irish music events, the Fleadh Ceoil, in 1999 and 2000. Enniscorthy was definitely on the agenda but that HOST TOWN TO POLAND sign had exerted its magical powers over the steering wheel. Somebody had suggested O'Faolain's as a likely bar, but true to form, we can't find it. It's probably a Polish wine bar by now.

So, instead, I'm glowering over a pint of Guinness (which doesn't even have a shamrock sculpted into the froth in the proper tourist-friendly fashion) trying to blot out the banal Ibiza thud coming out of the speakers which is destroying eardrums, brain cells and the will to live in equal measures. It's a huge place that has lured us in with a sign outside promising live music. Barmaids in cute matching outfits trip around with impossibly huge collections of empty glasses, guys already boozed to the hilt on cider (dear God, *cider*!) swarm around giggling gaggles of girls gulping from bottles of Smirnoff Ice, while

Russian agents in black bow ties lurk around in search of the entire population of Poland having a sly beverage in here.

I sit there looking at it all, and I think of Margaret Barry. There'd be none of this nonsense if Margaret Barry were here, that's for sure. The most enthralling singer I ever heard in my life, Margaret was a tinker, originally of Spanish-Italian stock, born to a family of travellers in Cork in 1917. Her grandfather Bob Thompson played the pipes, both her parents were street musicians (her dad played the banjo, her mother the harp), and at 14 Margaret herself was singing on the streets of Cork following the death of her mother, Maggie. Her father joined the circus and by the time she was 16 Margaret was travelling Ireland on a bicycle, living on her wits and earning money wherever she could.

Margaret would sing at fairs, football games, pubs, queues outside picture halls … anywhere crowds congregated, basically. She upgraded from bicycle to horse-drawn caravan, taught herself to play a crude style of five-string banjo, did a bit of step-dancing to draw in the crowds and sang everything from traditional songs from her family to stuff learned from records by John McCormack and other tenors. She is said to have learned 'My Lagan Love' listening to it through the open door of a record shop and the Leadbelly classic 'Goodnight Irene' from repeated plays on Radio Luxembourg. By the early 1950s, she'd come to the attention of the inveterate American folk song collector Alan Lomax, who took her first to London, where she gained greater fame, if not fortune, appearing at the Royal Albert Hall, and then on to New York's Carnegie Hall.

The other day I met a couple from Dublin who remembered Margaret Barry as a girl singing in the streets, and they still had diametrically opposed opinions of her. 'She was an institution, you'd often see her singing in the streets and she was wonderful,' said the woman. 'She was goddawful, I never thought she could sing,' said the guy. 'You just didn't understand her, she was singing in the traditional travelling style and she was mesmerising.' 'She was a joke, she was all over the place, I couldn't stand her.' 'Ah, you don't know what you're talking about, you've got no ears …' 'Your ears have been ruined by listening to that woman!' 'Dear God, will you listen to yourself!' Last time I saw them they were heading for the divorce courts, a fitting testament to the enduring, polarising potency of Margaret Barry.

I only ever saw her once … at a Sunday night ceilidh at the Woodenbridge Hotel, in Guildford. The Rakes were playing for the dancing, and when they took a break the compère, Mark Berry, stepped forward and, barely suppressing his boyish excitement, introduced – with rare deference – 'a very special, special surprise …

Margaret Barry and Michael Gorman'. Up stepped a large, impossibly fierce-looking woman in her fifties with a shock of tumbling black hair, a battered old banjo round her neck, and fewer teeth than Shane MacGowan. The story was that the strings on her banjo had originally started life as the brakes of her bicycle. Beside her, Michael Gorman – one of the great Sligo fiddle players – looked positively frail. Dressed smartly in suit and tie, hair Brylcreemed harshly straight across the back of his head in time-honoured fashion, he too appeared an austere figure.

They were an odd-looking couple to be sure, and there were some loud sniggers from the bikers who'd congregated at the back. Ill-disguised shockwaves went around the bar when they started to play. Margaret's banjo style was crude and ragged, contrasting sharply with Gorman's driving, earthy fiddle … and then she started to sing. To naïve, youthful ears conditioned to the thin impersonality of endless American singer-songwriters, she sounded like a hideous racket. Her voice was intense and full-blooded, soaring into a universe way beyond the banjo and fiddle. There was no subtlety, elegance or smoothness about her, her voice was impossibly intense, passionate, jagged and in-yer-face … and it scared me shitless. I'd never heard such a volcanic torrent of emotion from one singer before, or indeed since. Margaret Barry made her mark that night, and even the bikers were stunned into silence.

The Margaret Barry experience affected me deeply, but not neces-sarily in a good way. Our expectations of vocal performance are so shaped by pop culture, radio exposure and the desire for mass appeal that a singer with a style as raw and natural as Margaret was always going to be difficult to stomach. Easy listening she wasn't, but easy listening, surely, has always been the enemy. Her style was so far outside the realms of my normal musical horizons that when she finished, I didn't know whether to laugh or cry. So I sort of giggled, and generally sided with the biker view that she was one seriously weird lady who couldn't sing to save her life. Get her off, and let's get on with the next dance and see if we can't just pull some girls! That's an odious, tunnel-vision teenager for you, and the folk police should have shot me there and then. It's one of the most shameful episodes in my life, on a par with running with the bulls in Pamplona. But that was Ernest Hemingway's fault …

It was years later before I heard Margaret Barry again, and I didn't listen to her properly until, long after her death, Topic Records released its landmark *Voice Of The People* collections of traditional singers. Suddenly *that voice* launched itself out of the speakers and gripped me around the throat. The same disjointed banjo accompaniment, the same Michael Gorman darting around behind her, and the same wildly rich, undisciplined voice singing 'Farewell My Own Dear Native Land', a heartbreaking saga about emigration. In that one pained, broken performance she seemed to express the heartache suffered down the centuries resulting from emigration, Ireland's constant sorrow.

Reg Hall, who had played melodeon with The Rakes that night in Guildford, gave a superb talk about the traditional singers featured on *Voice Of The People* and Margaret Barry lived even more vividly in his warm and colourful descriptions of her. You've never really heard 'She Moved Through The Fair' until you've heard it sung by Margaret Barry. And if her version of 'The Factory Girl' doesn't rip you open, you have the skin of a rhinoceros. She gave her heart, body and soul to her songs, and I'm thinking of her now because I'm sitting in a soulless bar in Wexford remembering an extract of her talking to Alan Lomax on the album *I Sang Through The Fairs*. 'Wexford was the kind of country for laments,' she said, 'and for diddling … Wexford, Enniscorthy, that was the country for diddling.'

What I wouldn't give to hear some diddling now. I'd give anything to see her appear at the door, to stand before us with her cascading black hair and sing 'Her Mantle So Green' or 'The Galway Shawl' in that incredible, untutored, scary, vocal. The incorrigible gypsy in her soul will silence the whole wretched place. The horrendous thud of beats will flee instantly back to Ibiza from whence they came, the clinking glasses at the bar will shatter, the lads and lasses exchanging flirtatious inanities will be frozen to the spot, their mouths hitting the floor in amazement. And the Russian secret agents? They will fling their bow ties to the ground and dance on them.

It doesn't happen. Instead, we get a couple of guys with guitars singing covers of Radiohead, Coldplay and The Smiths. Frankly, it's not what the doctor ordered. I mean, if you're 19 and you're out on the pull drinking Alcopops on a Saturday night, you don't really want to be listening to two earnest young men singing the complete repertoire of the latest *Now That's What I Call Songs To Cut My Wrists To* compilation, do you? Whatever happened to all those fake Pogues bands? The response of the clientele to their irksome howling is predictable enough: they turn their backs on them and talk much louder among themselves to drown them out.

We make our excuses and head for a bar we noticed earlier. It had a window filled with Glasgow Celtic scarves and other green-and-white footie memorabilia. Can't imagine them drinking Alcopops in there. Surely there has to be a Pogues-a-like band belting out incomprehensible choruses, or some ballad singer with a fund of provocative rebel songs? There didn't seem to be any Russian secret agents on the door either, so it's probably full of Poles. But never underestimate the evil powers of the modern pub and the dreaded Ibiza beat. It's a poisonous combination. The next hour is spent padding round the back streets of Wexford, getting more and more lost on the way.

Passing the John Barry statue for the fourth time, hysteria is beginning to set in. So run this by me again, John. It's a wet Sunday afternoon in Wexford and you're bored, right? So you suddenly say 'I know what I'll do. I'll go to America and start a Navy!' Was that how it was, John? Then you wrote the theme to *The Magnificent Seven*, right? We then start humming *The Magnificent Seven* theme tune. Except we suddenly realise we're getting it mixed up with *The Great Escape*. Or is that the *Juke Box Jury* theme? Didn't John Barry write 'From Russia With Love' too? Hang on, doesn't that explain all the Russian agents standing in doorways all over the place?

Frankly, when you're lost in the back streets of a strange town at the dead of night there's only one thing to do: have a drink. Conveniently, a small bar appears up a side street next to us. It's one of those places you'd never find again if you were with Sherpa Tensing and your life depended on it. It's called Simon's Place and it looks worryingly shut. In fact it looks like it doesn't even have an entrance at all. But further investigation reveals a small side door and, even more excitingly, it's open. It seems rude not to go in.

There's a small conclave of lads at one end of the bar, while in the comfy seats under the dim lighting at the other end an intriguing cameo is being played out. A middle-aged man with no teeth and – by the looks of a face more crumpled than his trousers – no gums also, is pawing a woman too pissed to care. Then we see the walls, full of horse-racing pictures. There are pictures from Scottish, Welsh and English Grand Nationals and a lovely shot of Belmont King winning at Leopardstown and being led into the winning enclosure by a young lad. We look at the young lad in the pic and look at the lad behind the bar. Can they be one and the same? The boy in the pic looks about nine. The one behind the bar looks about 15. Could they possibly be … ?

'Simon Lambert Jnr' it says on the pic, and we are in 'Simon's Bar', *so* … 'Hi Simon,' we say, as Simon Lambert-Still-Jnr-But-Not-As-Jnr-As-He-Used-To-Be pours our Guinness. We talk about racing and drink some more and it strikes us this could win our Best Bar In Wexford award. I mean, it has racing and drinking … you haven't got a fiddle player hidden in the basement, have you, Simon? He moves aside to reveal a plaque on the wall, announcing Simon's Bar as winner of the 2001 Singing Pubs Award. 'It's very prestigious,' he says proudly.' There are over fifty pubs in Wexford and every year they hold this competition to decide which has the best singers – it's a big honour to win it.' Congratulations. 'Thanks. See, we get a lot of them working in the theatre up the road drinking here so we have some really good singers, y'know opera singers and the like.'

So this is a music pub, then? Simon ponders the question long and hard. 'I wouldn't say it was a music pub so much as a … *singing pub*.' There's a difference? 'Oh yeah. See, we don't advertise music or anything but we do have people that come in and like a sing and they'll often just get together and have a singsong. But you never know when it'll happen … there's nothing organised about it.' So what do they sing? 'Anything they want.' Like what? 'It might be opera, ballads, anything they fancy …' Oh. 'So what is it you're after, then?' Oh, anything really, Simon. Singing, traditional music …

A light suddenly goes on in Simon's head. 'Ah … I know what you're after … you want a bit of the ol' *Irish craic*, don't you?' Well, yeah … .'A bit of the ol' drink, a bit of the ol' session, a bit of the ol' craic.' Well, yeah … Simon's beaming now and shaking his head. 'It doesn't exist.' It doesn't? 'Noooo. We get 'em coming here all the time wanting some of the ol' craic, but that stuff's just for the tourists. It's not real. You don't get any of that stuff once the tourists have gone home. There's no such thing as the craic.'

I order another pint and contemplate a very short book …

Chapter two

WATERFORD: CHRISTY, ELVIS & OL' McDERMOTT

To be honest, Simon's words put a bit of a damper on the proceedings. '*So you're after a bit of the ol' Irish craic, are you? That's just for the tourists ...*' I don't want to be a tourist. Nobody ever wants to be a tourist, do they? They always want to find the bits the tourists never visit. That's where the art of marketing comes in. You sell some picturesque valley to tourists on the grounds that normal tourists will never find it. You see it in brochures all the time: 'DISCOVER ONE OF THE WORLD'S LAST UNSPOILT PLACES.' What, so you can go and spoil it?

Tourists, by definition, are generally a fairly obnoxious breed, patronisingly admiring natural landscapes and simple lifestyles while destroying them with their very presence. I really don't want to be a tourist. I haven't been coming to Ireland for twenty-five years to be a tourist. Maybe we should just turn right around and head back to Rosslare right now. But you know what they say ... never go back.

So instead we head for Waterford, the oldest city in Ireland. You know, where the glass is from. Well, I say glass, but what I mean is *crystal*. There's a gert big crystal factory in town, which they reckon is the biggest in the world. Driving along the quayside past the River Suir today, Waterford is teeming with people, and the parade of No Vacancies signs outside the B&Bs suggest there's no room at the inn. Someone on the boat was chuntering on about a light opera festival in Waterford. Maybe that's it. We come in search of Tommy Peoples ... will we end up with Gilbert & Sullivan?

Lord, give us a sign how we should proceed. And suddenly, He does. The sign says WATERFORD & TRAMORE RACES. There's a line under it announcing 'Craic On The Track' and that's good enough for me, squire, 'tis good enough for me.

Just a handful of miles south of Waterford, Tramore is a wondrous study in tack. It's a seaside town dripping in slot machines, fast food shops, candy floss, funfairs, juke boxes, Kiss-Me-Quick hats and buskers playing Christy Moore's 'Ordinary Man', Van Morrison's 'Brown-Eyed Girl' and − naturally − 'Fields Of Athenry' *ad nauseum*. No, Margate has nothing on Tramore. This is a major Irish family holiday resort of choice. The name is roughly translated as Big Strand (i.e. bloody great beach) and used to be a fishing hamlet until some bloke called Bartholomew Rivers got hold of it in 1785 and decided to transform it into Fun City.

I was last in Tramore over a decade ago. After a fortnight in a particularly isolated spot in Connemara, we'd closed in on the town as a final port of call in readiness for an early morning ferry out of Rosslare the next morning. Chilled and rested after conversing only with errant cows, bottles of Jamesons and the occasional incomprehensible farmer for a fortnight, Tramore came as a violent shock to the system. We'd got out of the car and instantly shrieking kids were landing on our heads, gangs of leering drunken lads bumped into us on their eternal quest for local totty and buskers, winos and beggars queued up for a hand-out. Still, when in Rome and all that …

We'd wandered into the first slot-machine palace we found and pretended to be having fun. Then, our toddler son − the one named after Kevin Keegan − started pressing knobs on the machines. We were just about to chide him when there was a dramatic explosion of noise. Bells rang, trumpets blazed, lights flashed … and a cascade of punts started tumbling out of the machine. Everything else seemed to stop as the coins kept a-coming and crowds gathered to watch the little boy being submerged in a treasure trove.

A man in a uniform came and stood beside us as we watched the pile grow, and I was waiting for his hand on my shoulder as we were marched off to meet the Gardai and be read the riot act about breaking Irish gaming laws. Instead he got to his hands and knees, spent several minutes scooping the bootie into a large bag, handed it to us with a wink and said, 'Congratulations, you have won the jackpot'. I've had a soft spot for Tramore ever since.

The town is a little more sophisticated these days, but not much. It now has candyfloss on tap and a proper amusement park with scary rides and everything. In the early nineties it was also home to the Celtworld Mythology Centre theme park, part-funded by an EU grant, but it closed after three years. But hey, the pubs look promising. There's a poster announcing the Tra-Fest Music Weekend, but hang on, read the small print, *always* read the small print. The festival is July and it's now, er, August.

There's more false optimism when a sign appears on a board outside a bar announcing 'ELVIS IMPERSONATOR – TONIGHT'. We can almost see the lip curling, the hips swivelling and some chubby bloke with comedy sideboards singing 'Return To Sender To Be Sure' and 'The Wonder Of Youse'. Do Irish Tom Jones impersonators sing 'The Green Green Grass Of Athenry'? So that's tonight's entertainment sorted … except this pub turns out to be the Heartbreak Hotel. We'd forgotten we're in Irish time now. So when they stick boards outside of bars announcing 'ELVIS IMPERSON-ATOR – TONIGHT' what they really mean is LAST NIGHT. And Elvis has left the building. Looks like we'll be lonesome tonight. Instead of following that dream we'll be crying in the chapel. Moral: always treat boards outside of pubs with suspicious minds.

The thing about this Elvis impersonator is that he seems to be booked to appear in every pub in Tramore over the next week. Well, every night except tonight. I mean, some days he's appearing in more than one pub per day. He's on a world tour of Tramore. So what *is* he doing today? What does an Elvis impersonator do on his day off anyway? Dress up as Michael Jackson? I met Jerry Lee Lewis' sister once. She's called Linda Gail Lewis and she's been married eight times ('but dahling, only to seven men'). One of her hubbies was a professional Elvis impersonator, who used to preen himself in front of the bedroom mirror singing 'Are You Lonesome Tonight?', admiring his quiff and imploring Linda Gail to call him The King. 'Daaarlin',' drawled Linda Gail, 'I *knew* Elvis and you ain't *nuthin'* like The King …'

Where's Linda Gail when you need her? She'd know how to find our disappearing Elvis impersonator. There's only one logical solu-tion: the Elvis impersonator has gone to the races. So off we go to Tramore Races, looking for an overweight jockey in a white suit, rhinestone cape, black sideburns and studded diamond rings. There's no sign, although he wouldn't be easy to spot in this crowd.

The first thing we encounter on course is a Tyrolean choir in full regalia, singing old traditional favourites like 'Annie's Song', 'What A Wonderful World' and, er, 'My Way'. The women are blonde with head scarves, pigtails and long frocks, and the men have colourful waistcoats, beer bellies and interesting neckerchiefs. Four little girls crouch in front of them with open mouths. I stand at the back and shout for 'Lonely Goatherd' from *The Sound Of Music*. They ignore me. Come on chaps, how about yodelling Frank Ifield's 'I Remember You'? Del Shannon's 'Swiss Maid'? Nothing. Then Chief Beer Belly squints and says: 'We are now going to sing "Fields Of Athenry".' No surprise there, then. But what *is* a surprise is that he has what sounds suspiciously like a *Manchester accent*. Dear Lord, what's that all about then? Time to move on ...

And so to the horses. There's little chance of missing any of the action at Tramore. The course is so small you can watch the horse boxes arriving, have some chit chat with the jockeys, give the horses a once-over in their stables, watch them parade around the enclosure, down a pint, give the contents of your wallet to a barrage of noisy bookies ('we'll take euros, Irish punts, sterling, travellers cheques, shirt buttons, anything ...' one told me) and join in a rousing Tyrolean chorus of 'Fields Of Athenry' without moving beyond a 20-yard radius. There's even an old chap playing a desultory jig on a creaky fiddle by the main gate. I stare at him hard. Surely Tommy Peoples hasn't resorted to *this*?

Rather recklessly, I toss a couple of euros (you can tell the racing hasn't started yet) into his proffered flat cap and ask his name. 'John,' he says, cackling through a toothless mouth. 'Where you from, John?' Another big cackle. 'Who taught you to play fiddle, John?' An even bigger explosion of cackling. 'What's gonna win the next race, John?' There's an eruption of noise as the Cackleometer hits meltdown. I give him another couple of euros and go backstage to study the horses. A crumpled man in a pork pie hat and ill-fitting suit is staring intently at the fine creatures being prepared for the next race. He greets me with a nod and a wink. I ask what he's looking for. 'Shit!' he says unceremoniously. Sorry mate, didn't mean to offend you ... 'No ... see, the thing is, them that shit before they run, run faster. Makes 'em lighter, see, and less stressed. It's all down to the shit. 'Tis obvious ...'

Armed with this insightful info, I search for manure and nod sagely as he draws my attention to an impressive, fresh pile sitting proudly beneath the tail of a horse bearing No 8. I head straight for the bookie and back No 7. I mean, you can study form, assess the jockey and measure the manure, but in the end it all boils down to one thing ... *does it have a good name*? There's a horse in the race called Traditional. It's got to be a sign, right? I spy a bookie offering 'the best odds in western Europe' and stake that evening's B&B money on Traditional coming in. The jockey, Paul Moloney, is wearing rather fetching yellow and black chevron silks and, I could be mistaken, but there is something of a jaunty strut about him as he makes his way into the enclosure to mount what I'm now confidently expecting to be a 10-1 winner. The course is so small that they run around it three times. Traditional romps home ahead of the field by at least thirty lengths. Unfortunately, he's still on his second circuit and the rest are on the third. Pagan Streams pips Dutch Lad to win the race, and it looks like we'll be sleeping in the car tonight. I'd have done better with Feargal commentating. Tomorrow's B&B money also goes up in horse manure, after a rash wager on the grannies' choice, Fosterandallen. It looks good in the paddock, but the harmonies are all over the place and it can't raise a chorus.

When in doubt, have a drink. Retiring to the bar to regroup and study form, a poster on the wall leaps out at me: AFTER THE RACES – CHRISTY MOORE TRIBUTE BAND. Somewhat psychologically scarred by the disappointments of the Elvis ads, I study the small print zealously. Nope, it's here all right, straight after the races today. A Christy Moore tribute band! There's gold in tham there hills! This is a major breakthrough.

You see, Christy is a personal hero. I used to go and watch him when he was a young, boozy, good-time, singalong merchant belting out the likes of 'The Raggle Taggle Gypsy', working the British folk clubs – in dank rooms above pubs with sawdust on the floors and everything – after jacking in his secure job at the Bank of Ireland. Christy was apparently such a superb bank teller that various big cheeses beseeched him to reverse his decision to quit, sacrificing all those lovely pension rights. 'The choice was simple,' says Christy in his own ingeniously unconventional autobiography *One Voice*: 'stay in Ballyhaunis, County Mayo for £8 a week, digs with Mrs Nester £5 a week, get turned down when asking fine things to dance in Toureen, or shag off to England where I could get £4 a night singing songs and backing jigs and reels, and there were beautiful women to be loved and friends to be made and goose feather beds and wide open fields with not a mortal sin in sight ...'

Originally from Newbridge, County Kildare – good solid horse racing country (the kidnapping of Shergar occurred close to where he was raised) – Moore relocated to the north of England and became a much-loved character on the UK folk scene. He was a celebrated rabble-rouser, too. He liked a drink in those days, did Christy, and almost anything else on offer. He looked like a cartoon cliché of an Irish navvy, with an impossibly ruddy face, big bushy beard, big physique, big voice, even bigger personality and the demeanour of a man who might spend Saturday afternoons wrestling at the local town hall and Saturday nights drinking at the working men's club ... and often confused the two. Even then, though, he could coax, cajole and caress an audience like no one else with a mix of lovely Irish songs like 'Curragh Of Kildare', 'Cunla', 'Rocky Road To Dublin' and 'Maid Of Athy', and the contemporary material of writers like Ewan MacColl, Ian Campbell and Brendan's brother Dominic Behan.

Christy fell in with the British folk *cognoscenti* of the day: people like Robin Hall & Jimmy MacGregor, The Watersons, Hamish Imlach, Bob & Carole Pegg and Mike Harding. In 1970 he recorded his first album *Paddy On The Road*, a primitive effort produced by Dominic Behan. Christy himself renounced it early on, but if you ever see an original copy, hang on to it for dear life – only 500 were issued and it's worth a few bob now. One way or another – whether it was singing 'Whiskey In The Jar', or drinking the pub dry of it afterwards – Christy made his mark on the English folk scene. But it's what he did when he left England in 1971 that stamped him as one of the true greats of Irish music.

Christy wanted to be more than the folk-club entertainer. He sang funny songs, and sad songs, and political songs, and chorus songs with a neat line in chat to boot. But he instinctively knew there was more to be gleaned from it all, something wholly deeper and more enduring. In London he'd listened to the ol' boys playing their reels, jigs, slow airs and songs in the pubs in Fulham, Cricklewood, Camden and Kilburn, and it always touched a nerve. He'd also heard the trail-blazing 1968 debut album by Sweeney's Men – a group that variously featured Joe Dolan, Andy Irvine, Johnny Moynihan, Terry Woods and Henry McCullough – and admired the way they'd merged the more familiar American folk blues style so popular in the early sixties with a distinctively home-grown Irish flavour. It was not Irish music of any popular perception, but it was real and exciting, it had verve, imagination and style, and it gave Christy plenty to think about.

He went home to Ireland to make his next album with Irish musicians, and gravitated to Prosperous, a village in Kildare, west of the Wicklow Mountains, a few miles from Naas. At Pat Dowling's pub, he got together with his old schoolfriend Donal Lunny – the man who'd originally taught him to play guitar – and they hooked up with Andy Irvine (Ireland's answer to Woody Guthrie), and the man popularly acclaimed as the best young uillean piper of his generation, Liam Og O'Flynn. They'd work out a song and then, with the venerable folk-recording pioneer Bill Leader, a Revox tape machine and two microphones in tow, they'd adjourn to the cellar of Christy's friend Andy Rynne's Georgian house to record it.

The end result was the LP *Prosperous*, a small step for records but a giant leap for Irish recordings. A million miles from the ballad groups and parlour songs that had essentially formed the face of Irish music for as long as anyone could remember, *Prosperous* took the suggestions offered by Sweeney's Men and sprinted off with them at a dynamic pace. Most Irish records – indeed, most folk records per se – had previously provided only rudimentary arrangements and predictably crude backings. Here, Liam O'Flynn's dextrous piping merged blissfully with Andy Irvine's mandolin and Donal Lunny's rhythmic bouzouki to form a complex, beautiful diversion for the voice of Christy Moore.

The band finished the record, but no one wanted to finish the adventure. So they just partied right on, calling themselves Planxty. It's a term of endearment used in the same way as *slainté*, a phrase primarily associated with the tunes of the blind harper Turlough O'Carolan, a seventeenth-century giant of Irish music history with his rich catalogue of gorgeous tunes in honour of the nobility who gave him food and lodging. Indeed, 'Planxty Irwin' was a keynote instrumental on the first official Planxty album, and a beautiful tune 'Tabhair Dom Do Lamh' (Give Me Your Hand) is tagged on to the end of 'Raggle Taggle Gipsy' to create a stunning overture to that dazzling self-titled album. Were I the Taioseach, I'd station Gardai at every port and airport specifically refusing visitors to leave Ireland without proof of purchase of a copy of that Planxty album, my favourite record of all time.

To all intents and purposes, Planxty were a rock band. They were young, inventive and irrepressible, with terrible haircuts and the air of rebels, hooked on the passion of their music and the potency of rhythm. Indeed, Messrs Moore, Lunny and Irvine were all children of the rock revolution who'd found their way into their own culture through a variety of paths. Donal and Christy had followed the example of many British folk singers before them who'd become intrigued by the roots of the folk and blues songs they'd flirted with in school skiffle bands. Andy Irvine simply thought he was Woody Guthrie (Dylan's 'Song For Woody' appears on the *Prosperous* album) and had been bumming round Eastern Europe prior to those fateful sessions at Pat Dowling's.

The joker in the pack, though, was Liam O'Flynn, a traditional musician of impeccable credentials who had been taught by three of the greatest uillean pipers of them all: Leo Rowsome; Willie Clancy; and Seamus Ennis. Ennis had even bequeathed his own beloved pipes to the gifted youngster. Another Kildare man, O'Flynn didn't have a silly haircut – it got a bit floppy at times but by nature he was a short, back and sides man – and he had the unimpeachable admiration of the traditional purists. His very presence alongside Christy Moore, Andy Irvine and Donal Lunny gave Planxty instant credibility and gravitas and they in turn supplied Irish traditional music with a brave new world and a new generation to enjoy it.

A seventies Celtic music boom of sorts followed, and even the more recent worldwide obsession with Irish musical culture resulting from *Riverdance, Lord Of The Dance*, et al, is still founded on what

Planxty achieved back in the day. Christy originally sang their first hit 'Cliffs Of Dooneen' – a song that Andy Rynne would sing at Pat Dowling's pub, and which featured on Christy's *Prosperous* album – extolling the beauty of a particular spot on the west coast of Ireland: 'You may travel far, far from your native home/Far away o'er the mountains, far away oe'r the foam/But of all the fine places that I've ever been/There is none can compare with the cliffs of Dooneen ...' Written down it may look like a case of bad cheese OD, and every pub singer sings it from Rosslare to Rathlin, but there is something irresistibly warming about it.

I'd love to tell you in detail exactly how beautiful the cliffs of Dooneen really are, but I've never actually found them. Once I drove up and down the coast of Clare for days in search of them, but all to no avail. It's not a heritage site, see. If there aren't coach loads of Americans and Germans hovering round it, it doesn't exist.

Christy Moore went on to many adventures after his two stints with Planxty. He was a founding member of Moving Hearts (the third greatest band in the history of the world, ever, after Planxty and the Bothy Band) which, gulp, mixed traditional song with thumping jazz-rock bass and drums and even an electric guitar. That was an education in itself: a loud, raucous band who attracted a loud, raucous audience. There were plenty of political overtones, as well as opportunities to dance your pants off, and you couldn't help but fear how Christy – whose forte is making an intimate, very personal connection with his audience – would be heard above it all. There'd be Keith Donald's searing sax, Davey Spillane's wailing pipes, Declan Sinnott's screaming guitar, Donal Lunny's pounding bouzouki ... and frenzied fans jumping up and down waving their knickers in the air. All of a sudden they'd stop and Christy, sweat dripping off him, would step meaningfully to the mic. An instant hush would descend. And, entirely unaccompanied, Christy would shut his eyes tight and quietly sing 'Irish Ways & Irish Laws', that stirring, emotive testament to the Irish spirit through centuries of occupation and oppression. It was an astonishing experience.

In pride and wonder I watched the rise of Christy Moore through the eighties. I saw him at Cambridge Folk Festival, Hammersmith Odeon and, most astonishing of all, the Royal Albert Hall. He walked on stage decked entirely in black, all biceps and pumping veins, in his granddad vest and Mike Tyson neck, looking like he'd come to dig up the Albert Hall, not play in it. He then proceeded to convert it into everyman's front room, holding a rapt audience with a bodhran solo one minute, inspiring huge gales of laughter with a song about *delirium tremens* the next, then turning them into an angry mob outraged by the injustices served out to victims of judicial abuse, then melting them with the seductive 'Nancy Spain', then a cover of Jackson Browne's 'After The Deluge', then an impromptu talking folk song ... before sending them home singing his own daddy of all choruses, 'Lisdoonvarna'.

Christy has fought his own demons all the way. He's had his conflicts with the booze and the odd chemical, and there have been times he may have behaved badly. He's upset a few along the way, too, as does anyone willing to put their head above the parapet. He was a vigorous anti-nuclear campaigner and a prominent figurehead of the nuclear-free village, festival and roadshow established at Carnsore Point in the extreme south east, just up the road from Wexford and Rosslare, in the late seventies. He never had any qualms about taking on the big guys. His own song 'They Never Came Home' became the subject of a High Court case in the eighties because it sided with the victims' families fighting for compensation over the fire at Dublin's Stardust Club, which killed 48 youngsters. The judge Frank Murphy ruled that a line in the song inferring the fire exits were chained was prejudicial to ongoing claim proceedings, and ordered the *Ordinary Man* album to be taken out of circulation and the offending song removed. The case cost him and his record company £100,000, but Christy has few regrets: 'I believe if they ban or censor or bring a song to court if must surely be touching a raw, raw nerve.'

Christy never held back when it came to politics, either. In 1979 he produced the *H-Block* album, in support of the protests of the Long Kesh H-block prisoners. Two of his most enduringly popular stage songs, 'Back Home In Derry' and 'McIlhatton' (glorifying a poitin brewer), were banned on the basis that they were written by the late MP, Bobby Sands, the first of the IRA hunger strikers to die in Belfast in 1981. Christy aligned himself with various republican causes, campaigned for the release of the Birmingham Six and the Guildford Four and can still stop any show as he bleakly recites the names of Jackie Duddy, Willie Nash, Gerry Donaghy, Willie McKinney and all the other Bloody Sunday victims on one of his simplest, yet most powerful songs of all, 'Minds Locked Shut'. His book *One Voice* boasts a nice line in anti-Thatcherism, too: 'When I saw her take tea with Pinochet and laud him for his support in the Falklands, I thought perhaps the poor lady might be totally mad. But that would be to trivialise her absolute danger to us all. I sense her spirit in Garvaghy Road, Brick Lane, Soho, Hungerford, Harrods and anywhere greed is seen to be good or violence is the answer.' Amen to that, Christy.

So yeah, Christy Moore's a personal hero of mine. We named our son after him – the one who's not named after Kevin Keegan. When I told Christy this, he was incredulous. 'You did not!' We did! 'Jeez, you did not!' Jeez, we did! 'You named your son after me?' We named our son after you. 'You did not!' We did! And so on for 45 minutes …

Once, we took little Christy to see big Christy at Hammersmith Odeon. Only seven at the time, he was sound asleep halfway through the second song. We woke him up to hear 'Joxter Goes To Stuttgart' because it's a funny football song – commemorating Ireland's famous World Cup victory against England when Ray Houghton scored and Jack Charlton became a saint – and the truth is that our own Christy is more into football than music, Irish or otherwise. Still, we took him backstage to meet his namesake after the show and Big Christy solemnly shook Little Christy's hand, enquired after his bodhran playing and engaged in some gentle banter about the footie. It gave me a real thrill.

Yet even that pales against the notion of a Christy Moore *tribute band* appearing at Tramore Races. Immediately the last race is over a lorry appears on the course and draws up in front of the main stand. Ah, this is it! The Christy Moore tribute band has arrived in style. There's what … eight of them? All in smart blue jackets and dark slacks and bow ties. Strange. And they are playing a bizarre assortment of jazz and populist hits. *Mighty* strange. With saxophones and clarinets and brassy stuff like that.

Something is amiss. I'm not sure which era Christy they are attempting to evoke, but unless it was the Christmas party when he was still working for the Bank of Ireland, I don't recall him ever performing 'Living La Vida Loca' or, indeed, 'Can't Buy Me Love'. I wander to the front, next to a couple of kids throwing mud at each other, and see a name on the drum kit: Brass & Co.

Clearly, this is not the Christy Moore tribute band. I walk away despondently, spitting on Brass & Co's lively interpretation of 'In The Mood', and forage deep in my pockets for the few last stray euros that have escaped the clutches of those nasty bookies for a compensatory pint. I was going to reclaim my earlier donation to John the Fiddler, but he'd long gone. Probably driven off in his Mercedes to get to Dublin in time for his flight to Buenos Aires. I wander into the Deise Bar, get a couple of pints in and notice there's a guy singing at the front. He's playing guitar. He doesn't have much hair. He's dressed in black. He's wearing a granddad vest. He has Mike Tyson's neck. He's singing 'Back Home In Derry'. He *is* the Christy Moore tribute band …

'I've come down from Cork with a hangover like a *house*,' says the Christy Moore tribute band, screwing his face up as he takes a sip from a pint. 'Uggh ... jeez, anyone got a real glass here? I just can't drink out of plastic.' He has a point. The beer does taste awful. In fact, the Christy Moore tribute band isn't at all bad. He does that impromptu scat singing that's Christy's trademark, he has the same mannerisms, he screws up his face in the same way, and huge sweat stains begin to appear under the armpits of his granddad vest. He does a passable impression all right, and gives the big songs a good belting. There's a ripple of applause when Ray Houghton scores in 'Joxter Goes To Stuttgart', and you wonder if Shane MacGowan and Kirsty MacColl impersonators will magically appear with him when he launches into 'Fairytale Of New York'.

I'm up front waving my plastic pint and giving him the thumbs-up by the time he hits 'Lisdoonvarna'. This is all going extremely well. Then he slows it all down for a moving version of the love song 'Nancy Spain'. As he reaches the end of it, there's an enormous roar of approval from the back. People are clapping and cheering and hugging each other in delight. The Christy Moore tribute band is taken aback. Even when Christy sings 'Nancy Spain' they don't react like this. The CMTB waves a hand, and gives a sheepish grin of acknowledgement of the acclaim. He's never had a reaction like this in his life. 'Thank you ... I ... er ... you're very kind ...' he mumbles towards the central core of this unexpected outbreak of hysteria. Then the truth dawns on him. Those cheering have their backs to him, and are avidly watching some hurling match on a TV at the rear of the bar.

The Christy Moore tribute band consults his songbook, and carries on with flattened ego. I want to talk to him and find out his name, but he seems to know more songs than Christy himself, and is showing no signs of exhaustion. For some reason, Mrs Colin is convinced his name is Bryan, but whoever heard of a Christy Moore tribute band called Bryan? I sidle up to a wise man at the bar. 'Yer man on stage, what's he called?' 'Yer man on stage? He's an ordinary man.' 'Well, I can see that, but what's his name?' 'An ordinary man ...' 'My wife thinks he's called Bryan ...' 'No, he's an ordinary man ...' ' "An Ordinary Man", good song that, he'll probably play it in a minute ... by the way, do you know the guy's name?' 'An ordinary man ...' 'Yes, but what's his name?' 'He's AN ORDINARY MAN!' I sense a communication breakdown, thank him for his time and make an undignified exit through the by-now rabid hurling fans at the back.

I leave singing 'An Ordinary Man'. It could be Christy's theme song, except he's got a dozen other theme songs. You hear it all the time from buskers and all those pub entertainers they dig out for the tourists. 'I'm an ordinary man, nothing special, nothing grand/I've had to work for everything I own ...' It's a working-class anthem of simple melody and plain message that has struck a particularly potent chord, not just with Christy Moore fans but with Irish audiences in general.

The way Christy tells it, he was emerging from Cleethorpes Winter Gardens after an indifferent gig one cold night in the mid-eighties when he was still on the drink, and a figure emerged in the darkness to thrust a cassette into his hand. The song he heard on it was 'An Ordinary Man'. Pretty soon he was performing it on stage, but he had no contact for the mysterious stranger who'd given him the tape and didn't have a clue who'd written it. Every performance of the song was accompanied by an appeal about the identity of the writer, because nobody seemed to know and there might be some royalties at the end of it. Cue hundreds of chancers claiming authorship. But eventually Peter Hames was located as the genuine author of the song.

Several months later, I am still trying to discover the true identity of Bryan, the Christy Moore tribute band. Chuck it into Google on the internet and what comes up? Apart from a couple of Dutchmen whose entire repertoire seems comprised of Moore material, there's just the one official tribute act ... some guy billing himself as 'An Ordinary Man'. Peter Hames has a lot to answer for.

But, right now, there are more important things to discover. Like, where's the craic tonight? The clear message of Tramore is no Elvis impersonator, no craic, so we follow the cars out of the racetrack and hope for the best. We end up heading west along the coast and, as night sets in, arrive in the lively town of Dungarvan, with its engaging square, striking quayside and tannery, and a bay swimming with oysters. Well, not *literally* obviously. Oysters don't swim, do they? They just sort of hang around seabeds in their shells and *cling*. Dungarvan is full of pearls like that. Just over a century ago, they also found a load of mammoth elephant bones here, and clearing them up proved to be quite a tusk.

Dungarvan's greatest moment, though, came in 1998 when the Tour de France came to town. That was when all the shop fronts were painted, and roads that residents had been complaining about for years were suddenly tarted up. The way they tell it, the opening skirmishes occurred in Dublin but the race proper started on the second stage when the riders set off from Enniscorthy, went through Waterford, had a scenic detour round Carrick-on-Suir, 'cos that's the home of Ireland's great cycling hero Sean Kelly, and then got down to the serious stuff when they saw the bunting at Dungarvan. As the riders sped out of Dungarvan en route to Youghal and Cork they hit The Sweep, a climb where the King Of The Mountains trophy could be won or lost. Well, the riders did have the small matter of the Pyrenees to contend with later in the tour, but in Dungarvan they know the truth – that 500ft summit on The Sweep was all-important.

But first things first: find a B&B. This is no easy matter in Dungavan after dark. Were there a lot of Polish cyclists in the Tour de France that year? 'House Full' signs materialise out of thin air as we approach, and even the hostel full of Austrian backpackers turns its nose up at our forlorn pleas for humble lodging. We trek halfway out of town and find a B&B with a 'Vacancies' sign. Ten minutes of furious knocking later, a man with an East European accent comes to the door. 'Got a double room for the night, squire?' 'Hello.' 'Yes, hello. Double room please.' 'I am guest.' 'That's nice. Double room, please.' 'I am not living. I answer door.' 'It says "Vacancies".' 'I am visiting.' 'Me too, sunshine.' 'It is night time.' 'Just pass the register, will you …'

We end up staying at an absurdly expensive guesthouse on the outskirts of town, run by a man wearing a Manchester United shirt. He shows us to our room and then spends 45 minutes regaling us with tales of the day Man U came to play Waterford, when Bobby Charlton, Denis Law and George Best were in the side. 'I still go across to Old Trafford whenever I can,' he says. 'They're great, United, aren't they?' I'm a Woking supporter actually. 'What sport's that then?' Football. 'Oh.' Yeah. 'I'm a United man, me. Through and through. Man and boy. Yer man Alex Ferguson, eh?' What about him? 'He's the man, right?' Right.

We escape in search of a session. Dungarvan, we are told, is a hotbed of traditional music and there are one or two likely pubs along the main street. See, there's a science to the search for the session. First check the walls. Posters, press cuttings, pictures, parish notices. Any clues here? Some sort of personal appeal from someone trying to track down the brain cells lost in Lisdoonvarna in the seventies, a photo of some old bloke with a tin whistle sticking out of his top pocket, unsightly marks you fondly imagine were sustained from the mass hysteria that ensued when somebody launched into the opening verse of 'Fields Of Athenry'. Then there's the décor. The barer the floors, the harder the chairs, the dodgier the loos, the better the potential. There are positively no juke boxes, dartboards, pool tables, one-arm bandits, wallpaper of any discernible colour, or quiz machines festooned with the faces of Chris Tarrant, Bob Monkhouse or, especially, Dave Lee Travis.

Then you check out the clientele. Once, you'd be drawn to wizened old men in a selection of comedy headgear and whiskers, but these days age – or indeed, sex – offers no clue. There's just the occasional oddly-shaped case subtly secreted behind a chair or the bar, a concealed wink or a glint in the eye as they greet one another and then sink into purposeful silence. There's none of the 'How's the mother-in-law, Cedric, still riding around on her broomstick?' which is the traditional greeting in English pubs. It's more of a respectful nod, then a glance at the landlord, swiftly followed by the efficient delivery of a foaming pint, and a long nesting process in a pre-ordained seat with no breath wasted on such trivialities as conversation.

Even more of a giveaway are the *empty* seats. It's a packed bar, pints are flying over your head on their way to some lucky customer at the back as if propelled by a magical homing instinct, and you really don't dare look down to discover exactly what it is that feels so squidgy under foot. And yet ... and *yet* ... there's a large table surrounded by empty seats at the back that nobody seems to have noticed. There is no 'Reserved' sign on it but we give it a large berth simply because everyone else does, and it remains empty. A hidden radar shield or maybe just the cold stares of the regulars instantly repel the occasional stray American who homes in on the empty seats.

Spot the empty seat and you know, by God you *know*, that sometime, somehow before this night is through, people will magically appear in the empty seats, brandishing fiddles, guitars, melodeons, whistles and the like, the drunks will suddenly get sober, the raucous conversations about the Rose Of Tralee will suddenly cease, and we will be in the midst of a session.

See, if you're looking for music in Irish pubs you might think a sign in the window announcing 'MUSIC HERE TONIGHT' would provide a decent clue. Let's face it, there aren't too many pubs in Ireland right now that *don't* have signs in the window announcing 'MUSIC HERE TONIGHT'. But there's music and there's *music*. And then there's 'Fields Of Athenry'. The sort we're after doesn't tend to advertise itself outside – or *inside,* come to that. You just have to look for the clues.

'This is the place,' I tell Mrs Colin confidently as we nestle in a corner of a particular dark, uninviting bar down a back alley that fits all the criteria. 'There'll be some wild music in here tonight, I can *smell* it ...' 'Nah, that's the dog shit on your shoe,' she says, unconvinced. After an hour watching the empty seats like hawks and most of the bar emptying fast, doubts creep in. It's not really session protocol but hell, I am English, so I nonchalantly approach the bar.

'When's the music start, mate?' 'Yer wha'?' 'Music? You know ... music. Any music?' 'Where?' 'Here.' 'When?' 'Tonight.' 'Music here

tonight?' 'Yeah.' 'No.' 'No, what?' 'No music tonight?' 'No music *ever*
… !' 'Are you sure?' 'We never have music here. The punters don't
like it.'

Considering the bar is empty, this sounds like a hollow claim.

'It's music you're wanting, is it?' Don't tell me, he's going to give
me Simon's line about *the ol'craic* and how it only exists to sucker in
gullible tourists. 'Is it the ol' craic you're after then?'

Here we go …

'Go to Beann A'Leanna's pub up the road, there'll be a bit of craic
up there, right enough …'

He's not wrong.

The party's already started by the time we make it to Beann
A'Leanna's. Half a dozen musicians of dramatically differing ages,
instruments, haircuts and fashion disasters are grouped in a semi-
circle, while the rest of us perch self-consciously on chairs around the
edge of the room talking in many tongues. It's like the United
Nations in here. There's a German couple trying to eat each other.
An Australian is zonked out on something a little fizzier than the
Guinness. And there's a woman climbing over chairs taking
photographs of every conceivable object in the room from every
conceivable angle … so she's obviously American. I half expect a
mass walkout when she starts flashing. It's bad manners to take
people's photographs without their consent … and a potential mine-
field to do it with musicians within the sacred conclave of a pub
session. But, as Simon says, pub sessions only exist for the tourists, so
what do they expect?

The musicians here seem a pretty laid-back bunch anyway, cheerily
trolling their way through a selection of dance tunes at a desultory
pace. A bunch of dancers rise without trace to twirl each other around
in chaotic fashion, and it threatens to end in tears as one couple land
on the lap of the flautist, flattening his bottle of Vodka Ice in the
process. Serves him right for drinking the stuff in a place like this, if
you ask me.

The dynamics are interesting. There's a young guy playing guitar in
a smart blue shirt with his hair in a ponytail, and a young girl barely
in her teens playing fiddle next to an elderly gent wearing a suit and
tie playing mouth organ. I note with satisfaction that he is drinking a
good solid pint of something black and frothy. Glad to see someone
is maintaining standards around here.

There are various assorted souls playing whistles, bodhrans and
accordions, but they all look to the large ruddy-faced guy in the
white sports shirt playing melodeon for their lead. His name is Mick
Dalton, a well-known character around these parts, as well as a fine

musician. 'Guess how old I am?' he says when I bump into him in the loo late into the night. 'Er … 55?' 'I'm 68!' he declares, triumphantly. Blimey, I say, how do you do it? 'Good music, good food, good drink and bad women!' he chortles. I ask if he's ever made a record. 'I had the chance,' he sighs, 'but it's a strange thing. I'll play all night here, I'll play for anyone … but if you were to put a microphone in front of me, I just couldn't play a note. That's odd, isn't it?'

We pause as a girl starts to sing. She's not good, but session protocol kicks in. If someone is invited to sing then they're accorded the total respect of the audience. They don't always get it – and this girl is perhaps less deserving than most – but as she embarks on a 58-verse ballad, nobody moves a muscle, least of all the other musicians. There's a burst of applause at the end, though it's probably out of relief more than genuine appreciation. A few more tunes from my new best mate Mick and his chums and then there's a bit of a kerfuffle from the bar area.

A small, red-faced old chap appears through the throng in granny specs, powder blue jacket and corduroy trousers and waving a walking stick. Again there is complete silence as he starts to sing a jaunty little ditty, and within seconds he has the place eating out of his hand. Even the American photographer stops snapping to have a listen. He holds a note, but more importantly he holds an audience, beaming at them as they hang on every word … before disappearing back into the crowd.

I find him at the bar. 'How old do you think I am?' he asks. 'Erm … 67?' 'I'm 70!' he announces, triumphantly. What is it with these people and age? I buy him a pint (the first law of being the audience at a session is buy the band a drink) and ask his name. 'I'm Ol' McDermott,' he says with an impossibly mischievous grin. 'What's your first name?' 'Ol' McDermott.' 'Yeah, but what's your first name?' 'Ol'.'

In ten minutes flat, he tells me his life story. He was a chef by trade. Spent much of his working life cooking at the Irish language school in Ring, but always loved to sing and picked up a load of songs on the way. He lives just outside Dungarvan, and is a regular at Beann A'Leanna – and most of the other music pubs in the area. A friend picks him up and drops him home afterwards, except for the other day when his friend couldn't make it and somebody else dropped him home. Trouble was this other guy wasn't his regular lift and dropped him on the wrong side of the road. As he crossed the road to his house a car mowed him down. That's why he's got the walking stick now.

'You think I'm a good singer?' says Ol' McDermott, his face getting redder and rounder by the second. I do, Ol', I do think you're a good singer.

His beam widens. 'Did ye say you're from England?' I did. 'Do they like good singers in England?' Oh they do, Ol', they do.

'Do they have good singers in England?' One or two, Ol', but none as good as you. That beam again. 'I think I should go to England.'

You should do that, Ol ... 'I'll do that ... I'll go to England and teach them all how to sing.' You do that, Ol'.

'I'll stay at your house ...'

Ol', I'll put the kettle on ...

Chapter three

RING, LIAM, GOATSKIN & THE GREAT
HURLING MYSTERY

'Wanna come upstairs and see my bodhran ... ?'
Now there's an offer you don't get every day ...
Naturally, I say yes. But then we *are* in a pub. It's always
hard to say 'No' in a pub. I have the hangover to prove it.

We haven't travelled far from Dungarvan. Okay, it's a fair cop, we
haven't travelled *anywhere* from Dungarvan. Yep, still here. Loved the
place so much we stayed another night. Just ... you know ... hanging
out looking for Tour de France stragglers. We'd asked where the craic
was and all signs had pointed to Ring, just a few miles up the road.
There's this pub in Ring, they'd said. Mooney's. It's Session City in
there, they'd said, and off we went.

Ring, or Ann Rinn to give it its proper name, does have a particular magic. It's Waterford's primary Gaeltacht Irish-speaking area –
introduced by the Deise tribe of Celts – with steep, narrow, bendy
swooping roads and tantalising glimpses of sumptuous scenery gradually giving way to an alluring dollop of ocean. Mooney's, an
imposing ranch-style bar, is perched impressively on the crest of a hill,
but somehow the promise of what might be further up the road drags
you on. More winding road, a modest supermarket of sorts, a smattering of B&Bs and you're curving round Dungarvan Harbour into
Helvick Head. A few boats, some random artefacts of a fishing
community, a smattering of shrewd houses hiding in the undergrowth, seabirds making swift, expertly pinpointed dives into the
water to emerge with something small and wriggling and a wind that
cuts you in two. On this day at least Helvick Head is a place for salu-
tary contemplation. Dangle your legs over the harbour wall, watch the
world stand still and elect to change your life. Decide to abandon the
vacuous high life and become a traffic warden. Decide to do something to benefit mankind and *kill* a traffic warden. Decide to sit here

for the next two weeks watching those seabirds – 'Oh, they'll be the *gannets*' I'm told later – practising dive-bombing the sea. Decide to sit here for two weeks training the gannets to dive-bomb traffic wardens. This, you feel, could indeed be a landmark life-changing moment that you will remember forever. Ten minutes later you've got acute hypothermia and can't feel your knees, you're so cold. Abort, abort. The gannets and traffic wardens can breathe more easily – for *now* – and Plan B is invoked. Go to Mooney's and get trollied. It's the only sensible option, frankly.

Mooney's *is* a glorious pub. Spacious, full of interesting alcoves and cackling guys bear-hugging one another. It does great walls. No room for pool tables, jukeboxes or pinball machines here; every inch is accounted for. Ancient road signs directing you to Gort and Kinvara elbow each other unceremoniously as they jostle for primary space with glamorous old tobacco advertisements from a more innocent age. One particularly eye-catching sign offers directions to Ring Health Centre. But a warning: follow it and you end up in the ladies' loo. There's an array of old Guinness posters of varying vintage, a campaign poster from a different century urging you to vote Sinn Fein candidate Seumas O'Cuillin and, most intriguingly, a framed programme from the 1899 All-Ireland Hurling Final programme. I look at it intently. This, I fondly imagine, marks a famous Waterford victory. Maybe there were a couple of Ring lads playing (or would they be banned for being Ringers?). On closer inspection, though, the match doesn't involve Waterford at all; it's between Tipperary and Wexford.

In time I become obsessed by this match. See, the records show that even though Tipperary held a resounding lead and were ultimately awarded the match, it was never finished. What could possibly have happened in 1899 to stop a vital hurling final? From the records it looks like Tipperary won every hurling title going in the late nineteenth century and all manner of ugly conspiracy theories begin to surface. Far from being a showcase of the cream of the county, the Tipperary team was represented by single parish and in 1899 this was Moycarkey. And when I say a single parish, it was more like a single village. And when I say a single village, it was more like a single pub: The Horse & Jockey. The story goes that long, long ago a horse lived there. With a jockey. The pair of them were so chuffed about this that they stuck a sign outside at the crossroads saying 'Horse & Jockey', in case anyone who happened to be passing suddenly felt the urge to engage the services of a horse and jockey. An inn was built there and they called it Horse & Jockey. It served stagecoach travellers and, in the 1790s, regularly served pints to one of Ireland's greatest heroes, Theobald Wolfe Tone, whose Society of United Irishmen held meetings there. After colluding with the French to support an Irish rebellion against the British government in 1798 he was tried for treason and sentenced to death, but committed suicide before the sentence could be carried out. A village emerged around the pub at the crossroads and that was called Horse & Jockey too. No tin-pot village either, not even in the 1890s. It had a sweet little hump-back bridge, a couple of threshing mills, a tailor, a cobbler and a post office … and it even had a railway station on the Thurles-Clonmel line. Even so, it was still a remarkable achievement by the Horse & Jockey boys to make it to the All-Ireland. They had to settle some fierce local rivalries en route, blowing away the likes of Drombane, Golden and Two-Mile-Borris to take the county crown; and then destroyed Clare in the Munster final. Then and only then did they make the trek to the All-Ireland final at Jones Road (now Croke Park) in big bad Dublin to take on the rascals from Wexford (who, knowing them, had probably smuggled a couple of giant Poles into their squad). As history shows, they triumphantly returned with the booty – a set of gold medals worth £25 – and you fondly imagine never had to buy a pint in the Horse & Jockey ever again. The village is still there in the north-east of Tipperary, just a few miles from Thurles, hugely proud of the team that brought it national fame and honour in 1899. Sadly, the railway station and the old hump-back bridge were demolished in the 1960s, but the inn remains in all its glory. They had quite a hooley there in 1999 to mark the centenary of the village's greatest triumph.

A monument was unveiled by two sons of the members of that victorious 1899 team, there was a pipe band, a special mass, loads of speeches … and a few ales. *'After the first 15 minutes the result was never in doubt,'* crows the plaque at Horse & Jockey. *'The victory exemplified their love of the ancient game of hurling and the unique sporting tradition of this locality. Their achievement challenges the youth of every generation to emulate them.'* Which is nice. What isn't explained is why it also says that the 1899 All-Ireland final was held on March 24, *1901*. They wouldn't have had a luxury team coach in those days and they might have taken the scenic route, but did it really take them *two years* to get to Dublin for the final? And what also wasn't mentioned at those centenary celebrations, even in hushed tones, was *what happened to Wexford* that day? Why didn't they finish the match? Did someone knobble their Quaker Oats on the morning of the game? Or maybe a plant in the Wexford team stuck some industrial chewing gum on all their hurling sticks, sorry *hurleys*? And perish the thought, but is it conceivable that they took a bung? I mean, I've been studying the history of those All-Ireland games, and there have been some highly peculiar occurrences along the way. The official reason given for the cancellation of the 1888 All-Ireland is 'the Gaelic invasion of the US'. You never see anything about *that* in the history books, do you? They did play the final in 1890 but the result stinks to high heaven. Wexford were narrowly beating Cork, but the Cork boys refused to play any more and walked off, claiming Wexford were using 'excessively rough play'. Aww, the poor wee lambs. Yet Cork – presumably represented that year by Diddums United – were awarded the title. Poor Wexford – hard but fair, I'd say – missed out again the following year in a battle royal with Kerry after the rules were changed, teams were reduced to 17-a-side, the points system was altered and half an hour extra time was added. If I was from Wexford I'd be screeching about conspiracy theories by now.

More mysteries followed in 1892 when Dublin walked off the pitch to concede their final against the whingers from Cork ten minutes before the end when there was only one goal in it. Were they trying Cork's own tactic, used so successfully against Wexford a couple of years earlier, crying that those rough Cork boys were being beastly and they were taking their ball and going home. Maybe they were frightened of their mams' reaction of if they were late home for their tea. 'Oh you're not going off to play that silly hurling again, are ye? Okay, I'll let ye go, but don't get yer shirt dirty and if yer late for yer tea I'll wrap that silly stick round yer neck!' More likely those big time johnnies from Dublin just *couldn't be arsed* to play any more.

The mysteries go on and on. In 1911 Limerick refused to play Kilkenny due to the state of the pitch and were replaced by Tipp. And in 1900, the year after Horse & Jockey's famous victory, Tipperary – by now represented by Two-Mile-Borris because H&J were presumably still celebrating last year's win – again won the title, taking apart Galway. But before being declared All-Ireland champions they had to play one more deciding match … against London! *London*? Now I'm no historian but I'm pretty damn sure London has never been in Ireland. Did the powers that be resent Tipp's dominance so much they brought in a team of cockneys to sort them out? You can well imagine the reaction of the London lads when invited to participate in this particular shebang. 'So this game … what ya call it? *Whoring*? So it's like a cross between footie, egg-chasing and hockey? And you get to wave sticks and whack balls at a bunch of Paddies? And drink Dublin dry afterwards? I'll have *summ-a-that*!' In the event they returned to the smoke with their hurleys between their legs, after Tipp teased them a bit, let them have the lead, and then came storming back with two goals in the last six minutes to defend the honour of the Gaels.

So yeah, I'd say it's reasonable to ask questions about that 1899 final and why Wexford didn't complete the match. In Mooney's they don't seem overly concerned about this possible stain on the proud name of hurling. But I do find one guy who seems to know what he's talking about. So I ask the question: Hurling. It's crooked, isn't it? 'What?' Come on, you can tell me ... it's bent. 'You're drunk!' Well, that's as maybe, but Tipperary played London in the 1900 final, what's *that* all about? 'Ah ...' he says, warming to the subject, 'that's Sam Maguire.' And he tells the story of one of Ireland's greatest sporting legends.

Sam Maguire was a Cork Protestant who emigrated to London in 1899 with his brothers, worked for the Post Office and was instrumental in setting up London's Gaelic Athletic Association. He led the London team to compete for the All-Irelands in four consecutive years – beating Cork in 1901 – and was also a revered patriot. He became close friends with Michael Collins and was a big player in the Irish republican movement in London; he returned to England in 1923 and died of TB four years later at the age of 48. The major Gaelic football trophy awarded in his name the following year remains the sport's ultimate accolade and there's even a Sam Maguire statue at his home town, Dunmanway.

Okay, that's all well and good, but why *did* Wexford withdraw from the field of play in that mysterious 1899 final with Tipperary? He muses for a second, clearly wondering if, after grappling with this dark and deadly secret for over a century, the time was now right to reveal the truth about dirty deeds off the pitch. Were they bribed? Knobbled? *Threatened*? 'I think you'll find,' he eventually says gravely, 'they were knackered.' *Knackered*? 'Yeah, knackered. See, they were getting their arses kicked and they just couldn't take any more. Just threw in the towel and said they'd had enough.' What? 'Well, they'd probably all got pissed up in Dublin the night before and had bad hangovers ...'

I make my excuses and gaze intently at other items on the Mooney's wonderwall. Comical old metal signs promoting Garry Owen plugs and Ritchie's fertilisers; random newspaper clippings dating back to 1866; a picture of Jonjo O'Neill winning the 1986 Cheltenham Gold Cup on Dawn Run; a battery of black and white photographs of old-time musicians and one lovely shot of Planxty where they all look about 12 years of age. I could spend all night in here gazing at these walls. In fact, I do spend all night in here gazing at these walls. 'Any music in here tonight, then?' I ask the barmaid. 'Well now,' she says pleasantly. 'There might be and there might not be.' Okay, thanks. 'No problem. You just never know, y'see ... there is nothing planned, but I'd say there might be a bit of craic later on ...'

There is certainly an air of anticipation and even celebration in the air as the pub fills up with a surprisingly young clientele and the pints flow. By midnight a trio has gathered in one of the alcoves with a banjo and two guitars to plunk out mostly American pieces like 'Singing The Blues' and 'Duelling Banjos'. They appear cheery enough but only about four people are listening. As it's already midnight we take a final, longing look around the walls and start the steep, dark climb back up the hill to our B&B and a chat about boxing with a landlord with a broken wrist. Best not ask how he did it. He used to be a boxing judge. Won an award for being the most consistent boxing judge at the 1988 Seoul Olympics, he says proudly. Wasn't Seoul the Olympics where there was all that fuss about judging at the boxing after a South Korean was awarded a fight on points against an American he didn't lay a glove on in the entire fight? 'So, what would you like for breakfast?'

The next day it's back to Dungarvan. Town Square. A pub they call *The Local*. And my new chum Donnchadh Gough offering me upstairs to see his bodhran. He leads me through the pub, but it turns out to be a never-ending journey. The pub is full and everybody in there is Donnchadh's best mate, keen to hear the latest adventures of Danu, the fine young traditional band with whom he beats his bodhran (he also plays uilleann pipes with Danu but sadly isn't offering to show me those). 'Must be great living above a pub,' I say as he bear-hugs a long-lost drinking buddy and concludes some unlikely anecdote involving a raucous bunch of Spaniards. 'Oh, I'm used to it,' he says, 'I was brought up in a pub. It's a great pub too. It's in Ring ... it's called Mooney's ...' *Mooney's?* 'Yeah. The family are still there. It's great for the music. We've some great sessions there. Jeez, we had a great session last night. Everyone was in ... what a night we had.' *Last* night? 'Yeah, it was wild!' In *Mooney's?* 'Yeah Mooney's, up at Ring. It was crazy.' What time did you start? 'Oh, I dunno. Late. After midnight ...' Oh. 'You should have been there, you'd have had such a good time. It was a great session all right. Shame you missed it ...' Yeah, isn't it just ...

I didn't like to tell him I *was* there, fretting about the highly dubious result in the 1899 All-Ireland hurling championship, listening to a trio desultorily playing American country songs. But I sneaked out, didn't I, to talk about boxing in the Seoul Olympics. Memo to the brain: nothing of note ever starts in Ireland before midnight. And when the tourists go to bed, the session gets going.

Donnchadh's first bodhran was a present from his neighbour, the singer Liam Clancy, when he was seven. 'I just got a notion for the music,' he says. 'One morning I was at home and there was the first Planxty album sitting on the record player and that did it for me.' You and me both, Donnchadh, you and me both … Almost impossible, in any case, to avoid traditional music in a pub like Mooney's, with its regular sessions and a trail of great musicians dropping by. Most of his family sang anyway and without really remembering how and why, he got sucked into shyly playing along when renowned visitors like Liam Clancy, Finbar Furey and Mary Bergin came along to play.

'I'd join in but you wouldn't hear me over a sheet of newspaper. I was so quiet, I never made a racket. My mum and dad had hundreds of records. The Bothy Band, Planxty, De Dannan, all that great stuff and Ring has a famous song tradition. There are a lot of singers from Ring and there was always a bit of a session going on at the pub, like. On Saturday nights we'd have great sessions. Mickey Dalton would come down and so on …' Mickey Dalton? My mate Mick? Me and Mick were only putting the world to rights at Beann A'Leanna's t'other night … do you know how old he is? 'Er …' 'He's 68! You wouldn't think it, would you?' 'Well, he's a great box player all right. But I haven't played tunes with him in a long time …'

I ask who his hero is as a bodhran player and he leaps in the air and launches himself at the sound system. 'I'll SHOW you … this is MY HERO!' He plays me an album by the brilliant tin whistle player Mary Bergin, accompanied by Alec Finn on bouzouki and Johnny 'Ringo' McDonagh on bodhran. 'I had this record and played along with it eight hours a day,' he gabbles. 'I had it on tape, vinyl and CD … it's lovely. Listen to that playing, it's so simple,' he says, grinning at McDonagh's gently lilting style. 'You can't beat it. It's so tasty and effective. It's the way the bodhran *should* be played and he was the first man to play it like that. But you know … I don't think kids listen to that stuff now. I was in Milltown Malbay this year and I couldn't believe it … all these kids beating the liberty out of the music. They're not listening to the music at all. Seamus Ennis said the best way to play bodhran is with *a pen knife*. And you know something? I tell you, he's *dead right*.'

Donnchadh is a big bloke. You don't expect it. I mean, bodhrans are small, round and cuddly and it does seem a bit odd to find such a huge geezer beating away on such a small object. The average bodhran is 18 inches in diameter but hey, size doesn't matter and you'd be amazed how many of the top bodhran players are big chaps. Tommy Hayes from Limerick. Tommy's a *sturdy* sort of chap. He does things on the bodhran you just wouldn't *believe*. They'd be dancing on the tables howling at the Moon when Tommy launched into one of his spectacular bodhran solos in his days with the band Stockton's Wing. Off he'd go, twirling both ends of his tipper (oo-er, missus!) o'er the skin, up and along the rim, working the crowd into a rhythmic frenzy.

They'd usually had a drink, mind, but Tommy can work an audience like no one else. And let's not even go near the unmentionable tricks he can play with a jew's harp, a couple of bones and a pair of spoons … Tommy, original percussionist with *Riverdance,* also did extraordinary things with the jazz music of John Coltrane. But not in *Riverdance.* John Coltrane wasn't in *Riverdance.*

Then there's Gino Lupari. I'm not saying he's big but he makes Giant Haystacks look like a privet hedge. You certainly wouldn't be advised to offer him outside for a sumo wrestle. A bit of a character, Gino. A bodhran player from Derry, he came to fame in the early nineties with the excellent Four Men And A Dog. Great name, but bands with great names are usually rubbish. I always wanted to see this band called Stanley Accrington & Third Division North but never did because with such a great name they were bound to be awful. Mind you, Half Man Half Biscuit weren't bad. That song about Dukla Prague's Away Kit was magnificent. And Four Men And A Dog not only had a good name, they were pretty hot on album titles too. Their first was called *Barking Mad.* Geddit? It won awards … and not just for being a good title. On stage you couldn't take your eyes off Gino Lupari. He had a habit of sticking his tongue out when he played bodhran. Amazing sight. The longest tongue in the history of tongues. It's probably in the records in some Guinness Book Of Tongues with pictures on loads of websites for tongue fetishists. A great bodhran player, charismatic front man, incorrigible joke teller, decent enough singer and even an occasional rapper. He was officially elected to the brotherhood of bodhran royalty when he started performing 'Wrap It Up', written by journalist Neil Johnston and the wonderful Tyrone guitarist Arty McGlynn. It's Gino's anthem. It could be the anthem of all bodhran players.

> 'At the pub and at the party
> I'm the session's heart and soul
> Hey it's me who puts the backbone
> Into Irish rock'n'roll
> You can keep your fiddle player
> Your banjo-picking man
> But the man who minds the goatskin
> Is the leader of the band …

> 'I'm the star of syncopation, I'm the statesman of the art
> Watch the dancers how they dig it
> They say who's the heavy dude?
> He's no moron on the bodhran, he's our Gino be goode!

So I'm giving you the message and I've got it right perhaps
The show is never over
'Til the fat man raps ...'

Quality.

So, the moral of this is if you want to play the bodhran, you have to eat all the pies.

Then again Kevin Conneff, bodhran player with The Chieftains ... there's nothing of him. And what of Ringo McDonagh, perhaps the most famous bodhran player in the land? He's spent many years spectacularly flexing his wrists with De Dannan and Arcady and is Ireland's celebrity bodhran player of choice, once played on a Phil Lynott record and strutted his stuff around the Europe's swankiest concert halls in Mike Oldfield's band. Mike Oldfield. Yeah, you remember him. Richard Branson's mate. *Tubular Bells. The Exorcist?* Remember the clinkety music playing when that little girl's head spins round and round and she starts vomiting green gunge everywhere? That was *Tubular Bells* by Mike Oldfield. Plenty have said his music made them feel like vomiting too. When Oldfield went on the road and wanted rhythm-with-a-difference, who did he call? Johnny 'Ringo' McDonagh. The very tiny Ringo McDonagh. Thin-as-a-pencil Ringo McDonagh. Ringo bought his first bodhran off some bloke in the street for ten bob and developed a revolutionary 'rimshot' technique playing along with that well-known Irish song, 'Ruby Don't Take Your Love To Town'. His mentor was Peadar Mercier, The Chieftains' bodhran player before Kevin Conneff. Peadar once told Ringo the bodhran represented the heartbeat in a mother's womb and he hasn't stopped playing since.

And yet the bodhran often gets a bad name in Irish traditional circles. Session musicians are full of stories about the curse of the bodhran. The poor bodhran player needs a tough skin. In fact he needs *two* tough skins. One for the bodhran, one for himself. You can't move in Irish music circles for cheap jokes about bodhran players. Stupid, they are. You really wouldn't want to hear them. Oh, okay then ...

'What do you call someone who hangs around with Irish musicians?'

'A bodhran player.'

'What do you call a bodhran player with a mobile phone?'

'An optimist!'

A guy walks into a pub with a plastic bag under his arm. 'What's that?' says the barman.

'Six pounds of Semtex.'

'Thanks be to Jaysus,' says the barman, 'I thought it was a bodhran!'

'What do bodhran players use for birth control?'

'Their personalities!'

'How do you know when there's a bodhran player at your front door?'

'The knocking gets faster and faster.'

'Why do bodhran players find it difficult to enter a room?'

'They never know when to come in.'

'What do you call a bodhran player with a broken wrist?'

'A huge improvement!'

'A fiddle-player in a pub was asked for a euro to help pay for the funeral of a local bodhran player. He said, "here's two euro ... bury another one".'

'Why is a bodhran player like a foot massage?'

'A foot massage bucks up the feet, and a bodhran player ...'

See, not funny are they? There's a whole website of this stuff and if you believe all you hear, mad-eyed bodhran players multiply before your very eyes, their accumulative thud swiftly obliterating fiddles, flutes, boxes and whistles. The sizable brigade of bodhran haters tell you with great glee that the literal translation of the word bodhran is 'deaf'. Then they look at you, knowingly, with the suspicion of a raised eyebrow, waiting for you to nod and mutter something like, 'That says it all really'. Those rascals at New York's *Village Voice* mag once memorably described bodhran playing as 'a goat's membrane being crudely assaulted by a no-brain'. If bodhran players were a nineteenth-century Cork hurling team they'd have thrown a hissy fit and stomped off the pitch long ago.

Yet if there's one instrument that defines the image of Irish music it's the much maligned bodhran. 'The heartbeat of Irish music' they tell you animatedly when they're trying to flog you one. You see them in all the tourist shops with their fancy shamrocks and Celtic designs painted colourfully across the skin. Yet there are a lot of misconceptions, too. The bodhran's origins are long lost in the mists of history. It developed from the humble family sieve, says one popular body of opinion, adapted as a result of the instinctive Celtic need to beat things and make a noise. Others feel it has rather more exotic roots in Africa or Arab traders or the Roman Empire. Others fervently argue it was used in ancient battles to inspire the warriors. One argument is that the word 'bodhran' is a corruption of 'bourine' – short for tambourine and therefore not Celtic at all. Historically similar types of frame drums exist all over the world, from China to Morocco, and Russia to Spain. Lots of theories, few hard facts. Nobody really seems to know where it came from – or indeed where it's going *to* – and its current eminence in traditional music circles does seem to be a relatively recent phenomenon.

Purists snort huffily at the absurdity of that scene in *Titanic* when Kate Winslet goes dashing off to the rough quarters with Leo DiCaprio and stumbles into a ceili in full swing, bodhrans beating as if their lives depend on it. Historically inaccurate, they say. In 1912 – when Cork were again being beaten in an All-Ireland hurling final by some more rough boys, this time from Kilkenny – it would have been unthinkable for a bodhran to be played socially in this way. Then the bodhran was used strictly for ceremonial purposes on one specific day, December 26, for the St Stephens Day rituals, when gangs of 'wrenboys' went from door to door singing the 'Wren Song' (or 'The King') in exchange for food and drink. The story goes that the humble wren, the smallest bird in all the land, had been regarded as 'the king of all birds' and was sacred to the Druids. But, hiding in a gorse bush from his enemies, St Stephen had been betrayed by the song of the wren and his followers had exacted revenge by deafening wrens to death with the beat of a bodhran on St Stephen's Day ever since. Traditionally the wren was hunted and killed on Christmas Day and presented for viewing to the neighbourhood the following day. In time they found less challenging things to do at Christmas, but the old 'wrenboy' custom survived for a while, despite the best efforts of the church to ban what became a thin excuse for a hoolie. But Irish emigrants spontaneously turning to their bodhrans as they grappled with icebergs in 1912 … it just wasn't gonna happen.

In fact, bodhrans didn't come into popular use until the 1960s when the folk revival gained momentum and Sean O'Riada explored folk history in radical fashion, reassessing Irish culture with traditional instruments in an orchestral mode with Ceoltoiri Chualann. O'Riada is one of the great figures of Irish musical history. A big, hard-drinking, quick-witted, well-educated, ambitious Cork man, he worked for Raidió Éireann, studied piano and violin, composed scores for symphony and chamber orchestras and was appointed music director at Dublin's Abbey Theatre. He first expressed his interest in traditional music in his score for the 1959 film *Mise Eire* (*I Am Ireland*), a documentary about the Irish war of independence, which hit a nerve in the national psyche, and established O'Riada's reputation as a trailblazing pioneer. Encouraged, O'Riada experimented with various line-ups and arrangements of traditional music before Ceoltoiri Chualann first took their bow, providing the music for *The Honey Spike* at the Abbey Theatre. Mainly playing harpsichord himself, his revolutionary arrangements of traditional songs and dance tunes had a profound effect on Irish music. A direct antidote to the old ceili bands, all playing in unison, Ceoltoiri Chualann developed complex harmonic arrangements to highlight individual musicians; it moved the goalposts and transported traditional music into a whole new arena. Precious few of the audience who came to see Ceoltoiri Chualann had ever seen a bodhran before and its inclusion with the orchestra – initially played by O'Riada himself and then by bones player Ronnie McShane – aroused much curiosity. Ceoltoiri Chualann's regular radio broadcasts and O'Riada's score for the 1961 movie *The Playboy Of The Western World,* starring Siobhan McKenna, added unprecedented weight to his stature and momentum to the growing interest in Irish traditional music. Not that O'Riada didn't have his critics. He was accused of exploiting traditional music and musicians for the benefit of his own ego and ambitions and Paddy Moloney, the young uillean piper who was his chief lieutenant in Ceoltoiri Chualann, believes much of the group dynamic resulted from the arguments that frequently flared between them. O'Riada's film score for the movies *Mise Eire* and *Playboy Of The Western World* were significant landmarks in a new era of cultural self-awareness that opened the door to the ensuing Irish folk revival.

When O'Riada was diverted by other challenges, Paddy Moloney picked up the baton, reassembled the nucleus of Ceoltoiri Chualann – Martin Fay, Sean Keane, Michel Tubridy and Sean Potts – and sped off with it. The name they selected for the new group was The Chieftains. As they prepared to record their first album, in 1962, Moloney searched high and low for an authentic old-school bodhran player who played with his fingers. His quest eventually took him to Castletown Geoghan, Co. Westmeath, to the door of Davy Fallon, a farmer already well into his seventies. It was a tricky conversation. There was no questioning Fallon's credentials, but there was a problem: Mrs Fallon. Davy's wife loathed the bodhran. With a vengeance. She told Davy he made a fool of himself every time he picked the thing up and refused to allow it in the house. She told him to get rid of it. So heavy of heart, poor old Davy took his beloved bodhran to – as far as Mrs Fallon was concerned – throw it in the dumper. In the best traditions of *Old Shep,* he just couldn't do it and hid the bodhran in the rafters of the farmhouse barn, beyond the view of the fierce Mrs Fallon. So Paddy and Garech Browne, the flam-boyant head of Claddagh Records, drove to Castletown Geoghan, and had a surreptitious whispered conversation with Davy on his doorstep. They waited outside while Davy thought on his feet and concocted a convincing alibi that would satisfy Mrs Fallon and then furtively made their way to the barn to rescue Davy's bodhran. They then found refuge in the house of a neighbour – who was sworn to secrecy – before Davy showed what he could do. 'Ah, he was a lovely old guy, Davy' says Moloney. 'He played with these big stumps of farmer's fingers but he was a great player and the whole thing turned into a session.' Davy subsequently managed to sneak away from his missus long enough to play on that first Chieftains album but it all got a bit trickier when they were invited to play on a television show in Belfast. It would take the mother of all deceptions to keep a trip to Belfast and a TV appearance quiet from the all-seeing eyes of Mrs Fallon and Péadar Mercier was recruited into The Chieftains in Davy's place.

The new sound of Ceoltoiri Chualann – and then The Chieftains – wrested control of traditional music from the prissy parlour rooms and the rigid unison ceili bands and an explosion of Irish folk music groups followed. Every single one of them featured a bodhran. Planxty had Christy Moore. De Dannan had Ringo McDonagh. The Bothy Band had Donal Lunny. Stockton's Wing had Tommy Hayes. The Fureys had Eddie Furey. Even Horslips, an electric band, had Eamonn Carr. And, of course, there were always the three dozen bodhran players hammering away in the corner at any session you care to name. Well, it's not like a set of pipes, which is like a do-it-yourself kit you have to construct every time you want to play and then howls out of tune at every change in the temperature. And it's not like a flute, where your cheeks puff up and you go red in the face and look like a prat when you play. And it's not like an accordion, which rather scarily looks like it's sprouting wings and is about to attack you like Rod Hull's emu on Parky that time. No, the bodhran's a cinch. Americans, Dutch, Norwegians, Japanese, Martians … they all come over to Ireland and go home with their bodhrans which have the shamrocks on to thrill and amaze their neighbours with their mastery of this unique instrument. Because it's so easy to play, *right*?

Hmmm … easy to play, improbably difficult to play *well*. 'If you're learning to play, it's practise, practise, practise,' says Donnchadh Gough back in Dungarvan. 'I tell you it's harder to teach than it is to play. I'm self-taught, which is great, but it means I can't teach anyone else how to play. You go to the States and they get you to do these workshops and they all come in and think you're gonna make them a bodhran genius in about ten minutes. You say something and they go "Oh well, I was looking at a Tommy Hayes video and this is the way he does it," or "Steafan Hannigan doesn't do it like that on his video" and I feel like saying "Why the fuck are you coming along to hear *me* then?' One place there was a guy sitting down with a pen and paper marking me. He had, like, four bodhrans himself and he was trying to tell me how to play! There's good money in teaching but you need patience and I don't have that ... 'specially with people I know that no matter what happens they're never gonna be worth a fuck ...'

There's a wonderful 1980 version of the comic song 'Lanigan's Ball' by The Bards. Chief Bard Diarmuid O'Leary met Christy Moore on the Holyhead ferry one day. They got tanked up together on brandy and Christy taught him 'Lanigan's Ball'. The Bards subsequently had a big Irish hit with it, but not without a significant adaptation featuring Ann O'Sullivan in the role of step-dancing 'Julia' who's sweet-talked into showing off her steps by a silver-tongued O'Leary tempting her with the beats of a bodhran. Or, as he rather seductively, whispers it, 'skin of the goat'. If there was ever a time the bodhran earned its place in modern Irish folklore this was it. It also brought home to everyone the reality of the instrument. It is indeed made from the skin of the goat. Most connoisseurs reckon it should be, at least, though plenty of alternatives have been tried. Donkeys, sheep, calves, greyhounds, horses – and once even a seal – but the makers all agree, nothing touches the goat. The thickness of the skin, durability, the resonance of sound it creates. Ah, but what type of goat? The brains of a generation have applied themselves to this one and Donnachadh Gough gets particularly passionate about it. 'A lot of them get their goatskins from abattoirs in Pakistan,' he says gravely. This is not good then, Donnachadh? 'No, they're bred goats, the skins aren't tough. You don't get a good sound out of them.' So where do you get your skins from, Donnachadh? Now hereby hangs a story. He knows this guy, see. He goes up into the Kerry mountains at the dead of night shooting wild goats and skins them himself. Good ol' goats, see. They've seen a bit of life, toughed it out through hard winters, run up and down a few mountains, survived the odd goat disease. This mystery man deals in nowt but the best goatskin. I'm wondering if I could meet this bloke, maybe accompany him one night on his work. Maybe go up into the mountains with him one night ... Donnachadh looks at me pityingly. 'No chance!' He has a point. I mean, I'm guessing here, but going up into the mountains at dead of night shooting wild goats is probably not entirely legal. Some other time then.

Before you can even think about playing a bodhran, though, you have to learn how to say it. They are very strict on this at Bodhran School. One incorrect syllable and you're drummed out. It's nowt to do with bods. Or bodes. Or boods. Or buds. Or bads. It's BOUGH. As in rhymes with sow, the female pig. Or cow. Pow-wow. Or now. Or row, as in argument. Or wow, as in exclamation of amazement. Add that to RAWN. As in brawn. Sean, as in Connery. Or lawn, as in grassy thing. Or pawn, as in things you flog to raise money, not porn as in dirty books. Bough-rawn, then.

Donnchadh Gough is still playing me Mary Bergin's *Feadog Stain* album, purring at Ringo McDonagh's crisp bodhran accompaniment as he pours the nineteenth cup of tea of the afternoon, talking about his charmed life. 'Being brought up in the pub I knew I'd never have to study that hard, know what I mean? I did a course at RTE and went all over the country with TV camera crews. Great buzz. Nice way to make a living. I never had any real thoughts of being a pro musician. Danu was my first band. Accident really. Donal (Clancy) and Daire (Bracken), Benny (McCarthy) and I met Tom and Eamonn (Doorley) playing at a pub in Dungarvan in 1994. Donal started playing with his dad (Liam Clancy) and Robbie (O'Connell) but the rest of us met up with Tom and Eamonn again at Lorient Festival in France. We recorded some tunes and it went on from there. Luck really ...'

I ask Donnchadh about Liam Clancy. Does he still live in the area? 'Yeah, just up the road from Mooney's ...' Liam is one of the great legends of Irish music. For many years Tommy Makem and the Clancy Brothers were the face of Irish music. For many years they WERE Irish music, synonymous with booming ballads, Aran sweaters and the big chorus songs everyone sings when they're pissed – 'Jug O'Punch', 'Whiskey In The Jar', 'The Holy Ground', 'Wild Rover', 'The Parting Glass', et al. The Clancys and, later, The Dubliners were the international flagship for Irish ballad groups long before anyone else got there. They were the toast of New York, topping the bill at Carnegie Hall on numerous occasions, making top-selling albums, adored by Dylan and the rest of that sixties wave of American folk royalty. On St Patrick's Night in 1961 it is estimated that fifty million people watched their appearance on *The Ed Sullivan Show*. The following day they got an invite to the White House. They even discovered Barbra Streisand. Sort of. She was sleeping on people's floors until she got a spot on one of their shows. So the Clancy Brothers ... we're talking serious fame here.

So how is Liam, Donnchadh? 'Liam, he's great, y'know. You wanna talk to him?' Before I can answer he's on the phone. 'Liam ... how's it going? I got this writer guy here from England. He wants to come and interview you ... I'll put him on ...' Ten minutes later I'm driving back to Ring. Up the hill, round the windy roads, past Mooney's to Liam Clancy's house.

Now I must admit I'm a bit nervous here. Liam is a legend all right after all. But it's more than that. In the true traditions of revolution, those of us fired by the new generation of exciting instrumental bands that arose in the 1970s were programmed to despise what had gone before. And to love Planxty, the Bothy Band, De Dannan, Stockton's

Wing, Horslips, Moving Hearts and all was to hate the Clancy Brothers, Dubliners, Wolfe Tones and that whole generation of ballad groups. *Our* bands had risen to destroy those bands with their simplistic arrangements, crude singing and lowest common denominator populism. Nobody *I* liked would be heard dead yelling 'Fine gal, y'are' and destroying floorboards with the heel of their boots as they pounded out the rhythm. I mean, these people positively encouraged *hand-clapping*! Christy Moore was ready to dive into the audience to sort out anyone who dared to handclap a Planxty rhythm and upset the subtle balance of the band's own rhythmic interplay. *Our* bands had long hair. Those bands wore caps. *Our* bands were young. Those bands were middle-aged. *Our* bands wore tatty jeans and scruffy tee shirts. Those bands wore slacks and Aran sweaters. *Our* bands were instrumentally challenging. Those bands were so basic it was embarrassing.

That was the perception anyway. It was a view totally eradicated years later with the emergence of Shane MacGowan and The Pogues, emerging from the charred carnage of punk rock to embody the raw, emotional spirit of the Clancy Brothers and Dubliners. The Pogues' thing was direct full-on communication with their audience. No frills, no instrumental virtuosity, no subtlety … just old-fashioned choruses rammed down your throat at a rate of knots and a generous helping of those old ballads we'd so reviled to hammer home their affinity. In the course of it you realised that yep, Shane was right. Uncomplicated boozy chorus songs they may be, but these were really good songs. And we'd done the Clancys and Dubliners a great disservice. But not before I'd written a load of guff in different organs slagging them off. Not that I expected Liam to remember or care about anything I'd written about him, and there was a time when the Clancys were regarded as fair game for a bit of sport. 'Four adult jumpers singing about dead fishermen!' was Billy Connolly's description. But musicians are funny. When you dismiss someone's entire career with a few damning smart-arse phrases that sounded great when you tried them out in the pub, you never quite know what the reaction will be.

I still occasionally bump into people at the most unlikely places - acid house raves, hip hop gigs, clubbing nights, Albanian rock festivals, that sort of thing - who approach waving crumpled bits of print demanding an explanation for some mauling I'd given their band in a long defunct magazine in 1979. Unsavoury stories would invariably emerge. My review had hit so hard they'd hoofed it down to Helvick Head to contemplate the meaning of life and ended up jacking in music and becoming traffic wardens instead. Their families couldn't stand the shame inflicted by my caustic pen and had left home and changed their names.

Suitably enraged, the wounded party had come searching for me with a blow-torch but had been headed off at the pass and incarcerated in a mental asylum, where they'd been rotting in abject misery for the last 20 years. The only thing they could do there was sit and plot hideous revenge. The cunning plan, they told me with a hollow laugh, was to convince the doctors they were finally safe enough to be allowed to resume their place in society. Free at last, they'd tracked me down and, clutching the offending review, they'd smile in a Jack Nicholson sort of way, and ask if we could go somewhere to talk…

So yeah, I'm a tad nervous walking up Liam Clancy's long drive …

The door is open. Which is a bit scary. I mean, I'm not even certain I'm in the right place, but, encouraged by a glimpse of a guitar within, I creep inside, half expecting the door to slam behind me and a disembodied voice to say 'Glad you could make it, Mr Irwin, I've been expecting you …' Paranoid? Moi?

In fact, Liam is as nice as pie. He sits me down, furnishes me with coffee and tells me I'm in the first solar house in Ireland. It was about twenty years ago and he'd had enough of America, basically. 'Oil prices were going through the roof, things were looking very dicey on the international scene, so I came here where I can be self-sufficient. It gets away from the need for Sellafield. I can grow my own vegetables, put some fish in the pool if need be so I'll have fresh food and the world can kiss my arse.'

One of life's natural storytellers, he's swiftly into anecdote mode. 'Oh yeah, we had some fun times all right back in the ol' days,' he's saying. 'We did TV shows with all sorts of people. I remember being on one show with Liberace. You know Liberace? He was there, all sparkles and spangles and candelabra and he came over to me and put his hand on my shoulder and … *my flesh just crawled*. And I looked up and there was this incredible smile and those teeth that only Americans have and he said "*Oh mah Gaddd* … your sweaters are jus' sooooo *be-yeewwt-ti-full*. I just wish I'd started out wearing somethin' so … *simple!*"'

Ah yes, the sweaters. You don't track far into the history of Irish music without encountering the sweaters. You don't get *anywhere* into the history of the Clancy Brothers without encountering them. Those big white roll-necked Aran jumpers were so key to the image of the Clancy Brothers – and by proxy all Irish music – that lazy commentators still use it as a catch-all description for ballad singers.

Liam re-tells the story of *those jumpers* with good grace. Tom and Pat Clancy had emigrated to Canada to pursue a career in acting in the late forties. By the early fifties they'd wound up in New York, staging plays at the Cherry Lane Theater in Greenwich Village. Liam, the youngest of the family, followed them to New York in 1955, as did his good friend Tommy Makem. They'd met after Liam, the youngest of eleven children, had hooked up with an extravagant – some said *eccentric* – American called Diane Hamilton, who was in Ireland on a song-collecting mission. Liam didn't know it then, but Hamilton wasn't her real name; she was actually a Guggenheim, one of the wealthiest and most famous families in America. They headed for Keady, in Co. Armagh, the home of Sarah Makem, a traditional singer with a huge repertoire of songs. In fact, one of Sarah's songs, 'As I Roved Out', ended up as the title music in a landmark fifties BBC radio series. Liam and Sarah Makem's son, Tommy Makem, hit it off. They had music in common for one thing. There was always plenty of music back home in the Clancy household in Carrick-on-Suir, Tipperary, just as there was at the Makems' home in the north. But they both also had thespian aspirations – Liam had already directed and starred in a stage version of *Playboy Of The Western World* – and they both headed for America, their heads full of dreams of becoming Hollywood stars. But they were diverted. Reunited with the elder Clancy boys in New York, Liam found himself helping his brother Pat run America's first Irish music label, Tradition Records, funded by the extraordinary Diane Guggenheim. They also ran their own Greenwich Village theater company, Cherry Lane Productions, putting on some ambitious works like *Othello* and Sean O'Casey's *The Plough And The Stars*. Purely as a fund-raising exercise, they hit on the idea of maximising use of the theater by staying on at the end of the productions to stage midnight folk concerts. Somehow out of the mayhem, the legend of the Clancy Brothers & Tommy Makem emerged. Liam has no illusions about their quality. He describes his own guitar playing then as the 'boxing glove method' and cheerfully admits their singing was just plain embarrassing. Yet they made a connection. The concerts became a pivotal haunt for the emergent Greenwich Village folk scene which descended on their concerts in force. Apart from the resolutely teetotal Tommy Makem, they drank plenty and partied hard with their new chums, who included legends and mini-legends like Rambling Jack Elliott, Sonny Terry & Brownie McGhee, Paul Clayton, Phil Ochs, Carolyn Hester, Peter LaFarge, Pete Seeger, Josh White and Bob Dylan. A Bob Dylan quote – 'Liam Clancy is the best ballad singer I ever heard in my life' – appears proudly on the cover of Liam's autobiography *Memoirs Of An Irish Troubadour*, though Liam has the good grace to be slightly embarrassed about this. Then again, Dylan did service his girlfriend Kathy behind his back. 'Oh, we were good friends in the early days, we used to hang out a lot,' he says of Dylan. 'Sometimes we'd stay up all night singing. Even later on. We were all together. There was the Rolling Stones, George Harrison, Eric Clapton and Dylan. We put a guitar in Bob's hand and he said "Oh man, I don't do that any more". I said "Don't come that with me, let's have a song!" So he started to play something but he couldn't remember the words, so Ronnie Wood takes over and starts up playing "Rosin The Bow" and we were all there singing it with him. Which proves these rock stars are all the same. Give them a few beers and all they want to do is sing an Irish folk song.'

The Clancy Brothers got a manager, started touring the States, opened for Lenny Bruce and became the toast of New York. But back home in Carrick-on-Suir, Tipperary, Mrs Clancy was worried about the well-being of her sons across the Atlantic. Especially with it being winter. She knitted three cream Aran jumpers for her boys. Then she thoughtfully knitted another one for Tommy Makem 'cos she thought he might feel the cold too. She posted them off to New York and they were gratefully received. It *was* cold at nights, especially when they played their draughty midnight gigs and they all ended up wearing the jumpers on stage. Their manager wasn't slow to recognise the benefits of a homely image represented by four Irish lads wearing cosy jumpers knitted by their mam and suggested it might be an idea to wear those matching jumpers on *The Ed Sullivan Show*. That was how every piss-take of an Irish folksinger for the next thirty years involved an Aran jumper. Not that Liam has any complaints. The jumpers were a key selling point … so much so that at the height of their fame they were offered a million-dollar advance for the franchise of an American company to manufacture Aran jumpers in their name. They refused. Er … why?

'Of course it was a temptation. It was a huge amount of money and it was a million just as an advance. We talked about it long and hard but were we going to turn on the people of Connemara and Kerry who made these things? Were we going into *competition* with them? We just couldn't do it, it wouldn't have been right. And I'm very proud now that we didn't do it.'

He's philosophical about the ridicule heaped on the Clancy Brothers by idiots like me. 'We were young, ebullient and full of excitement and had a ballsy way of singing which became very popular. But there were a lot of imitators and it became a cliché and in the end it became a bit of a joke. All these bands with three chords belting out drinking songs in a pub. We did resent it at first, then we just laughed.' You didn't feel usurped by the likes of Planxty and all the instrumental bands who came up in the seventies and maybe contributed to your decline? 'Not at all. I had great pride in them. They were creating a musical tapestry beyond anything I'd heard. Irish music hasn't evolved historically the way other countries had done because, well, a lot of it was because of the British government and oppression. So we had to try and catch up. Sean O'Riada was the father of that type of music and he wrote for an orchestra. Nobody had ever done that before. And suddenly you had young groups who weren't classically trained playing traditional music with no dots. I have no problem with the way Irish music has evolved. If things don't evolve they stagnate and become museum pieces and you might as well stuff them. Songs are ghosts out there in the ether waiting ...

'I came back to Ireland from America in 1963 and the fleadh ceoils had started and the musicianship in the country was amazing. Girls could go into bars for the first time and it was free love, free music. The oppression that had characterised Ireland had lifted, the shackles were off. And it was great fun. I remember touring here and waking up in my hotel and all the housemaids were round the bed going "'Tis, 'tisn't, 'tis, 'tisn't!" And playing the Ulster Hall in Belfast trying to get through the crowds to the limo and I suddenly feel a jab in my arse and I turn around and there's a teenage girl with a safety pin and my blood on it! And she's looking at it saying "Is that *real*?"

'No, I never had any resentment about any of the younger bands. I love the instrumental side of Irish music ... I see it as holding on to a great tradition. I still love a great night in the pub, a good session with good musicians with their heads down and the spark is jumping out of them. Even though they're playing for themselves and nobody else, it's still very, very exciting. In this country we have a very healthy, thriving tradition.'

Somebody at Mooney's had told me this bizarre story that Liam Clancy was planning to make a record and go on tour with fellow Tipperary chorus merchant, and the king of all reprobates, Shane MacGowan. I'd assumed it was the drink talking. The notion of the rabble-rousing old punk rocker and the dignified veteran of the Aran jumper sharing a stage just seemed too preposterous to mention. But I mention it anyway. Liam instantly starts chortling. But he's not laughing at the absurdity of the idea, but the memory of the meeting they'd had to discuss it ...

The way he tells it, the idea came from Terry Woods, Shane's old Pogues colleague, who suggested that he, MacGowan, Liam and Dubliners singer Ronnie Drew might get something together. A meeting was arranged at Liam's house ... 'Jeez, that was amazing.

Shane sat there for about four hours with this bottle of White Russian. I came into the room and he was chopping out a line. He looked up at me like a little child caught in the act, then he said "Leeeemmm … yewww wanna try some MAAARCHING POWDER?" The thing is Ronnie, Terry and I … none of us drink. Or do *anything* like that …

'Then he starts having a go at me. "Leem, Leem, yew never recorded my song, Leem? Why didn't you record my song?" "What song was that, Shane?" " 'Wild Majestic Shannon'. I fucking wrote it fer yew!" I told him I couldn't understand a word of it because it was so fast. "Okay," he says, "I'll write it out for you, Leeem." So he starts writing. Half an hour later he's got half a line written down and he passes it to me and says, "Is that okay, or do you want the rest of it?". Actually I do intend to record it. I love the song, but I did tell him there's one change I'll have to make, I don't like the word "babe" in a song. It sticks in my craw. Shane says, "All right, Leeem!" '

So will the four of you do anything together? 'Oh, I dunno. It's trying to fit it in, that's the problem.' If you did go on the road together, what would you call yourselves?

'We'll be a boy band. We'll call ourselves *The Marching Powder Boys!*'

Driving away from Liam's later I remember a question I'd meant to ask. *Where is Tommy Peoples?* Part of the purpose of this pilgrimage is to track down Tommy, a personal hero and undisputed god of the fiddle who'd been keeping his head down for 20 years. To get anywhere near the heart of Irish music and understand this whole craic thing it seems imperative to find him.

In truth the search isn't going well. Partly because I'm having so much fun I keep forgetting I'm looking for him. But when in doubt and all that, so another pint in Mooney's it is then. This bar is clearly the font of all knowledge. They will know in here, for sure, how to find Tommy Peoples. For once, though, Mooney's is deserted. Just some old guy supping quietly in one corner of the wall of fame. I sidle up and ask him if he knows Tommy Peoples and where I might find him.

He looks at me suspiciously. 'Tommy Peoples, you say?' I nod encouragingly. 'Tommy Peoples…' he muses, staring at the wall…' Now where have I heard that name…' I start to offer clues but he's not listening. 'I'd say he's a Tipp man.' No, he's… 'I'm sure he's a Tipp man. One of that hurling team. Didn't he play in that 1899 all-Ireland final? Y'know, the one when Wexford got knackered and walked off. If you're looking for Tommy Peoples son, I'd say you need to head for Tipperary.'

Never argue with a confident man, so Tipp it is. After all, it's not a long way to Tipperary…

Chapter four

TIPPERARY, KILKENNY & GALWAY: WE'LL ALWAYS HAVE WINKLES

An essential thing to do when you're driving through Ireland is to sort out the soundtrack. The people, the countryside, the music … they are one and the same, and when you have those three ingredients in the same place at the same time you get somewhere close to the soul of the nation. If it's the dramatic, rugged cliffs of Donegal, then you need to be playing Tommy Peoples at his bow-scraping best. If it's the rolling hills of Clare, you might go for the lyrical fiddle work of Martin Hayes. If it's Galway, you need to be wallowing in the sumptuous voice of Dolores Keane. If it's Cork, then you could do a lot worse than Jimmy Crowley, with that mischievous accent, singing about the devil's drink, Johnny Jump-Up cider, and the devil's game, pool. And if you're stuck between an armada of lorries trying to negotiate the streets of a brash city like Limerick, then just swallow your pride, stick on The Dubliners and have a good bellow, 'Wild Rover' and all.

So I point the car at Tipperary and listen to that popular traditional Irish band Bob Marley & The Wailers. Sod it, Muhammad Ali was an Irishman, so I reckon Bob was too. Well, so legend has it. His grandmother was called Birdie Grady, and her dad Abe had emigrated from Ireland. That's what my mate in Mooney's reckons, and I'd trust him with my life.

Then, just at the point I decide I want 'No Woman No Cry' played at my funeral (it could be quite soon, if I spend too many more nights in Mooney's), a sign saying 'Mahon Falls' suddenly drags me off the beaten track into the dark Comeragh Mountains. It's cold and a bit spooky and there's a lake, Crotty, that's apparently named after a highwayman. How can you resist a country that names lakes after highwaymen, eh? I'm wondering about embarking on an assault on the nearest mountain peak when two tweed-laden hikers come bounding over. 'What ho! Lovely morning, eh?' barks the guy, with exaggerated cheeriness, in a stage Home Counties voice. It's not a lovely morning at all. It's cold enough to freeze your knackers off and it's starting to drizzle and I have this overwhelming urge to rip his ridiculous necker-chief off, feed it to the waterfall, drop my pants and tell him to kiss my arse. Instead, I say 'Yes, lovely morning' and slope back to the car.

My first stop today is Carrick-on-Suir, home of the Clancy Brothers and 'host town to Slovakia'. Liam Clancy had talked eloquently of Carrick and its bloody history, notably at the hands of a marauding Cromwell, and the later terrors inflicted by the Black and Tans, not to mention the Christian Brothers. As a kid Liam played in the ruins of the Norman castle, observing the drunks, oddballs and misfits who populated the town. They reckon Anne Boleyn was born here too but every other town you visit in Ireland claims that, so don't put it in your history essays, just in case.

Today all is quiet in Carrick. Well, more like *comatose*. Still, it's good to be in Tipperary. I had a premeditated plan for arrival in the county, which would double as an interesting survey and show me up as an odious smart-ass. So I bound up to a lady juggling with onions outside a greengrocer's and, rather fetchingly, I feel, start to sing 'It's a Long Way to Tipperary'. She looks at me, aghast.

'Who wrote that song?' I inquire cheerily. There's panic in her eyes, and I can see her thinking 'Nutter in the street, why do I always get the nutter in the street?' She continues to stare at me so I give her another burst of the chorus as encouragement. 'Yes, I've heard that song before,' she says cautiously. 'Ah, but do you know who wrote it?' She shakes her head with the firmness of one who doesn't know or care. I tell her anyway. Jack Judge, a music-hall performer from Oldbury in the English Midlands, wrote 'It's a Long Way To Tipperary' in 1912. 'Oh, interesting …' she says, edging away.

But I won't be deterred, and tell the onion lady the story of Jack Judge and how he was in a pub shouting the odds when some bloke from Birmingham bet him five bob he couldn't write a song in a day and perform it on stage in Stalybridge the following night. So the next day, Jack sat down for a lunchtime pint at the New Market Inn in Stalybridge, knocked out 'It's a Long Way to Tipperary', dragged in a mate to write the musical score, sang it that night at the Grand Theatre, and went home five bob richer.

The song was later popularised by the Australian music-hall star Florrie Forde – the Vera Lynn of her day – and subsequently adopted as a theme tune by the mainly Irish 7th Battalion of the Connacht Rangers Regiment. At the outset of the Great War the British Army marched into battle singing Jack Judge's song-in-a-day. 'That's nice,' says my clearly impressed new friend. But do you wanna know the weirdest thing of all? 'Erm ... okay.'

Jack had never set foot in Tipperary or *anywhere else in Ireland* when he wrote it! I mean, his parents were Irish, but Jack himself didn't really have a clue how far it was to Tipperary. 'Well, he doesn't say where it's a long way *from*, does he? When he says it's a long way to Tipperary, where is he starting from, can you tell me that?' Well, no. To be honest I wasn't expecting supplementary questions. I only know all this anyway because the criminally underrated English singer-songwriter Bill Caddick wrote a brilliant song called 'Writing Of Tipperary' which cleverly knits together the story of Jack Judge with a description of the events leading to the First World War.

'And there's one other thing,' says my newfound conversational companion, bolshie all of a sudden. 'What?' I say, somewhat affronted. 'It's all very interesting all right but this isn't Tipperary.' 'Well, I know that, it's Carrick-on-Suir, but that's *County* Tipperary, right?' 'Well now, there lies a story ...' she says. 'Part of Carrick is in Tipperary right enough, but part of it is in Waterford.' Don't tell me, we're in the bit that's in Waterford. 'We're in the bit that's in Waterford ...'

I head on to the bit that's in Tipperary and relax in Sean Kelly Square. You have to give respect to a place that names its lakes after highwaymen and its squares after cyclists. Sean Kelly was a star of the Tour de France through the 1980s, winning several stages. He obviously could have done with a bit more practice riding up and down The Sweep outside Dungarvan, 'cos while he was hot stuff in the sprints he wasn't much cop in the mountains. Not like Dublin's Stephen Roche. Rochey – as we cycle people like to call him – was a demon in the sprints but on a good day he could skip up mountains too and in 1987 he did what no other Irishman – or Englishman come to that – has ever done: he went and won the Tour de France. Rochey, bless him, now runs cycling camps in Majorca, gives unintelligible commentaries on Eurosport where they talk about wine all the time and – the greatest accolade of all – is the subject of a suitably celebratory Jimmy Crowley ballad.

Still, Sean Kelly has a town square named after him, though as town squares go, it's not enormous. In fact, in a *Who's Who* of Town Squares, it probably wouldn't even merit a footnote. Still, I'm standing on one side of it gazing into a sports shop window festooned with Arsenal shirts when the local drunk wielding an empty bottle of vodka lurches across the street into my path. He sees me jabbering into my dictaphone about Stephen Roche and Sean Kelly and reaches the obvious conclusion.

'Youse the focken' taxman?' 'Er no.' 'Yes y'are. Taxmen always have them pocken' machines to add up the numbers cos youse too pocken brainless to do it in y'head.' 'I'm not a taxman.' 'Why youse got that pocken thing then?' 'I'm looking for singers.' He brightens considerably. 'Oh, pocken singers, is it? Youse looking for pocken singers?' 'Yes, you know any singers?' 'Patsy in the pub, she's a pocken singer. She's a pocken *great* singer. And I'm a singer … I'm a pocken great singer, too, me, I am.' 'You are?' 'Oh yeah, I'm pocken great, ask anyone.' Luckily, there's no one round to ask. Then he makes me an offer I can't refuse. 'Youse wanna hear me sing?'

Oh I do, I do. The guy – he calls himself Carrick Dennis – is reeking of something that smells suspiciously like detergent, his eyes are darting round his head at an alarming rate, he has a manic toothless grin, and is swaying so much I fear the soggy unlit roll-up he's removed from his mouth will at any minute end up embedded in my nostrils. But let's not pre-judge. I still have vivid memories of a similarly unstable hiccupping wino who'd lurched up to me on Wimbledon Station late one night. He'd wobbled around in front of me for a bit blowing intoxicating fumes in my face, steadied himself, wagged a finger at me, removed his cap, gobbed something unspeakable which landed in a green blob at my feet and launched into song. 'Please allow me to introduce myself, I'm a man of wealth and taste, I've been around a long, long year, stolen many a man's soul and faith …' He'd then delivered the most compelling, word-perfect version of 'Sympathy For The Devil' this side of Mick Jagger, including all the 'whoo whoos' and 'oh yeahs'. It was amazing. At the end he bowed extravagantly, returned his cap crookedly to his head and staggered back into the night never to be seen again.

So I'm looking forward to hearing Carrick Dennis, wondering if I'll get a reprise of 'Sympathy For The Devil' or will it be something a little more native? Christy Moore's song about the DTs, maybe? Jimmy Crowley's 'Ballad Of Stephen Roche'? 'Seven Drunken Nights'? 'It's A Long Way To Tipperary'? Or, joy of joys, 'Fields Of Athenry'? But Carrick Dennis has something more cunning up his sleeve. He's planning a little audience participation. 'Have you pocken heard of Elvis pocken Presley?' 'Yep Dennis, I certainly have.' 'You know a song called "In The Ghetto"?' 'On a cold and grey Chicago morn … ? That one, Dennis?' 'Aye, that's the one. We're not far from the ghetto here, y'know,' he cackles. 'It's where I pocken live!' He's chortling at a disturbing decibel level now and grabbing me by the arm dragging me into the centre of Sean Kelly Square. 'C'mon, let's pocken sing In The Pocken Ghetto.' He gives me the vodka bottle to hold, coughs half his lungs up to clear his throat, puts his arm round me for support and we're all set. 'As the snow falls … on a cold and grey Chicago morn …'

My good lady Mrs Colin, who'd been in a nearby store buying essential rations of chocolate, emerges bearing gifts to find her beloved waving a bottle of vodka, wrapped around Carrick Dennis and swaying together in the middle of Sean Kelly Square impersonating the Everly Brothers impersonating Elvis Presley belting out the second verse of 'In The Ghetto' at disturbing-the-peace volume. 'Take a look at you and me, are we too blind to see? Or do we simply turn our heads and walk the other way?'

She tosses a couple of cents in our direction, simply turns her head and walks the other way.

Back at Mooney's, they had recommended a music pub in Carrick called Drowsey Maggie's. We find it a mile or so out of Carrick, brightly decorated in yellow and blue. Inevitably, it's shut. Or it pretends to be. I have visions of a rare ol' session going on inside, full of rampaging fiddles and accordions, and then someone peeks out the window. 'Stop playing! Pull down the shutters! Lock the doors! Not a sound! It's that nutter who was singing "In The Ghetto" with Carrick Dennis in Sean Kelly Square and he's coming this way! Pretend we're not open!'

Luckily, I can take a hint, so it's back on the road again. We head for Cashel, where one of the guidebooks suggested we'd find a bit of sport. I'm not sure how far it is because the Irish have this amusing game they like to play with visitors, randomly switching between miles and kilometres on the road signs just to confuse them, but I strategically replace Bob Marley on the car cassette with The Pogues. It's only right and proper. We are, after all, in Shane MacGowan territory.

Sometimes, late at night and three sheets to the wind, I'll collar whoever is around and wants a bit of an argument into a debate about the nature of genius. Elvis Presley: genius or not genius? Love him to bits, but no way. Surely genius is the manifestation of an acute vision, the ability to go beyond the beyond. He was a great singer, a charismatic personality, a good-looking guy, but essentially Elvis just got lucky. He was in the right place at the right time. If not him it'd have been somebody else. You know … Carl Perkins, or Freddy Garrity, or somebody.

Was Sinatra a genius? He has more of a shout, actually. I was never struck on him personally, but didn't he change the whole nature of vocals when he started fannying around with timing and started singing when he felt like it, making the bands fit in around him? Was that going beyond the beyond, or was he just pissed? Spike Milligan? Yes, oh yes. Miles Davis? Probably. Billy Connolly? Perhaps. Louis

Armstrong? Definitely. Dylan, clearly. Lennon, obviously. McCartney, good lord, no … a gifted but functional tunesmith. And Shane MacGowan: yes, yes, a thousand times yes.

The descriptive qualities and sheer range of Shane's lyricism put him up there with the very finest, even before we begin to analyse his unique ability to knit the inherently romantic and sentimental heritage of Irish song with anger, attitude, danger and all the other things that make him appear like a saloon-bar chancer wading around in a treasure chest of rich music and colourful experiences. Listen to Shane sing 'A Pair Of Brown Eyes'. It has everything … a boozer, a war, a love story … a whole movie unfolds before your eyes. It's a flawed genius, certainly – as Liam Clancy and the rest of the Marching Powder Boys will vouch – but isn't the gene that lures him repeatedly along the precipice also the very thing that fuels his amazing talent? The same self-destructive gene of brilliance, in fact, that also drove Dylan Thomas, Luke Kelly and Brendan Behan. Like them, it may prevent Shane living to a ripe old age, but you'd never really want to see him singing sensible songs with a full set of teeth and a sensible haircut, would you?

Yet I always get howled down when I make these claims about Shane being the greatest songwriter of his generation. Even now, people often think he's a con man. They see the gaps in his teeth, they hear his slow estuary drawl and they discover he went to Westminster School, and they decide he's a charlatan. They assume he's really a spoilt rich kid who assumed the persona of a drunk Irishman to glean credibility as a punk rocker. Probably a teetotaller, they say. Probably never been to Ireland in his life, they say. They say wrong.

Shane spent the first six years of his life living with assorted relatives in a small Co. Tipperary farmhouse owned by his Uncle John. His mother was a model – she once met the great poet Patrick Kavanagh – and she was also a dancer and singer of traditional songs. A lot of the stuff that featured in the early Pogues repertoire came from his childhood. And his dad? ' A drinker and a gambler,' according to Shane. Both parents got jobs in England, but Shane stayed on his Uncle John's farm in Tipperary until it was time to start school. That's when he joined his parents in England and at one point, incredibly, was earmarked for the priesthood. He did indeed go to the ultra-posh Westminster School, but it was a scholarship job and he didn't last long, kicked out after being caught carrying dope.

I first met Shane MacGowan after the split of his punk band the Nipple Erectors, when he'd just formed The Pogues – or Pogue Mahone (famously translated as 'Kiss My Arse') as they were then called. He was working in a record shop just off Tottenham Court

Road in London and I wandered in one day, introduced myself and asked if I could arrange an interview with the band. Shane, who was reading a book at the time, looked blank for a second, then nodded and mumbled something totally incomprehensible. 'Sorry, I didn't catch that.' He mumbled again, even more incomprehensibly. 'Erm ... sorry, Shane. I ... er ... didn't quite er ... hear ...' 'ARE YOU FARKINN DEFF?' he yelled. 'THERE'S A BOOZER NEXT TO LONDON BRIDGE – BE THERE TOMORROW NIGHT!'

There was indeed a boozer in a murky back street next to London Bridge and it was rocking by the time I arrived. No, I mean literally, it was *rocking*. It was rocking so much I thought it was going to tumble right over into the Thames. God knows how long Pogue Mahone had been in residence but they all seemed hopelessly out of it, charging round the bar and filling my tape recorder with ear-splitting claims about their greatness while a hapless photographer tried to coax them outside to pose for the sleeve of their debut single. He failed, just as I failed to get much sense out of them.

Spider Stacey was welded to the bar talking bollocks while Gentleman Jem Finer earnestly attempted to be the sensible one. Shane actually seemed one of the more sober of this wild bunch, though he got very stroppy every time anyone attempted to haul him outside to have his picture taken. 'I AIN'T FARKING MOVING ... OKAAAAY?' Totally unfazed by the disconcerting sight of the band's bass player, Cait O'Riordan, dancing on the table in front of him in black fishnets, swearing like a docker, spilling beer over anyone in spitting distance and chanting 'I WANNA BE ON THE COVER OF *SMASH HITS*. I WANNA BE A LEGEND. I WANNA MARRY EDWYN COLLINS' into my tape recorder, Shane wavered between joyous cackles and moroseness, repeatedly toasting the health of one of his heroes, Luke Kelly of The Dubliners, who'd died the previous day.

I met him again a few years later when The Pogues were on the crest of a wave, well-established as manic performers on and offstage, when Spider used to beat his head with a tray, Shane sprayed unintelligible oaths all over the stage and the pogoing audiences were even more pissed than the band. There had been loads of press at the time that Shane had seen the light and had given up drinking. I was a bit taken aback to find him partaking liberally from a tumbler of wine.

'I thought you'd given up the drink, Shane,' I said. 'Yeah, I have,' he said. 'What's that, then?' I said, indicating the vat of wine he was consuming in copious quantities. 'This? It's only wine. Wine don't count.' For all that, he was funny, coherent, warm, charming even, happy to explain the genesis of his songs and ridiculing my comment that I preferred his version of 'A Pair Of Brown Eyes' to Christy

Moore's. 'That's just stupid,' he said. 'Christy is a much better singer than me, his version is much better than mine. It's *obvious*.'

Shane talked about Irish music and literature with real relish, and intently discussed the history of Irish music from Michael Coleman to The Clancy Brothers, The Dubliners, Planxty, Bothy Band, Moving Hearts, Clannad and all. He put The Pogues into Irish music context, saying they were based on the old ceili band format of strict beats, designed for dancing rather than head music. A recent addition to The Pogues, Terry Woods – who'd been a founder member of the folk-rock band Steeleye Span – was also there that night, talking about a love of the music re-ignited by playing sessions at a small pub in Cavan.

'You'd go in on a Saturday night and all of a sudden there'd be old guys with fiddles and accordions and they had *real working hands*,' he said. 'They'd been out in the fields working every day and they'd just go to the pub to play and have a few pints and a laugh and there was none of this "You played the wrong fucken *note!*" Once the session starts you don't stop, and it doesn't matter if you play *48 wrong fucken notes*.' Yet what I remember most about it was the warmth and respect with which Shane talked about The Dubliners and his pride in having just made a hit single – 'Irish Rover' – with them. And that's what I'm listening to as we pull into Cashel.

Ah, I remember Cashel. It's impossible to forget that bloody great rock all lit up like a Christmas tree in the centre of town. I've never stopped here before though. All those Americans with their posh cameras, flashing around the old chapel, and the inevitable traffic jam halting that mad dash back for the Rosslare ferry put me right off. Still, the *Rough Guide To Irish Music* informs me that while Cashel is indeed a tourist trap, Feehan's is a good place for music so we take the plunge and book in at a modest B&B.

'Oh, it's the music you're after, is it?' says the inevitably inquisitive landlady. 'Yeah, I'm trying to track down this great fiddle player, Tommy Peoples ...' 'Tommy Peoples, y'say? I know a Tommy Little, he's my cousin's youngest, that wouldn't be him now, would it?' 'Does he play fiddle?' 'No, I don't think so but I do remember him having piano lessons when he was younger. Lovely boy, he was then. Had this cheeky little smile. Now he does something in computers in Limerick, I think, so it probably wouldn't be him, would it?'

We dine at a pub near Feehan's. Well, I say *dine*. A big woman with blonde ringlets frogmarches us to the back of a long bar where we can't do any harm and she can keep an eye on us. She deposits us on tall stools and thrusts a couple of menus in our hands. 'Soup's off, steak's off, no chicken goujets, I'd have the fish if I were you but make it snappy, the chef goes home at eight!' There is major consternation when Mrs Colin elects for two starters rather than a main course. Managers are called, chefs are consulted, the local tourist board invited in as mediators and the Rock of Cashel begins to crumble. Madame Blondie eventually, reluctantly, noisily relents and we get away with the two starters thing, but everybody stares. I later have a disturbing dream involving the waitress's secret life as a leather-clad, whip-wielding dominatrix in the sin bins of Cashel. Sorry, did I write that out loud? I shouldn't say such things, Cashel being such a religious place and all.

We are plotting our escape through the gauntlet of glares with Mrs Colin dubbed forever in Cashel as 'The Woman Who Had Two Starters' when there's a flurry of activity at the front of the bar. It's a bloke with a violin case. Either that, or he's come to mow us down, wreaking vengeance for some previous humiliation at the hands of Mrs Dominatrix. There is a long preamble as he extricates his fiddle and lovingly polishes it before being joined by a guitarist. They then spend the next twenty minutes deep in conversation – probably debating the rumour that there was someone in the pub who'd asked for two starters – before embarking on a desultory reel.

The locals seem to regard their presence as an inconvenience and merely raise their conversation levels to counter the music, and the whole exercise seems pointless. Maybe the LIVE TRADITIONAL MUSIC sign in the window may have coaxed in the odd thirsty American returning from a hard day at the Rock with the camcorder, but if this is the craic, I want my money back. As discreetly as possible we barge through the crowds at the bar and, with a sympathetic nod to the musicians, make a dash for the door. The look from the two poor buggers with the instruments suggests that for half a sixpence they'd come with us. Presumably they get a few bob for their troubles but what price humiliation?

Liberated, we head for the main attraction: Feehan's. It's a decent sized bar that offers, from the outside at least, plenty of character. It has a pleasingly ornate front that appears to suggest that, as well as serving you copious amounts of Guinness, it will additionally furnish you with groceries while also operating as a funeral parlour. Yep, you can still find Irish bars that double as supermarkets, post offices, garages, ironmongers and, in this case, a greengrocers and funeral parlour. So we march in, confidently expecting to confront a seething mass of drunken revellers while a band blazes away on pipes, flutes, fiddles and accordions in front of a blazing fire in the corner. And we find ... *stillness*.

A pair of ol' boys at the bar turn round to stare sullenly at us as if to say 'No two starters for you HERE, sunshine', while a couple in the corner are exploring each other's tonsils with rapacious enthusiasm and won't notice if the Rock of Cashel itself comes crashing into the pub. The earth looks like it's already about to move for them. The only other people in are a group of lads who look about 12, staring at a telly showing Newcastle thrashing the pants off West Ham. 'Any music tonight, then?' I ask the barman optimistically. Without taking his eyes off Shearer's assault on the West Ham goal he shakes his head and points me back in the direction of the bar of the Dominatrix. I start explaining we've just come from there and it was crap and the *Rough Guide To Irish Music* says Feehan's is THE place to be in Cashel, but his eyes are already glazing over. That'll be an early night then.

So the next day we head on north. But to where? Thurles is up the road, and I vaguely remember somebody back in Dungarvan saying there was a great music pub in Thurles that only opens on a Thursday night. But this is a Wednesday, there's not a race meeting in sight, and after the Cashel experience the whole notion of hanging around Tipperary for another day on such a vague promise seems too ridiculous to contemplate. Kilkenny is a possibility. It's a great place, Kilkenny. It poses as a tourist trap with its cute narrow streets, its fancy arts and crafts shops, its array of historic castles, cathedrals and abbeys, its medieval past, its endless arty festivals and its history as the seat of Irish parliament in the seventeenth century. Yet scrape off the surface and Kilkenny is as mad as a frog. The home of Smithwicks Brewery, it has a pub on every corner and an anecdote in every one.

It was in Kilkenny in 1999 that I had my first close encounter with hurling. I was with Martin Hayes, the great Clare fiddle player, and he'd been telling me about the chain of events that had transformed his life and career. Brought up in the dancing stronghold of East Clare, he was taught to play by his father PJ Hayes, who in the 1950s featured with Martin's uncle Paddy Canny on one of the first LPs of traditional music ever recorded in Ireland. PJ played with the Tulla Ceili Band and Martin was just 14 when, suited and booted, he joined them too. Groomed in the clearly defined strict tempo traditional style of that area of Clare, Martin was the golden boy, hugely admired in the local community. And then he followed a familiar path, expanding his horizons with a trip to the States ... and went completely off the rails. In Chicago, he grew his hair, set his sights on fame and fortune and *experimented*. Profusely. He formed a jazz-rock fusion band, acquired a taste for loud rock music and even louder parties, picked up jobs in all manner of dodgy bar bands. And when the band stopped playing, he carried on drinking. He abused the music and abused himself and there was scarcely a pub wall in Chicago he hadn't been scraped off.

Out of luck, out of control, he reached the age of 30 and overnight decided to change his life. 'I quit drinking, quit smoking, quit eating meat and changed my life irreversibly. It was very empowering. I can now go to bed knowing whatever party is out there I've been to one twice as good!' he told me. He's been a strict teetotaller and vegetarian ever since, and the result of this absolution was dramatic. In 1995 he recorded an album of solo fiddle music. It was primarily for his own benefit, a personal cleansing of his musical soul, going back to basics with the music he was brought up with in Clare. He expected to sell just a handful of copies, mostly to loyal family and friends back home. In fact that simply stripped-down instrumental album of traditional tunes had a mesmerising sway and it sold in vast quantities. And, accompanied by another former Chicago party king and born-again teetotaller and non-smoker, guitarist Dennis Cahill, he gradually established a reputation as one of the most beguiling live performers of Irish music.

Now settled in Seattle, where he has his own studio, Hayes was back in Ireland for his annual tour with Cahill when I met him prior to a show at St Canice's Cathedral at the top of the hill as part of one of the arts festivals they seem to hold every week in Kilkenny. With his tangled hair, granddad glasses and wry humour, Martin is one of the most laid-back characters you could ever wish to meet. He's been there, seen that, done it all, and you can't imagine anything disturbing the mellow flow of his benign temperament. Except this day he was *fretting*. The complicated requirements of the support band delayed his soundcheck, things kept going wrong and by his standards Martin was getting agitated (he tutted once or twice and may even have grimaced). He also kept looking at his watch. 'You okay, Martin?' I said. 'The match,' he said, 'I've got to see the match.' And then it all fell into place. The yellow and black bunting decorating the streets of Kilkenny had not been stuck up as a personal welcome to Martin Hayes, but as a celebration of Kilkenny's progress in the All-Ireland hurling championship. Today was the semi-final in Dublin. And today Kilkenny played Clare.

Familiarised with the urgency of the situation, I'd assumed the role of roadie-in-chief, tour manager and aggressive bastard. 'Come on, outta the way, Mr Hayes has an important appointment and he can't be late,' I said shirtily as the support band arse around with a keyboard straight out of Rick Wakeman's attic, and an xylophone painted a bizarre shade of green. The support band got locked in a cupboard, Martin and Dennis whipped through the quickest soundcheck known to mankind, and we hit the pub running. By this time, though, Kilkenny were already ahead and you could barely see the telly for the cheering fans. I applauded with them, until I noticed Martin – devout Clare man and all – crumpling visibly next to me. I switched allegiances immediately.

'It's tribal this game,' he was saying through clenched teeth, 'pure tribal.' I saw what he meant. The play is fast and furious. There is none of this posing and prancing around you get with footie or egg-chasing. Bodies fly around all over the place and some of the stuff makes you wince, but there's no time to roll around in front of the camera, they just get up and get on with a game played at breakneck speed. I was totally gripped.

A couple of pints down the road, I was screeching 'Go Clare go' and, on the basis of the briefest summary of the rules from Martin, I'm roundly abusing the ref (do they call them refs?) for a series of increasingly ludicrous decisions. It worked, too. Clare scored, and Martin and I danced around the pub hugging each other in front of a pub of stony-faced Kilkenny fans in their black-and-yellow-striped shirts. I instinctively threw a few shapes, duck walked among them, thrust an avalanche of V-signs into their faces and launched into a chorus of 'You're not singing any more' but Martin shushed me. Protocol. Respect for the opposition. Especially when you're in Kilkenny, and you're being paid to play a concert for them tonight.

Still, the natives were getting restless and agitated with their own side. 'Jayzus, that kid spends too much time on the juice, that's his trouble,' said one of the locals knowledgably as a Kilkenny player fumbled his hurley. 'Yep, he's crap alright,' I said sympathetically, always ready to wind up the opposition. 'He's a farmer and he's always having a jar … look at him … he was out on the piss last night,' the local explains. Really? How do you know? 'I was out on the piss with him.'

In the event Kilkenny narrowly won the match (though they went on to lose the final to Cork) and everyone was very grown up and shook hands and told us we were unlucky but at the end of the day, Brian, hurling's the winner. But I could tell Martin was gutted. And I'll still tell anyone who'll listen that the ref must have taken a back-hander. And Clare are *my* hurling team forever and ever amen.

Yet, ever the trouper, Martin clambered back up the hill to the cathedral, gallantly embarked on one of his hilariously surreal intro-ductions, congratulated the audience on their victory, and gobbled up their hearts with a joyously intuitive display of fiddle playing. He is a master musician, but it's more than that. Ably supported by the percussive strength of Cahill's guitar, he connects with the soul rather than the head, and you really don't have to be a fan of Irish music or indeed folk music to connect with it.

'What we do,' he told me, 'is we go to the core of the music and the tunes. There is a tendency in music to embellish and decorate before you know what you're decorating so I always work my way backward to first find out what's there. It's like a door painted with forty coats of paint and you just keep on painting it until you wonder what was there in the first place and you strip it down to the wood. It might not need painting at all and if it does then the painting must be a very delicate operation. That's the way I feel about Irish music. You go to hear the music not the musician.'

There was a man in a suit and tie at the back of that cathedral in Kilkenny. He had a Latin American complexion and, I've got to be honest, he looked a bit shifty. When he accosted Martin and Dennis at the end of the concert, I began to get a little worried. They shook hands, but Martin was frowning and Dennis was looking ill. Suddenly, Latino Man was marching them off to a big minibus thing in the car park.

I went running to their rescue, suspecting foul play, anticipating a 'Top Irish Musician Kidnapped By Bandito In Kilkenny' headline in the next day's *Irish Times*. The bandito headed me off at the pass. 'Gutaa everrinkkk,' he said, a tad sinisterly, I think. So maybe I was going to be kidnapped too, just like yer man McCarthy? Then Martin introduced me to the Venezuelan ambassador to Ireland. Or it might have been Peru. Or Ecuador. Or Bolivia. Somewhere like that.

So into his posh people carrier we piled, while he played us the latest folk music from Venezuela (or Peru, or Ecuador, or Bolivia) on his state of the art in-car entertainment system as he drove around Kilkenny showing us the sights. 'We will go see summerthink errmaazzink, I think,' he said, squealing around the back streets like Schumacher. 'We mersttt be quikk ... eet starts at meednight.' He mounted the pavement, parked abruptly where it looked highly illegal to park (diplomatic immunity, I guess) and ushered us out into the crowds grouping around a car park where a makeshift stage had been erected. There was music and suddenly, amid cheers, a massive waterfall was sprayed into the night air.

I was wondering what the hell was happening, but then a child's face gradually came into focus in the middle of the waterfall. Followed by a disembodied child's voice. 'What I am praying for in the new Millennium is world peace for all ...' It was the weirdest bloody thing I'd ever seen. There were faces of all ages, colours and cultures projected on to the water cascading into the sky, and their voices offering their hopes and dreams for the twenty-first century. There were local school kids, priests, politicians, mothers, hoteliers ... all human life was here.

Some of their testimonials were profoundly moving. One girl

hoped her granny would recover from cancer. Plenty wanted to see a peaceful resolution in the north. Others were more comical. There were a few up for winning the lotto. Some were keen on bringing the All-Ireland back to Kilkenny. And one lad wanted to spend quality time with Andrea Corr. Join the queue, mate, join the queue. In the flow of the water, it looked like their faces were moving. Eerie, but deeply impressive. Then, as suddenly as it started, the sound went off, the images ceased and we watched the water disappear before our very eyes. The Venezuelan ambassador marched us back to his people-carrier, stopped at a takeaway for supper and deposited us back at our hotel. I clasped him to my bosom and promised to spend next year's holiday in Venezuela. Or Peru. Or Ecuador. Or Bolivia.

I was also in Kilkenny a few months ago, as it happens, after wangling myself on to an Irish Ferries press trip. Strangely, though, we didn't travel across by ferry, but by plane, with hundreds of travel journalists arriving from all corners of Britain. Landing in Dublin from Heathrow, I was mystified to discover no sign of any Irish Ferries staff. I wandered around the airport for a bit and then remembered this was Ireland and found the bar. There they all were, sinking Guinness to their heart's content, seemingly oblivious to the fact that a coach was waiting to take us to Kilkenny. A couple of pints and I enquire who we're waiting for before we head for Kilkenny. 'Oh, the bloke who's organising it, he missed the plane.'

When he finally arrived we had another couple of drinks and a good chortle over him missing the plane, hearing some involved, unlikely explanation about a lorry and a milk cart, then finally rounded up the stragglers. We were halfway across Dublin before realising we'd left a couple of journos behind, and turned back to the airport. Suitably reassembled we once more set off for Kilkenny, but within the hour the immortal cry came: 'Anyone fancy a drink?' And before you knew it, we'd stopped for lunch and a quick livener.

After finally making it to Kilkenny, we end up in the splendid four-teenth-century Kytelers Inn, greeted by a convivial barman who employs full RADA training to tell the engrossing story of the original householder's daughter Dame Alice le Kyteler. The father, a wealthy merchant, had built the house in Kieran St in 1300 and his daughter Alice duly inherited it. Beautiful and wealthy, if a tad eccentric, Alice had no trouble attracting men. Unfortunately, they all seemed to have the same problem – they kept dying. She lost four husbands in all, and all in mysterious circumstances.

When the fourth, an obscenely rich man called John Le Poer, was evidently dying without any doctor able to offer medical explanation, folks began to suspect Alice might have been sticking summat nasty into his porridge, or whatever they had for breakfast in Kilkenny in the 1300s. Mr Le Poer's family started making enquiries, breaking into another house owned by Alice and discovered all manner of mysterious potions. They presented their evidence to the local bishop who accused Dame Alice of witchcraft. Suitably aggrieved by the very idea, Alice called on a few favours (apart from the alleged dabblings with the dark side, she was a professional money-lender) and had the bishop thrown in prison.

Yet, being a bishop, he had some powerful pals, too, and after they'd sprung him, he made damn sure Alice was charged with witchcraft. An infamous trial followed resulting in a conviction, not only for Alice, but also her son William, her maid Petronilla, and several friends. She was sentenced to be burned at the stake. But the night before she was due to be burned, a friendly jailer aided her escape and she fled to England never to be heard of again. It's probably bollocks, but that RADA training is fantastic, and that barman has us eating out of his hand by the end of it.

So, why not? I like Kilkenny. Let's go to Kytelers and, if we can't find any music, we'll just go hear about Dame Alice again. Which way to Kilkenny? 'You missed it. There was a turn to Kilkenny 20 miles back,' announces Mrs Colin solemnly. 'Why didn't you tell me?' 'Oh, I never interrupt an anecdote ...'

It's at this point I realise we've also missed Cork. And Limerick. Ireland's second and third largest cities. I can't imagine how that happened. Ah, never mind. Nobody will notice. There's no going back now. I have the scent of craic in my nostrils. We're getting close to the west coast heartlands of Kerry, Clare and Galway, the traditional epicentres of Irish music.

I remember somebody saying there's a thriving scene in Limerick these days, but I can't quite eradicate the memory of driving through the city late one night *en route* for Connemara and being chased through the High Street by a gang of evil-looking skinheads waving and gesticulating. The car was bumping all over the place as I put my foot down trying to escape. When I eventually did get clear of them I stopped the car, got out to take some deep breaths to recover from the traumatic ordeal ... and realised they'd been trying to warn me I had a flat tyre. It was just like that time in America when I'd got off the wrong subway on my way to the New York Fleadh. It was dusk as I cut through some back streets past a gang of nine-foot-tall dudes lurking with intent on the corner, and I realised I was in Harlem. Isn't this the place folk are shot on sight, no questions asked? I quickened my step as a shadow loomed behind me and I could hear a heavy footstep getting closer. I froze as a huge hand gripped my shoulder. I swung round to find a huge brother – shaved head, tattoos, white T-shirt, the whole bit – staring hard at me. 'Hey, dude, you could get hurt,' he said. 'I could?' I said shakily. 'Yeah, your shoe-lace is undone. You wanna tie that up. You could trip over and hurt yourself *baaaad*.' So Harlem's all right, okay? And those Globetrotters were magic. I still won't stop at Limerick, though.

After the shambles of Cashel, I decide it's time to get smart and take some advice. I call De Dannan founder and bouzouki player Alec Finn, possessor of the scariest haircut in Galway. I remember Alec living in some sort of a castle. I went there once. He had this incredible life-sized model of a bird of prey, a falcon or kestrel or some such, sitting on a perch. I was fascinated by it, and stared at it for minutes. It looked so real. Eventually I prodded it to see what it was made of. The bloody thing flapped its wings, started squawking and nearly bit my finger off. I've been terrified of birds ever since.

De Dannan started in sessions. They were the ultimate session band. Alec, a Yorkshireman by birth – though not a lot of people know that – would be the man to call to find out what's going on in Galway. Maybe he'll invite us to his castle. 'Actually,' he says, when I get through to him, 'I'm a bit out of touch right now.' He has a house in France and that's where he spends most of his time these days. He's about to fly out there now, as it happens. 'It's the climate in Ireland, y'know?' he says. 'It's so damp it gets in your bones.' Before he goes he does recommend a session run by a whistle player in a haunted castle. 'Sounds good, where is it?' 'Tipperary.' 'Ah, I've just come from there. Anywhere in Galway?'

He muses for a second … 'What day is it? Right, yes, I've got it! There's a great session they have on tonight down there in Kinvara. The pub is called Green's. It's a beautiful spot. They have some great players down there, you'll love it. Tell 'em I sent you.' 'You sure it's on tonight, Alec?' 'Oh God, yes, it's written in stone …'

Kinvara it is then. To the south of Galway Bay, Kinvara is a picture postcard that's sprung to life. It's so quiet you want to tippy-toe around the fisherman's cottages grouped around Kinvara harbour and the thatched cottages laying off the main road. It's not even host town to Thailand or the Caymans or the Scilly Isles or *anywhere*, that's how special it is.

Ambling sedately around the place I wonder why some maps and books spell Kinvara with two Rs. Not that it matters. The proper Irish name is Cinn Mhara, meaning 'Head Of The Sea'. I'm pondering all this, gazing in the window of a cheery music shop at the front of the harbour. A shame it's shut, but I soon discover why. The guy who runs it is in the pub, which is where I meet him. He's an English guitarist called Stuart. 'I was just driving past here one day,' he's saying, 'and you know what it's like when you do a double take? I just couldn't believe how good it looked. I slammed on my brakes, reversed down into the harbour here, got out the car and I haven't left since.'

It's a lovely spot all right and it gets lovelier by the minute as we while away the afternoon in the bar putting the world to rights. Eventually, though, it's time to find a B&B and prepare for tonight's session.

'What session's that then?' asks Stuart.

'Green's. Always a session at Green's tonight. Written in stone, it is.'

He looks at me strangely. 'Green's? Tonight? No, that was *last* night. Jeez, what a session we had in there last night. There's been some great sessions in Green's all right. You get them all. You know John Prine? He's here a lot. He spends most of the summers here. Great session with him at Green's the other day ...'

'But not tonight?'

'No, definitely not tonight.'

'I'll kill Alec Finn ...'

'But there are other places. The Auld Plaid Shawl might have something on, and I think Winkles has a session tonight ...'

After a complicated procedure at the B&B ('knock three times, ask for Alice, do a backwards somersault and come and find the landlady doing her shopping in the supermarket up the road') we enter Green's. You know, just in case. 'Any music tonight?' I ask the barmaid hopefully. 'Not tonight, but we had a great sesh ...' '*Last* night ... yes, I heard.'

But even without any music, Green's is a magnificent place. You never see pubs like this any more in Britain. Sloping shelves behind the bar are jammed tight with all manner of spirits, from absinthe to suspiciously strange-looking concoctions of local whiskey. There's a low roof, cosy alcoves, and posters all over the walls and ceiling offering their own feast of entertainment. There's a big advertisement for the 1982 Lisdoonvarna Festival, and brown-edged pictures of everyone from Jackson Browne, UB40 and Seamus Ennis to Classix Nouveaux, Micho Russell, Dave Edmunds and John Otway. Oh, and look up: there's a John Prine T-shirt, a Grand Ole Opry poster and a flag for the Cambodian Celtic Club. 'You never know what's gonna happen in this place,' says the barmaid, 'you know, there might be a session later on, you just never can tell.' Which sounds like waiting for a kettle to boil, so we decided to gamble instead on Winkle's up the road, knowing that, as soon as we are out of sight, John Prine and an army of fiddle players and pipers will dive into Green's for a session they'll be talking about in here for years to come.

But we'll always have Winkles. This bar has none of the romantic old-school character of Green's. Skulking away up a side street next to the square, it looks pokily nondescript from the outside. Inside, there's a surprisingly vast bar, but if I'm going to spend any time in this place, those revolting red walls have to go. No absinthe, John Prine T-shirts or intimacy on tap here. But Winkles does have one big advantage over Green's – a small sign promising TRADITIONAL MUSIC TONIGHT. The main attraction even has a name: Mad Yanks.

Sadly, they don't have a watch. A chap could get drunk waiting for a session to start in Kinvara. Instruments are strewn promisingly around the place, but nobody shows much interest in picking them up and playing them, and most of the entertainment is centred on a drunk at the bar incomprehensibly, but endlessly, haranguing a young bloke with long hair minding his own business. Eventually the long-haired bloke abandons ship and gets up and stomps out. He's probably off to Green's, where he'll doubtless be dancing on the ceiling later with John Prine.

The Winkles drunk observes his exit with a triumphant bark of parting expletives and then swivels round to survey the rest of the sparsely populated bar in search of fresh meat. Mrs Colin and I keep our heads down, closely examining the beer-mats and I'm pretty thankful I had a haircut before I left home. Slowly, but *painfully* slowly, the bar begins to fill up, and at the sort of time most drinking establishments are stacking chairs on tables and yelling 'You lot not got homes to go to?' a fiddle player, a flautist and a whistle player assemble in front of the bar and start to play.

Eileen, a big blonde woman from Chicago who'd been roaring round Winkles all night like one of the cast of *Starlight Express* and, it turns out, plays a mean bodhran, soon joins them. She also plays guitar. When Stuart turns up with a mandolin, she plays that too. And when the music stops, she sings too, delivering a lovely performance of 'Stor Mo Chroi' that's disturbed only by the sound of text messaging. I can't imagine what the text messages are saying: 'CU @ Greens – GR8 SESH WITH J PRINE' maybe? But hey, suddenly Winkles is full, the band are letting rip, the drinks are going down well, so who needs Green's anyway? Things are shaping up nicely for a long, lively night. That's when they play the Irish national anthem. Everyone stands up, they shut the bar, stools get put on tables and we all go home. On the way back to the B&B, I make a sly detour back to the harbour and peer into Green's. It's shut too. Tonight at least I can rest easy. Satisfied that Kinvara sleeps, I can sleep too.

Chapter five

KERRY: THE FLEADH, BILL CLINTON & AN ITALIAN ROSE

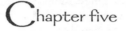

It's morning, it's sunny and here we are busy doing nothing, armed with all the essential fuel to get you through those strange few hours in Ireland before the pubs open: a croissant, a cup of coffee and a newspaper. Kinvara Harbour looks divine, the mood is tranquil and I think I could spend the rest of my life here. I am just about deciding I *will* spend the rest of my life here when something suddenly leaps out of the pages and biffs me on the nose: 'THE ROSE OF TRALEE FESTIVAL – THIS WEEK.'

There had been no real game plan on this trip and with the first life-giving sip of coffee I'd contemplated maybe a few days of gentle ambling around Galway, taking in the glorious Gaeltacht area of Connemara. But this changed everything. I mean … *The Rose Of Tralee*. We're talking Kerry. Drinks. Music. Laughs. Tacky glamour. And horse racing. We've hit the jackpot here. There's only one way to go … head for Kerry and don't spare the horses.

I'd been hooked on the Rose of Tralee for many years since a holiday in Glenbeigh, a sleepy little spot where even the sheep walked on tippy-toe for fear of breaching the peace. The only traffic jams were caused by the cows on their way for a game of chess in the field over the way or a couple of tractors camped in the middle of the road discussing what they had for their tea last night. One morning I turned on the local radio station expecting the usual exciting parish notices and bulletins about lost bicycles, errant cattle and the price of peat, when the announcer said: 'THERE'S MAYHEM ON THE STREETS OF TRALEE.' *There is?* This, I had to see.

Not so much a beauty pageant, more a mad insight into the Irish at play. More than that it's conclusive proof that – as The Chieftains' large catalogue of fusion albums invariably suggests, and the ancestry of Muhammad Ali undoubtedly proves – the entire world is Irish. The rules are simple, if blurred. Anybody can enter to be the Rose of Tralee. *Anybody*. As long as they're female, aged between 18 and 26, unmarried, have no children and have some Irish blood. Even a teensy bit. So that's anybody really, then. You win 5,000 euro, a nice tiara, some Waterford crystal thingy, swanky shopping trips, a ride round Tralee racecourse in a horse-drawn cart … and you become the focal point of an event that, in true Irish tradition, has become one great big street party. And yes, the radio station is right, there is indeed mayhem on the streets of Tralee as the hoolie begins and the little town is overrun with the colourful array of misfits, chancers, opportunists, lost souls, impromptu entertainers and undiscovered legends who descend from who knows where to events like this. It's not something exclusive to Tralee or even Ireland. I once caught the last bus out of Penzance to attend the annual May Day celebrations in the Cornish town of Padstow. Halfway there the driver stopped the bus and said 'Anyone fancy a drink?' and we all piled out into a pub. By the time we reached Padstow the whole bus was ratted and had turned into a mobile festival of people juggling, doing three-card tricks, singing, dancing, making bunny rabbits out of balloons, performing one-man interpretations of 'The Scottish Play', and making lifelong friendships that end when we get off the bus. When the Rose is on, Tralee feels like a bus ride from Penzance to Padstow.

The journey down towards Kerry is relatively uneventful. Well, it is if you count getting hopelessly lost and then being stuck in a noisy traffic jam that's formed behind a man in a white coat pushing a large harp on wheels down the centre of the road a regular occurrence. It's probably somebody writing a book about pushing a harp round Ireland – best ignore it. And once again trying to circumnavigate the Limerick lorry hell we are kept entertained by the news that Ireland have become world champions at Aussie Rules football. Well, why *wouldn't* they be? Apparently the players all paid for their own trip out to Melbourne after qualifying for the finals by beating England and Scotland, and once there, they took out New Zealand and Australia to reach a grand final against Papua New Guinea. Even the chat-show hosts are a bit non-plussed by this latest triumph. You don't see a lot of kids in parks playing Aussie Rules to be fair. It's the refs and all that camp flag waving. That'd put anyone off.

Still, a national triumph is a national triumph and one station manages to track down a reporter at the event. The stadium was basically empty, he said, apart from a few scattered Papua New Guinea fans encouraging their team – affectionately known as 'the mozzies' – chanting something along the lines of 'Kaikam ol, na givim ol malary'. Which roughly translated means 'Bite them and give them malaria'. Which is nice. After they'd lost and the Irish captain Michael Johnson made a speech in Gaelic that nobody understood, the mozzies blamed their defeat on the cold weather. They don't tell you that on *Neighbours*, do they? Not a word about Australia's abysmal failure. How can you lose to Ireland in a sport that has the name of your own country on it? It wouldn't happen in America. The Yanks knew what they were doing when they launched baseball's 'World Series' and didn't bother inviting anyone else to take part. They're not stupid. Let other nations compete in the 'World Series' and before you know it the Irish will gatecrash the party and be whacking home runs and hurling curve balls at your goolies.

While musing all this and looking for the first 'IRELAND – AUSSIE RULES WORLD CHAMPIONS' sign being erected we somehow get lost. I blame the harp. Before we know it we are going in the wrong direction entirely and following the Shannon up to Lough Derg. At this point something rings a bell. Somebody in Kinvara had said there was a pub on Lough Derg that provided an orgy of traditional music. We pull up by the side of the road. Cases are opened, pockets are emptied and the floor of the car is scoured for the scraggy bit of paper on which I'd scribbled this vital information. At last – carefully preserved in an old Aero wrapper cunningly concealed under the brake pedal – I find it. The Piper's Inn at Killaloe. Killaloe is a pleasant little town nestling on the banks of the lovely Lough Derg, dominated by the impressive twelfth-century St Flannan's Cathedral. It also has a significant footnote in Irish history as the birthplace – in 940AD – of the ancient king Brian Boru.

The Piper's Inn is a big yellow pub up a side road leading up a hill a mile or so out of town. It looks promising, partly because it has a big sign saying 'Traditional Music.' There's also another sign saying TONIGHT LIVE: THE BREEDER'S CUP. This elicits a mixed reaction. The Breeder's Cup is a big American horse race meeting. Is it also the name of an Irish traditional band? I pop my hand round the door. 'Any music on tonight, mate?' The guy behind the bar looks at me blankly and starts scratching his chin. 'Music?' 'Yes. Music. Any on tonight?' His brow furrows and he looks at his watch. Why do people do that? It's not like I was asking the time. 'I'd say,' he says eventually, 'there might very well be a possibility of a bit of music right enough.' 'Is that a definite yes?' 'Oh yes, I'd say so … *definitely maybe*.' 'You mean Oasis are on?' 'What?' 'Never mind … see you later.' Not entirely filled with confidence, we climb the hill and book into a guesthouse up the road.

A couple of hours later, we're back in The Piper's Inn watching the

Breeder's Cup on a telly in the corner of the bar. The Piper's Inn breaks all the session bar rules. There's the telly for one thing. There's also a pool table, a cigarette machine, fruit machines, Pringles, the lot. Yet this is countered by some corking walls. There's some glorious pictures of old pipers … there's a gorgeous one of the Ballinahinch piper and fiddle player Martin Rochford; there are some nice shots of various Rowsomes; Bernard Delaney; Pat Mitchell; Willie Clancy; Liam O'Flynn; loads of unidentified ancient pipers all with moustaches; a drawing of the Loughrea flute player Paddy Carty. In pride of place near the telly there's a plaque to Tony Keegan, who apparently established The Piper's Inn as a centre for traditional musicians between 1978–1987. 'Any music tonight?' I ask again. 'Oh, I'd say so,' says a different barman. 'Later though … after the racing.' Fair enough, we settle in with the punters poring over their papers roaring at the telly showing events from the Arlington course in Chicago. I search the room. There's got to be a bookie in the house. A bloke in a flat clap and a lopsided grin sits himself down to watch the big race. 'What are you on?' I say. 'You're very kind, I'll have a large Jamesons,' he says, patting my knee. 'No, what I meant was … what horse have you backed?' I say, delivering the whiskey. 'I know,' he says with a wink. 'I'm on Rock Of Gibraltar. You know, the big feller's horse.' 'The big feller?' 'Alex Ferguson. Manchester United manager. He owns the horse. He's got the luck of Old Ned with him, that feller.' It's a tense race. Mr Jameson's face turns a whiter shade of pale as the commentator shouts 'Rock Of Gibraltar is LAST' at regular intervals and with such ill-concealed glee he must be a Liverpool fan. He's on his knees on the floor as they approach the last furlong and The Rock is still ambling along behind everyone else. 'Don't worry,' I tell him, 'Alex's teams always score the winner in injury time'. And as I say it, The Rock wakes up. You can see him stepping up a gear, picking off the horses in front of him with an irresistible surge. He steams through the field and it looks like he's timed his run to perfection as the winning post approaches and he bears down on the leader, Domedriver. My friend the Jameson drinker is now yelling at the screen, digging his fingernails into my arm. 'He's gonna do it,' he's yelling, 'the bastid's really gonna do it!' I'm screaming too, but that's more to do with the fingernails in my arm. Then it's as if time stops still. Rock Of Gibraltar is still pounding along but the winning post is hurtling forward faster and Domedriver is still in front. 'DOMEDRIVER WINS IT' shouts the Liverpool fan triumphantly. My new friend is sobbing. 'Pocken nag … pocken Alex Ferguson … pocken Yanks … pocken Aiden O'Brien … pocken hell.' 'Would another Jameson help?' 'That would be grand. You're very kind.'

Racing over, I'm waiting for the musicians to move in. Not a sign. After an hour I ask the barman if we're likely to hear any music tonight. He looks at his watch. 'It's awful late,' he says. 'I'd say they won't be coming on account of the fog.' I look outside. Fog? You call this fog? In England we call this a bit misty, matey. My own theory is that the musicians had all put their life savings on Domedriver in the big race and were by now walking across Lough Derg. It's only just gone midnight so the night is young and we head into town to check out the rest of the action. Killaloe is a confusing place. There's a lovely seventeenth-century stone bridge in the middle of it that absolutely begs you to cross it. And when you do it's like you've crossed into another town. That's maybe because you *have* crossed into another town. It's called Ballina. The upmarket array of restaurants and pubs along the waterfront, like the picture postcard pub Goosers, with its thatched roof and cosy interior, suggest this is the posh side of the water. Naturally we scarper back across the bridge to Killaloe right away. We know our place.

Two pubs face each other in the town square. We can hear music drifting from both but the mist has now given way to a downpour of rain so instant decisions have to be made. We dive into the one on the left because it's closer. Inside there's a fat man singing 'Somewhere Over The Rainbow' unaccompanied, but he's no Judy Garland and the way he keeps burping and winking at us leads me to believe he may have had a drink. Then his wife – no Twiggy herself – bursts in through the door with a face like thunder, drenches us as she shakes her umbrella, marches up to him, snaps his ear between her fingers and drags him off into the angry night.

Nobody bats an eyelid and a slight, dark-haired girl called Siobhan clambers shyly on to a stool and, with the merest token attempt at tuning her guitar, sets off on an introspective performance of the busker's songbook. A Suzanne Vega here, a Michelle Shocked there, an REM song for surprise impact … but the packed pub shows her even less respect than they did the fat guy singing Judy Garland. A lot of people have their backs to her staring intently at the telly above the bar. The telly isn't actually switched on but nobody seems to notice or care. You have to feel for Siobhan. There she is pouring her heart out (well, Suzanne Vega's heart to be precise) while a group of soggy drinkers sit a few feet from her discussing what they are going to do with their winnings from the Breeders Cup. I wonder about starting a book on which song she'll do next. I have a mind's eye fiver on 'Big Yellow Taxi'. A few promising strums and I raise it to a tenner. But she's such a tease, this Siobhan, she's thrown in a joker and the bookies are laughing. Instead of 'Big Yellow Taxi' she's singing 'Lakes

Of Pontchartain'. It's a song about New Orleans, but its theme of alienation in a strange land has touched a particularly sensitive chord in Irish hearts and if the lost soul who falls in love with the Creole girl in the song wasn't originally Irish, he's sure been naturalised now. Christy Moore first popularised the song here, but Paul Brady may have recorded the definitive version, even taking the title of his landmark *Welcome Here Kind Stranger* album from a line in the song. It's one of my favourite songs in the history of the world ever and I decide I want it played at my funeral … straight after 'No Woman No Cry'.

I have no problem with Siobhan singing 'Lakes Of Pontchartrain' – indeed, I applaud enthusiastically when she starts it – but when she changes the words I'm enraged. The 'pretty Creole girl' of popular legend has been bafflingly replaced by a 'handsome Creole boy' though his hair somewhat worryingly still 'in black ringlets fell' and he's still singing about a lover far away at sea. What have you changed it into, Siobhan, *a gay anthem*? 'Why change it, Siobhan?' I'm yelling. 'You are a storyteller. You may even be assuming the role of the hero in the story. That doesn't give you license to change their sex and destroy the song. Great singers like Dolores Keane, Sinead O'Connor and Cara Dillon have no problem narrating the part of a man and if playing a role makes you feel uncomfortable, DON'T SING IT!' I yell at her.

Well, I would have done, but she wouldn't have heard me over the chatter of the punters. Plus the fact that Mrs Colin had me in an armlock, had stuffed a gag in my mouth and was marching me outside. Not that Siobhan is the first to change a lyric gratuitously. I still seethe every time I hear the Fureys' version of the stunning anti-war song 'No Man's Land', Eric Bogle's graphic reaction to his visit to the war grave of a 19-year-old soldier. Not only did the Fureys change Bogle's title to 'Green Fields Of France', they misheard the original and changed the line 'in mute witness stand' to 'mute in the sand'. Which made no sense whatsoever. 'That's what the folk process is all about,' says Mrs Colin, steering me into Walsh's bar.

Walsh's is a 'Fields Of Athenry' bar if ever I saw one. You can always tell. A guy with a banjo and a checked shirt at the front for a start. A packed, raucous pub baying for a big chorus. I can't see the floor but there's probably sawdust on it. There's a guy singing 'Stand By Me' and I join in lustily. 'Stand By Me' is the only song with its own fan club. It's true. There's a whole group of people who scour the world for different versions of the song and have meetings where they play newly discovered versions, discuss the lyrics and drink a toast to Ben E. King. 'Sing "Fields Of Athenry",' I shout. 'We've done it twice already,' says the banjo man. Instead, they burst into a bluegrass version of 'Last Thing On My Mind' and I retreat to the back of the pub with a glass of orange juice.

I shout some more for 'Fields Of Athenry' but Banjo Man is having none of it. 'We played it twice already!' 'But I missed it!' 'That'll teach you to be late ...'

Next morning we're up with the larks and hit the road to Tralee. It's a long haul – a journey that takes about four hours. Three hours of that are spent motionless in a traffic jam in Limerick. We also stop for a coffee in the jaw-droppingly cute village of Adare. It's all thatched cottages, wonderful stone walls, delicate bridges, ancient churches and small, comely pubs you feel you've marched out of the busy confusion of Limerick and stumbled into a film set in nineteenth-century Cornwall. Dear Lord, it even has a thirteenth-century castle. Still, no time to gawp, we've got a Rose to find.

Tralee, host town to El Salvador, feels a lot bigger than I remember it. That's probably because it *is* a lot bigger than when I remember it. It is the capital of Kerry after all and it does have a windmill. It's probably an exaggeration to say there's mayhem on the streets of Tralee today but it's lively enough. You keep tripping over the buskers but there's always a smart upwardly mobile woman in a tartan skirt and subtly highlighted auburn hair to catch you and flog you a raffle ticket. 'What do I win?' I ask as she sweet-talks me. 'You get flown over to England for a weekend in a top hotel in London and see all the sights, all expenses paid.' 'But I live in London.' 'That's all right, we can pick you up in Dublin.' 'Eh?' 'There are some other prizes ... a cuddly toy, a hamper, Westlife's *Greatest Hits* ...' 'No trips to meet Tommy Peoples?' 'Who?' 'It doesn't matter ... I think I'll pass ...'

'Oh and there's a VIP trip to Tralee Races ...'

'How much are the tickets?'

'Three euro each.'

'I'll take five ...'

The biggest tent west of Glastonbury – sorry, The *Dome* – leaves you in no doubt where the centre of activities will be come the unveiling of the new Rose of Tralee, but there's no shortage of additional activity in the town. There's a bit of trouble at t'mill too. Last night 10,000 people were expected to attend a big open-air concert due to be held in Tralee town centre in Denny St, the highlight of which was to be a concert by Phil Coulter, performing with a 20-piece orchestra. Dear Phil Coulter, a man whose credits stretched from writing Sandie Shaw's Eurovision Song Contest winner 'Puppet On A String' to producing Planxty to doing something or other with the Bay City Rollers to writing the deeply affecting 'The Town I

Love So Well' about his home city, Derry. Twenty-eight would-be
Rose of Tralees and numerous dignitaries had tripped around the
stage at the opening ceremony and it had also been used for a 'light,
fire, sound and water show' but the technical people apparently took
one look at the size of Phil's orchestra, shook their heads solemnly
and declared the stage could collapse at the first wayward stroke of a
cello. There's steam coming out of the garish Radio Kerry mobile
studio parked prominently in the middle of Tralee as distraught Phil
Coulter fans phone in to register their distress, while irate mums are
on the phone instantly when it's suggested the concert will now take
place tonight, elbowing out the scheduled gig by pop bands D'Side
and Six, winners of the Irish version of *Popstars*. Then there's the
thorny question of *Rose Idol*, Tralee's very own mini *Pop Idol* competition. The hallowed name of Louis Walsh has been mentioned in
dispatches and those hapless souls who've entered aren't too chuffed
to find neither sight nor sound of the man who discovered Boyzone
on the judging panel. 'It's a mess all right,' says a Radio Kerry caller,
'if I was the organiser I wouldn't know what to do for the best.' Me
neither. Definitely time for a drink.

We cross a square where there's all manner of shenanigans afoot.
There's a huge lorry with a portable stage attached containing a hairy
guitar band who look and sound like they've walked straight out of
1974. The singer's making all the shapes like he's Bono. Well, more
Francis Rossi really. There's also a guitarist who looks so like Brian
May I wonder if he's Anita Dobson. His party piece is a Jimi Hendrix-
style assault on 'Amazing Grace' that goes on for about twenty years.
A couple of little girls are bopping excitedly and a Japanese family are
having a fight with helium balloons but interest in the band swiftly
subsides as a vigorous argument breaks out between a woman who's
trying to park her car in the square and an impatient bunch of
jobsworths trying to make themselves heard above the rock band, the
car revving, the shrieks of the Japanese family and the torrent of abuse
from the lady in the car. As they rant at each other something extraordinary happens. A giant black and yellow snake emerges from the
ground and starts to envelop the woman in the car. She takes one look
at this ghastly monstrosity getting bigger in front of her eyes and
reverses hard. She mows down a couple of cones, demolishes a
defenceless bush and smashes into a brick wall. The men in yellow
coats are gesticulating and waving, but their voices are lost in the car
revs and the guitarist whacking up the feedback, and she's away in a
screech of breaks, hurtling in the direction of the Radio Kerry bus.

After she's gone the black and yellow snake continues to grow, gradually enveloping the whole square. A crowd has gathered to watch it come to life, gasping as it sucks in breath. Even the band are on automatic pilot, abandoning the Pete Townshend windmill guitar rhythms and going easy on the wah wah pedal as they gaze at the ballooning monster, its colourful body now sneaking round the whole perimeter of the square. I find myself gawping at it, standing next to a weird guy wearing a scary mask and a Kerry hat while waving a Brazil flag when a little girl skips gleefully in front of us. 'Mummy, can I have a ride on the Go Kart track?' Oh, so *that's* what it is.

We adjourn to Willy Darcy's Corner bar for a freshener, where the sudden influx of customers fleeing from the giant inflatable snake and Brian May and his mates howling outside is handled with admirable coolness by a blonde woman with a London accent. Between serving heavy metal fans, Go Kart competitors, Radio Kerry groupies and Rose growers, she tells me her story. Originally from Islington, she moved to Ireland with her family 35 years ago when she was ten to take over a farm in Listowel. 'I hated it,' she says. 'I didn't speak for the first ten years. It was so … *quiet* here then. It just felt so strange. I didn't feel I belonged here at all. But Ireland has changed so much. The changes have been incredible. Now it's so … *busy*.' And now you love it, right? 'I do yes, although … I went back to London for the first time last year with my four kids and it still felt like going home.' I wanted to know more about how she felt about those changes, what effect the roar of the 'Celtic Tiger' and an apparently buoyant economy and mass tourism had had on the true soul of the nation. I wanted to know why the potato, the country's celebrated national produce, costs three times as much in Ireland as it does in Britain. I wanted to have a good old rant with her about the evils of capitalism and the reality of a country with a rampantly healthy economy also being named in one recent report as neck and neck with Sweden as the most expensive country in Europe. Instead, a chap suspiciously dressed in a suit (inflatable Go-Kart circuit hirer-outer? Heavy metal band manager? Radio Kerry big cheese? Pub inspector?) asks for a pint of cider and a bowl of mushroom soup and I never see her again.

The real Rose of Tralee was Mary O'Sullivan, a poor servant girl from Brogue Lane, Tralee, who was, 'lovely and fair as the rose of the summer'. It was the middle of the nineteenth century and she was 17 and in service as a children's nanny at the large home of the Mulchinocks, the wealthy merchant family who owned much of the area. Their eldest son William Pembroke Mulchinock took an instant shine to her and they embarked on a love affair that's entranced Kerry ever since, but didn't impress the Mulchinock family. William proposed but, with a deep class and religious divide between them, it was a wedding that could never happen. What he should have done was say 'To hell with your small-minded bourgeois conventions, I am marrying this girl whether you like it or not and bugger the consequences – we're off to live in a tent in Kinvara, bye forever!' Foolishly William didn't do that. Instead he wrote her a song, 'Rose of Tralee'. Bad move. Legend has it that Mary didn't like music. In fact, the O' Sullivan family regarded it as a curse. Whenever anyone in her family died, the story goes, ghostly music filled the air.

Here the story gets a bit confused. In some versions the shame brought on the Mulchinock family by the news of William's affair with a papist servant caused him to leave Ireland in disgrace and go into exile in India, where he became a war correspondent or joined the Army, depending on who you believe. Another more dramatic slant suggests he fled Ireland to escape a murder charge after a street fight ended in tragedy. Six years later, in 1849, he returned to Tralee after friends in high places had finally smoothed out his little local difficulty, resolving that the first thing he'd do would be to find Mary O'Sullivan and marry her. First, though, he called in at the King's Arms in Rock St for a glass of cognac, and asked the landlord why the curtains were shut. 'A mark of respect,' said the landlord, 'there's a funeral today.' 'Oh?' said William. 'Who died?' 'It's very sad,' said the landlord, 'a beautiful girl just died of tuberculosis … a girl from Brogue Lane called Mary O'Sullivan. They called her the Rose of Tralee.'

William wrote another verse to his song, married a woman called Alice and emigrated to America. But, the story goes on, he couldn't get Mary out of his system. The marriage failed, William took refuge in drink, returned to Tralee and died in 1864 at the age of 44, a broken man. He was buried next to Mary at Clogherbrien. It's a nice story, anyway, though it's probably a load of old rubbish. Certainly the notion that William Mulchinock himself originally wrote 'The Rose of Tralee' seems to be dispelled by the official songwriting credits to C. Mordaunt Spencer (lyrics) and Charles Glover (music), who published it in London in 1845. If William Mulchinock was the original author his descendants might want to enquire about 150 years of royalties. Much favoured by the great Irish tenors Josef Locke and John McCormack, it's a song that's come to define Tralee and, my God, don't we get sick of hearing it today …

The Rose of Tralee competition was first staged in 1959 when a Dublin girl, Alice O'Sullivan, came out on top, but its tradition of celebrating the international culture of Irishness was truly established the following year, when Teresa Kenny from Chicago won. Since then the winners have come from all over the world, with entrants turning up from all sorts of places claiming an unlikely Irish ancestry. It's half the fun. Listening to the Dubai Rose explaining how her great grand-father emigrated from Sligo and that's why she can now play 'Danny Boy' on the tin whistle is a joy. None of your 'I want to travel and work with children and animals' here either. Miss World, this is not. These girls have jobs like occupational therapists, biologists, architects, solicitors, computer wizards, civil engineers, teachers and gardai. Christy Moore sings a very funny song – which he swears is based on a true event that happened to Donal Lunny – about being arrested one night by a former Rose of Tralee.

Apart from parading around in their posh frocks (no swimsuits here), they are expected not only to swap jokes with MC Marty Whelan (the days when Terry Wogan and Gay Byrne were the princes of Tralee are sadly gone), but to perform a little party piece too. There's always a good smattering of Irish dancing, a bit of harp playing, the odd weepy slow air on the fiddle, plenty of would-be pop singers covering Elton John and Rod Stewart, and loads of bad poetry. Very occasionally you get something out of left field … a cheer-leading dance from Texas, a spot of juggling from New Zealand, a bit of stand-up comedy, one or two ventriloquists and one girl who did the splits and tore her frock.

Last year's winner, Perth Rose Lisa Manning, a boutique manageress, recited a poem written by her mother based on Romeo and Juliet and shocked the audience by rather racily revealing a tattoo of a panther on her ankle. It's a big deal to Tralee this festival – and be warned, there's a big hike in accommodation prices when it's on – though it attracts some entertaining debate too. There are perennial rows about funding and a couple of years ago there was a splintering in the organisation, resulting in an attempt to set up a rival competi-tion which, if nothing else, inspired the headline 'War of the Roses'. It was amusingly suggested the splinter faction should adopt the song 'Paper Roses' as its theme. Then there's the rivalry between the Rose of Tralee and the Miss Ireland contest. Miss Ireland Yvonne Ellard was even moved to call an RTE phone-in show to complain that Rose of Tralee was getting all the attention while Miss Ireland was ignored. 'The Rose of Tralee is still in the fifties,' ranted Yvonne. 'All these girls going "I have distant relations in Ireland and I love this country so much even though I've only visited it twice". It's crap!'

But what we really want to know, of course, is who will win this year? There's a lot of publicity about the first Italian entry, Tamara Gervasoni, though the hot favourite is 18-year-old Alaskan-born Claire Roche, not least because she plays harp and fiddle and does

Irish dancing as well. More than that, Claire writes her own songs and is a keen public speaker. So if she doesn't wind up as Rose of Tralee you might see her at next year's Eurovision or maybe running for president. Law student Zena Al-Nazer, the daughter of a surgeon from Jordan and a nurse who left Bantry twenty-five years ago, represents Dubai and is well-backed, though I have a flutter on the first-ever Luxembourg rose Yvonne Lintner, a student in Vienna. When it comes to the crunch, the Texan rose Ashley Childers, a Tai Chi expert who bounces around in a cowboy hat and sings a Shania Twain song looks like she's stolen it from under all their noses. There are plucky musical turns from Claire Roche and the UK rose, Nicola Norris, a student from Derby, but amid the usual hail of whoops and tears, the tiara goes to Italy's Tamara Gervasoni.

An interesting character is Tamara. A 22-year-old telemarketing agent, she was born in Sligo, but her dad's Italian and growing up she lived in Africa, Greece, Spain, Iran, Iraq and Russia, as well as Italy and Ireland. I meet her the next afternoon at the races at Ballybeggan Park. Well, when I say *meet* her, I wave at her and she waves back as she passes me on a horse and cart on her lap of honour round the racecourse. 'I am very happy to be here, I love horses, I've always loved horses … I mean, I *really* love horses,' she says in such a strong Irish accent you do wonder where exactly the Italian connection comes into it. Tamara's a popular winner and with her love of horses looks set to be a fine ambassador for Irishness as she embarks on her tour of duty as the new Rose of Tralee. It's a tour that takes an unexpected turn a few months later when she has to temporarily hang up her tiara while battling an eating disorder.

But it's too expensive to hang around in Tralee long at this time of the year and there's plenty more going on in this neck of the woods. Kerry – 'The Kingdom' – is a wonder to behold. Avoid Killarney at all costs – a plastic Paddy's paradise – but travel round the Ring of Kerry and prepare to be amazed. A 100-mile round trip, it guides you across scary passes, mysterious valleys, dramatic cliff tops, rolling peatland, endless craft shops and cute villages … just ignore the army of American tourists and the heritage souvenir opportunities blocking your path and you'll be fine.

So we wind up heading further and further south and eventually end up in Kenmare. Now, there's no two ways about this. Kenmare is posh. You can tell it's posh because there are no 'Host Town To …' signs here. And if there were they'd be for the Isle Of Wight or Monaco. But while it may not be hosting any special Olympians, it is going full tilt for those all-important Best Kept Town In Ireland awards. Set picturesquely at the mouth of the River Sheen, it is historically associated with lace-making, a legacy of the famine when nuns from a local convent introduced it as a way of creating work for local girls. These days we are talking a jewel in the ring of Kerry and gateway to the Beara Peninsula and the place is crawling with trendy restaurants and fancy hotels.

We opt for the most downmarket B&B we can find on the edge of town and dine at a flamboyant bar/restaurant called Casey's, mainly because we can see the diners being entertained by a singer who looks a dead cert to perform 'Fields Of Athenry'. Or at least 'As I Leave Behind Neidin'. Neidin is the Irish name for Kenmare and 'As I Leave Behind Neidin', famously recorded by Mary Black, was written by Jimmy MacCarthy here after a visit to the *Cibeal Cinise* festival held here every Whitsun.

The singer at Casey's – Dan O'Sullivan – looks like he's fresh from a stint at Butlin's Holiday Camp. He bounds on grinning and addresses the scattered diners with 'Hey, where youse all from?' London, mate! ('London … what a wonderful city.') Winchester? ('Winchester in England? Oh how beautiful!') Chicago! ('The windy city! How wonderful!') Holland. ('Wow Holland! Fair play to youse …') He performs a rudimentary selection of songs by Christy Moore and Eric Bogle before asking if anyone has any requests. 'FIELDS OF ATHENRY' I holler, emboldened by some surprisingly potent red wine. He ignores me and does 'Tell Me Ma', much to the delight of the over-excitable Dutch woman at the front, who kicks off her shoes and dances an extravagant jig that ends up in a painful collision with the Russian shot-putter waitress. 'SING FIELDS OF ATHENRY,' I shout again and Dan goes into 'Black Velvet Band'. He finishes it, stares at me hard and says 'I think I heard somebody earlier request this one …' And yep, he's off … '*Low lie the fields of Athenry, where once we watched the small free birds fly …*'

It's at this point I start speculating how many other people are singing 'Fields Of Athenry' tonight throughout Ireland. Or indeed how many other people are singing this song tonight throughout Kenmare. I leap up, shake Dan Sullivan's hand vigorously on my way out and set off on a pub crawl of Kenmare to find out. The first place I come to is the long bar at Moeran's where a guy with silver hair and khaki slacks is singing 'Tell Me Ma'. I've barely had time to order a pint before a familiar melody comes floating along the bar … '*By a lonely prison wall I heard a young girl calling/Michael they have taken you away/For you stole Trevelyan's corn …*' Well done, Moeran's, got it in one, you've passed the 'Fields Of Athenry' test. I move on to Foley's where a bald-headed man with a beard and a harmonica round his neck is playing a Johnny Cash medley. 'FIELDS OF ATHENRY,' I shout more in hope than expectation and the guy abandons 'A Boy Named Sue' for 'Our love was on the wing/we had dreams and songs to sing/It's so lonely round the fields of Athenry ...' The hatrick! Well done, Foley's!

The pub crawl goes on. Mickey Ned's Bar, McCarthy's and, er, a few others. In the end I count six different performances of 'Fields Of Athenry' ... but a couple of them could have been by me.

The next day we get lost again, finding ourselves heading south into Cork and arriving in the middle of a picture postcard with the name Glengarriff on it. We take tea at a church overlooking Garinish Bay and fall into conversation with a local philosopher. 'The differences between the English and the Irish are defined by their sports,' he explains. 'The English play cricket, which is a game of patience, and the Irish play hurling, which is a game of passion. No wonder we've been fighting for hundreds of years ...'

That's quite a thought to ponder as we enjoy the unaccustomed sunshine, admire the glorious views and wonder if we have time to get the boat out to Garnish Island. Probably not. It's tempting to make for the Sugarloaf Mountain and maybe indulge ourselves by heading round the bay to Bantry but ... well, it's the wrong direction, frankly. So we turn the car around and drive back north to Kerry, which has plenty of picture postcard scenes of its own.

Yet it's not just the breathtaking scenery that makes Kerry so special. There's a strange mysticism about it and oddness abounds. Fleeing from Killarney as fast as my VW Beetle could carry me one time I saw a sign to Black Valley and, on impulse, swung the car off the main road. The road narrowed to a track almost immediately and then dropped with such an unexpected steepness it felt like the Pepsi Max at Blackpool all over again. We quickly realised why it was called Black Valley; it got darker and darker as we drove deeper and deeper into the bowels of the earth and the track almost became invisible. I know it's silly, but the still darkness and the sheer depths to which we were sinking was genuinely eerie. At such times you start believing in leprechauns and little people as we continued to descend for what seemed like hours, expecting to see a sign for Australia any time. We didn't see a soul. Just a few cows and a bunch of goats in the hills in the distance who fled as soon as they saw us, clearly believing we were bodhran makers searching for fresh skin. Lakes, waterfalls, streams, bogs, silhouettes of charging goats ... that's all we saw for miles and miles and miles as driving rain added to the hazards. And then the yellow light went on to warn me the petrol tank was running on empty. Mrs Colin and I were just about to draw lots to decide whose arm we'd eat first to help us survive here at the bottom of the world when the track started rising.

We crawled up the ensuing miasma of hills and bridges (my little Beetle was never too keen on hills) watching the fuel needle settle resolutely on zero. A couple of crossroads and we tossed a coin and turned right. A sign to Glencar raised our spirits and suddenly, through the swirling mist, we saw lights. We drew closer. A hotel! We rubbed our eyes, suspecting a mirage, and then dashed inside before it went away. The bar was teeming. People were singing, hugging each other and laughing like drains the way you do when you've been drinking for three days. I ordered the biggest brandy in the house and asked the barman if there was any room at the inn. He tossed us a room key and let us get on with it. We had dinner – every packet of crisps they had in the place – and, exhausted by the trauma inflicted by Black Valley, retired to our room, trying to blot out the din from the bar.

We were up early next morning (10am) and crept downstairs for breakfast. There was not a soul to be seen. We found the restaurant. It was totally deserted. All the chairs were upside down on the tables. It was completely silent. We found the kitchen. Not a soul to be seen. We went to the front door. Locked. We rang the bell at reception several times. Nothing. We wandered the length and breadth of the hotel for signs of life. Absolutely nothing. We went into the kitchen and looked longingly at the coffee pot, wandering if we dared. Nobody came. We rang the bell again. Nothing. It seemed incredible. Last night you couldn't *move* in here. Where had everybody gone? Or did we imagine it? We went on one final circuit of the hotel, banging on doors and shouting 'Is anybody there?' rather pathetically. Finally a door creaked open and a girl who looked about 15 going on 45 blearily poked her head out. 'Is it breakfast you're after?' 'Well ... only if it's not too much bother ...' 'No bother,' she groaned, emerging in slippers and dressing gown, wincing as she collided with a sharp shaft of sunlight. 'Jeez, I've got a head like a cow's udder,' she said, leaving us with a curious image of what that might be like. 'Bit of a party last night then?' I said weakly. 'Is it the full Irish breakfast you want then?' she said through narrowed eyes. 'That'll be lovely, thanks,' we said, rescuing chairs from table tops and finding our own cutlery. We had breakfast, paid, checked out and fled without another word exchanged. It put me in mind of the Hotel California ... you know, 'you can check out any time you like, but you can never leave'. I've been back to that area of Kerry several times since but have never been able to locate that ghost hotel that saved our lives but wasn't keen to give us breakfast.

Then there's Killorglin. A small market town to the north west of Killarney along the Laune River at the gateway of the gorgeous

Iveragh Peninsula. A largely agricultural community, it's pretty, but mostly pretty unspectacular. Until Puck Fair Weekend. Ireland loves its festivals. There are festivals all over the country virtually every weekend … craft festivals, literary festivals, poetry festivals, busking festivals, food festivals, arts festivals. Any excuse for a party really. Yet the strangest of them all is surely that weekend in August when Killorglin holds the Puck Fair.

This is a seriously strange event. I mean, *seriously* strange. There's all sorts of theories about pre-Christian worship of the Celtic sun god Lugh, pagan symbols of fertility and superstitions about horned animals representing gods with supernatural powers. But I prefer the suggestion that it all stems from the seventeenth century when the hated Cromwell ran amok through Ireland, ruthlessly devastating Drogheda and Wexford before heading west. The story goes that the people of Killorglin were warned of Cromwell's advance by a fleeing herd of goats at McGillicuddy Reeks. Of course it may have been that Cromwell was just after a bodhran but thereafter Killorglin canonised goats, and have marked their gratitude ever since by going up into the McGillicuddy Mountains and catching the best-looking goat with the biggest horns they can find. They spend a couple of weeks sprucing him up, stick him in a cage and put him on a float and then they all dress up as Celtic warriors and lead him on a bizarre parade around the town. When they reach the town square a pre-selected schoolgirl puts a crown over his horns and officially declares him King Puck.

The cage is then winched on to a platform overlooking the town, where he remains for three days, observing his new subjects getting royally pissed for the duration. So pissed, in fact, the whole ritual is now sponsored by Guinness. Once populated mostly by travellers and serving as a market for horses and cattle, the Puck weekend is now a major event in the Irish calendar, an orgy of singing, dancing and general merrymaking that's extraordinary, even by Irish standards. When the last man falls in a heap by the side of the road, King Puck is levered back from his throne in the sky, given a hearty meal and returned to the mountain from whence he came. He'll have a bit of explaining to do to Mrs Goat when he gets home too. 'You'll never guess what happened to me.' 'Aw, Puck off!'

This is a momentous week to be in Kerry. Always a hotspot for visitors, the county is playing host not only to the Rose of Tralee, but the Fleadh Cheoil na h'Eireann. Literally translated as 'a feast of music', the Fleadh was first staged in Monaghan in 1952, following a trial run organised the previous year in Mullingar by the newly formed Comhaltas Ceoltoiri Eireann, a coalition of musicians and enthusiasts dedicated to promoting the music. Originally designed as a means for the like-minded to get together and play and talk and drink, it has become Irish music's most renowned travelling show. Its central focus is the all-Ireland titles in a mind-boggling array of disciplines in a broad range of age groups at which emergent talents are judged on everything from war pipes to lilting to ceili groups to mouth organ to storytelling. Each year it is held in a different town that is subsequently instantly recognisable by a haggard exterior, the unmarked graves of a trillion dead bodhrans, some stray bunting in a back street that nobody could be arsed to take down and wizened old men shaking their heads muttering 'Never again'. Every musician who ever played a pub session, every scholar of the Irish tradition, every daft bugger in search of the craic has an invisible homing device round their necks that drags them kicking and screaming to the Fleadh Cheoil.

There are plenty of impostors, of course. Fleadhs of various sizes, shapes and descriptions go on all year around Ireland and the word has been commandeered as a means of putting a Celtic spin – however spurious – on festivals in the UK and America. The London Fleadh became an event at which you need to get up early in the morning to find much of an Irish representation on the bill. But there is only one Fleadh Cheoil and it's being held here and now in Listowel in the county of Kerry. So let's find that N69 and off we go. Here I would surely find Tommy Peoples.

To be frank we could have thought this through a bit more. By now it's Saturday and the Fleadh has been in full swing for several days. It's an event that attracts people from all over the world – 200,000 is the estimate this year – and quite apart from the usual mass of tourists and professional drinkers who can sniff a party at a hundred miles, an estimated 10,000 musicians turn up at the event every year. That's an awful lot of people to be accommodated in one small market town in Kerry. And we're bowling up there on a Saturday afternoon expecting to waltz in unannounced and find a nice en suite B&B. 'You're going to the Fleadh?' said someone in Tralee. 'And you think you'll find somewhere to stay, d'ya? I'm telling you now, you won't find anywhere within 20 miles of the place to stay. They booked everything out months ago. You might as well stay here.' We'd found an advert in one of the papers for accommodation above a pub in the centre of Listowel for Fleadh weekend, and a quick call ascertained they indeed had spare accommodation ... the third hammock on the left in the loft was still going if we didn't mind sharing with a Scandinavian reggae band, the Horse & Jockey hurling team and a large family of bats. Only 100 euro a night.

Interested? We say no ta, we'll pass ... and head for Listowel on a wing and a prayer.

The traffic starts building about 10 miles out of Listowel. Cars abandoned at sod-this-for-a-game-of-rhubarb-I-need-a-drink angles on grass verges and chancers scrawling 'CAR PARK HERE – 10 EURO EACH' on scrubby bits of cardboard and directing people into fields otherwise occupied by mystified cattle. We crawl closer and the cars are piled ever more erratically by the side of the road, barriers appear as if from nowhere and the gardai wander among the motionless traffic chortling heartily to themselves but skilfully not showing it to the frustrated motorists. 'What's the hold-up, officer?' asks an American in a hire care. 'Ah, 'tis the Fleadh,' says the garde. 'The whaaat?' 'The fleadh.' 'The flarrrrr? What in hell is that?' 'It's erm ... they have music and y'know, a bit of a party.' 'How long will the traffic jam last?' 'About three months I reckon ...'

A shield of cones block all roads into Listowel while gardai patiently indicate the ring road and hug themselves with laughter when I ask if there are any guest houses in the vicinity that might have room for a couple of little 'uns. We crawl round to the Ballybunion road and optimistically stop at a B&B a couple of miles out of town. A woman is shaking her head at us through the window before we've even stopped the car and the process is repeated every couple of hundred yards. Mostly they have 'No Vacancies' signs up, but the more sadistic deliberately leave them off, take an age to answer the door, pretend to go away and inspect their bookings and then gravely tell you they've been fully booked for this weekend since last April. As you limp back up the path you can hear them splitting their sides at the folly of the stupid tourists who think they can just roll up during the Fleadh and expect to find accommodation. 'You really should have booked up a long time ago,' scolds one landlady who is surely a retired headmistress. 'Do you know where we might find some accommodation?' 'You might be lucky and find somewhere in Tralee.' 'But we've just come from Tralee.' 'Ah, you'll know the way then.'

It's tea-time by the time we arrive at the seaside town of Ballybunion a dozen or so miles from Listowel. 'Oh look, there's hundreds of places to stay here,' I say brightly, trying to lift the spirits of a disheartened Mrs Colin, who'd been counselling advance booking for several days. The Ballybunion branch of Sadistic B&Bs R Us are even more cruel than the Listowel branch. 'Ah yes, we have lots of rooms available.' 'Great,' we say, congratulating ourselves on our fine fortune. 'Unfortunately, none of them are available tonight.' We dump the car by the sea and wander around the town looking for clues. A sign suddenly appears in the window of a pub saying 'LATE

CANCELLATION – ROOMS AVAILABLE.' From nowhere, there's a stampede of Austrians with rucksacks, who've all apparently developed a rakish thirst. After being trampled on we approach the barman. 'You have a room?' 'Oh,' he says, with cod concern. 'It's just this minute gone. Some Austrians. Nice people.' We order a drink and contemplate the next move. A night in the car or shall we toss a coin to decide whether to try our luck north or south?

A couple of guys start chatting. 'Looking for a room, are you? We've been here all afternoon trying. Everywhere's booked but we've got our spies out …' At that moment his mobile rings. 'Really?' he whispers into it. 'Up by the golf course? Along the beach? Up the hill? Cliff top? Two rooms? What's the name of it again?' About a dozen of us strain to hear the answer from the disembodied voice at the other end of the phone, but he's already out of the door with the rest of the pub in hot pursuit. Me and Mrs Colin among them. 'He said something about a golf course along the beach,' I say as we sprint to the car. This is the kind of sport they should be including in their Special Olympics – Finding A Room In Ballybunion During The Fleadh. Austria are clearly the world champions. We follow the beach, drive up the hill and locate a very fancy golf course and see the guest house. It looks divine. A huge place overlooking the Atlantic Ocean and the golf course and more importantly it has a VACANCIES sign up. We approach cautiously for fear of Austrian backpackers lurking in the undergrowth waiting to pounce and knock on the door.

'It's just the two of you, is it?' says the silver-haired lady who answers. 'That's a pity.' 'Why?' 'Well, I did have a room but somebody called just a couple of minutes ago to reserve it. I think they were Austrian.' We slope back to the car, tails between legs. 'But you might try Bridget.' 'Bridget?' 'Yes, top of the hill, turn left, third house on the right. You can't miss it.' If anything is guaranteed to get me lost it's the words 'You can't miss it' and half an hour later we're still driving around the cliffs of Ballybunion knocking on people's doors asking for Bridget.

'Bridget … would that be Bridget Moss now?' 'I don't know …' 'Is she the blonde woman from Kilrush?' 'I really don't know …' 'Would she be the schoolteacher?' 'I'm sorry I don't …' 'Now why would you be wanting Bridget Moss anyway?' 'Well, we need a room to stay for the night and somebody said she might have one.' 'Oh, it's a room you're after, is it?' 'Yes,' we say hopefully. She scratches her head. 'Now I wouldn't want to get you worried but that might be a bit difficult, there's the Fleadh on at Listowel, you see.' 'Yes, so I heard.'

'I'll tell you what, I'll give Mary a call.' 'Mary?' 'Yes. Mary sometimes lets out rooms, I'll give her a call now' and with an encouraging wink she ushers us into her sitting room, beckons us to sit down, plies us with biscuits and calls Mary. 'Mary … hello Mary, it's Joan. How are you, Mary? Oh that's good. Yes, not too bad, thanks. Tom's had a bit of trouble with his hip but he's on the mend … yes, you must come over for a coffee … haven't seen you for an age … now when was it? … Ah, that's it, the quiz night … wasn't that a scream? … I know … this weather …' She suddenly remembers she has visitors. 'The thing is Mary, I was wondering, do you still let out rooms to visitors? I've got a couple here from England who were looking for a place to stay but because of the Fleadh and all, everything is booked up here.' We waited with baited breath and she looks intently at us, frowning. 'Yes, they seem nice enough.' She leans over to us whispering 'She wants to know if you look like decent!' Then she returns to the phone. 'No, you're all right Mary, they say they're house-trained!' Peals of laughter. 'Shall I send them over then, Mary? Okay, they'll be with you in about ten minutes. I'll tell them you'll meet them by the garage.'

Joan then spends the next 15 minutes drawing a map so intricate it includes detailed scale diagrams of inlets, side roads, cliff faces and corner shops. 'If you see the Bill Clinton statue you'll know you've gone straight on when you should have turned left.' 'Bill Clinton, Joan?' 'Bill Clinton? The *Monica Lewinsky* Bill Clinton?' 'Yes. He had a round of golf on the course up the road here a few years back so they built him a statue.'

Waving us off, she said, 'Don't forget, if you see that Bill Clinton statue you've gone too far.' First thing we see is the Bill Clinton statue. Forty-five tortured minutes later we find Mary, who must have been standing outside the garage for at least an hour, but doesn't bear a grudge. 'Oh well, Irish time,' she keeps saying, nudging a sheepdog sleeping on the floor alongside her to wake up. 'It's that house up there,' she says, pointing at a dot in the sky. 'I said I'd meet you here 'cos you'd never find it on your own. Follow me.' She gets into her car and roars off on a narrow track up the hill. I follow. And then the dog appears. Irish canines are loopy. Most dogs chase cats or rabbits or sticks of wood. Irish dogs terrorise cars. There you are driving leisurely along some back lane admiring the beautiful views and suddenly there'll be an horrific noise as a huge dog leaps out in front of you barking for Ireland. You judder to a halt for fear of mowing him down and sit there for about twenty minutes with the dog staring you out until a little old lady wanders out beaming, whisks the dog into her arms, tells you he wouldn't hurt a fly and waves you on your way.

Mary's dog's speciality is racing cars up steep hills. His cunning trick is to sneak in front of you at the start and occupying the centre of the track making overtaking impossible. When he stops for a rest you gingerly try to edge the car around him, but just as you think you've made it he's up and barking and leaping around in front of the windscreen. By the time we're halfway up the hill Mary is long out of sight and as the path diverts into an alternative selection of houses we have absolutely no idea which way to go. The dog does, of course, but he's not telling and sits there staring at us, amused by our stupidity. A quarter of an hour later Mary comes looking for us. 'He'd get out of the way, you know,' she says, nuzzling the dog. 'He wouldn't let you run him over. He's not stupid.' I knew that.

She leads us to a large house with a breathtaking panoramic view of the Shannon Estuary and explains she usually lets it out for block holiday bookings only, but is renting out individual rooms on a daily basis for the duration of the Fleadh. 'So how many others are booked in tonight?' 'Oh, just you.' We head back into Ballybunion and contemplate a second assault on Listowel. There is a shuttle bus service that promises to get you into Listowel tonight, but slyly makes no promises about getting you back again. Besides, I'm getting to like Ballybunion now. I want to find a pub full of Austrians and make faces at them.

Sadly we've just missed the Ballybunion Busking Competition. How good would that have been? An endless parade of hairy monsters all singing 'Fields Of Athenry', 'Ordinary Man' and 'Black Is The Colour'. And we've also missed the annual Bachelors Festival. I wonder for a minute if this might refer to the sixties vocal group and search the pubs for a clean-cut, well-scrubbed trio singing 'Charmaine' and 'I Believe' in perfect harmony. No joy. The lads wandering round with tongues hanging out suggests it's a festival for the maritally challenged. Maybe that's why the Austrians are in town.

We're also a couple of weeks early for the first Ballybunion Mussels & Music festival. At first I misread this and think it means *muscles*, and assume it's some kind of extension of the Bachelors Festival. Maybe they put the bachelors on an intensive weight-training course and bring them back for a couple of weeks and see if they can't pull a few tractors through the town to add to their eligibility. Then I hear Abba's 'Dancing Queen', followed by Village People's 'YMCA' being piped out of one of the amusement arcades and start wondering about this place. Bachelors, muscles, Abba and there's a guy with a moustache over the road too … is Ballybunion the gay capital of Ireland? But no, we're talking Molly Malone-style mussels. So the idea is you come to Ballybunion for the weekend, have a laugh and a sing-song with Brendan Grace, rock out to Picture House, mince around to an Abba tribute band and gorge yourself on mussels all weekend.

We find a pub, settle down in a corner and wait for the topless bachelors to come sashaying along the bar. Instead we get a bald man in a checked shirt with a small guitar and a big grin giving the punters what they want. 'You may know this one, please join in ...' he says and he's straight into it ... 'Beside a prison wall I heard a young man caww-aww-awww-llling ... Mary they have taken me away ...' Yep, first song on it's jackpot time, 'Fields Of Athenry'. This bloke takes no prisoners. Problem is, how do you follow it? We listen to tuneless versions of 'Norwegian Wood' and 'The Town I Love So Well'. When he winks at the ladies and starts playing 'Annie's Song' it's definitely time to cut our losses and embark on the search for the beach road, the garage, the mad dog and our new home in the sky.

We're up early the next day ready for another assault on the Fleadh. Early enough to make it through Listowel's barricades and find a dusty old building site on the outskirts of town where a man in a yellow jacket relieves us of 10 euro. Mid-morning and the streets are already rammed. What they're rammed with is an entirely different matter. Ghost-like figures are holding surreal conversations with lamp posts and the painful squints and suppressed groans at the first glint of sunlight breaking through the clouds suggest not everyone found a nice house to stay in last night. 'Excuse me,' apologises one young guy stinking of cider and stale cigarettes, as he staggers into me, 'I haven't slept for three days.' The odd abandoned sleeping bag and ashen-faced ghoul slumped in side streets indicate he's not the only one.

Every few yards you find huddles of people and in the middle of them there'll be a couple of fiddles and an accordion vigorously belting out some jig. Stallholders are still setting up pitches to flog you everything from bodhrans to tin whistles to novelty balloons to tacky T-shirts and groups of youngsters marching purposefully along the road clutching flute, fiddle and accordion cases with anxious parents trotting behind tell you that the competitions being held in schools and halls all over town are already well underway. An irresistible burst of diddley-i breaks out in Church St and I suddenly find myself in the midst of an impromptu ceili. Even without a drink the fumes of the week-long reverie swiftly seep into your system and suddenly I find myself linking arms with a sylph-like woman from Belfast and a 20-stone bearded Dutchman. To hell with it, I'm there, kicking legs, waving arms, sending big fat bearded Dutchmen round my little finger. Eat your heart out Michael Flatley.

There's a crash on the floor and the innards of something small and battery-driven are trampled underfoot. That'll be my dictaphone then. This is bad news. When the dance is over I look at the ugly mangled remains of tape, battery and dictaphone metal, rescue what I can for a decent burial and reflect that the death of the dictaphone also signals the demise of the one true record I have of the trip. The bottom line is you can discount everything I've written so far as unreliable evidence. And while you're at it you might as well discount everything else I write hereon in, too. A man without a dictaphone is a man in need of a very good memory.

It's nearly lunchtime so we adjourn to Mai Fitz's bar. There, various pockets of sessions are beginning to stir and it's uncomfortably hot. The conservatory at the back, though, is deserted apart from a couple of guys trying to fix a telly hanging from the roof and we settle down for the first pint of the day. A guy with a bodhran comes and sits next to me and we gaze in wonder at the barmen desperately trying to get the telly to work. 'There's a big game on today,' says my new companion. 'Kerry and Cork in the All-Ireland football semi-final, that'll be a cracking game all right.' A Kerry man, right? 'Noooo, I'm Cork, but don't tell anyone around here. Thought we'd have a few tunes and watch the match here.' Not if Laurel & Hardy trying to get the telly working have anything to do with it, mate. They've managed to get a picture but the sun is directly on the screen so nobody can see a thing. A home-made blind is hastily erected but this fails to do the trick and as our two heroes jiggle the telly around it comes flying off its hinges. I brace myself for the crash as it hits the floor, but it pitches into the ample stomach of the guy at the top of the ladder. His arms wrap around it, bending him over double and there's a classic freeze-frame moment as he wobbles around on a ladder, puffing his cheeks out furiously as he hangs on to the telly for dear life. For a second it looks like the ladder will topple and I'm wondering which will hit the ground first, the telly or the fat man, and if my mate's bodhran will survive the impact. If it happens it'll knock the Dictaphone Incident off tomorrow's front pages, that's for sure.

Then the music starts. An accordion player has appeared on my left and is instantly into a tune and the bodhran player on my right quickly joins in enthusiastically. In no time at all two fiddle players, a couple of flutes, three fiddles and a battalion of bodhran players have magically appeared and are giving it almighty stick. And there's me right in the middle of them, grinning inanely, tapping my foot, feeling like a complete lemon. A few bystanders watch curiously from the wings and even the telly technicians temporarily abandon their bid to bring us the Kerry-Cork game to wonder who the guy in the middle of the session is and why is he clutching a dead dictaphone? 'Will yer give us a song?' says my mate, the bodhran player as the onslaught of tunes shows the first signs of abating after about three quarters of an hour. 'What?' 'A song. I think we'd all like to hear a song ...' Nods of approval and agreement all round. 'No, I er ...' Panicking, I contemplate the options. A coughing fit? Pretend I'm Austrian and don't speak English? An attack of amnesia and can't remember any words? An urgent appointment at the dentist? 'No, I don't really, er, you know, singing isn't, like, no, erm ... must go, *bye*!'

Outside Listowel is creaking at the seams. If there are indeed 200,000 people they all seem to be heading for the town square, where a large stage has been erected for various concerts and displays of Irish dancing. I can see the legendary Galway accordion player Joe Burke in the middle of a session with his wife and fellow accordionist Anne Conroy, and the Kilfenora Ceili Band played a concert in the square last night, but this is a people's event, the antithesis of the celebrity-driven festival. In one corner of the square there are about a dozen flute players with, right in the middle of them, a monk in full habit. I battle through the throng to the opposite corner and find a group of new-agers, matted hair and all, pounding furiously on bongos and howling unnervingly. The main singer is dancing around trying to get people to join in. I step back nervously. 'C'mon, you all know the chorus,' he yells as he unleashes another blood-curdling roar. It sounds vaguely familiar and one or two other people join in. A girl starts dancing with them. Their ranks swell until there's about thirty people jumping around, yelling the same words over and over again. I strain hard to listen to those words. 'Loooooooooolyyyyyyyyyyyyythefeeyaldsofaaveeenryyyyy' and the penny suddenly drops. My God, they're singing 'The Fields Of Athenry'. Is desecrating 'The Fields Of Athenry' a capital offence in Kerry? Sid Vicious murdering 'My Way' has got nothing on this.

We find John B Keane's bar in William Street. John B – author, dramatist, journalist, wit, raconteur, bodhran enthusiast, publican, social livewire and Listowel legend – was a central figure at last year's Fleadh, also staged here. (Listowel likes the Fleadh, this is the thirteenth year it's been held here.) Sadly, at the age of 73, he died in May during Listowel Literary Week and is clearly sorely missed. 'Oh, John B would have loved this,' says a guy I find myself wedged up against at the bar. 'He loved the Fleadh, he really did. I mean, he was a great writer an' all but he loved the craic, so he did. If he was here now he'd be out here having a chat, leading everyone in a tune. He was a great man, John B. A character and a half he was. Sure, they don't make 'em like that any more.' The next day I go out and buy *The Bodhran Makers*, John B's insightful story of the indomitable spirit of Irish farmworkers and their battles with the church in the 1950s.

After that it all becomes a bit of a blur. More bars, more sessions, more hugging complete strangers and telling them your life story. We're in one pub slightly out of town near the car park buried in tents enjoying relative respite from the frenzy going on elsewhere, listening to an uillean piper. The pipes have been conspicuous by their absence in these sessions though, given that they are notoriously temperamental – and in a drunken sauna who can blame them? Especially when they are virtually impossible to play sober let alone with serious drink inside you. He's playing a beautiful, heartbreaking lament and the mood inside the pub is wonderfully mellow and sanguine, in contrast to the carnage outside. A middle-aged barman sits back on his stool surveying the benign scene with calm contentment. Then there's the sound of a glass breaking, voices raised, yells and two guys are pummelling each other to pieces. In a flash our laidback barman is on top of the bar and in one leap dives over the heads of a group of innocent drinkers and lands on top of the two fighting. Before you can blink the guy on top is hurtling head first out of the door, the other is dusted down and the barman has vaulted back over the bar to resume his quiet Sunday night at the Fleadh. 'Can I get anyone a drink?' he asks politely while the rest of us gaze at the Listowel Superhero and wonder what he did with his cape.

We wade through the human wreckage of the Listowel night, stopping to take in a few more of the huddled street sessions you still find every few yards and eventually make it back to the building site where we left the car. The same car park attendant is on duty, though his yellow jacket is a bit grubbier. 'You've had a long day,' I say, 'don't you ever sleep?' 'At the Fleadh,' he says gravely, 'nobody sleeps.' He' s wrong though. When I eventually find my car beneath a carpet of dust, there's a guy snoring on the floor beside it. I try to rouse him but Yellow Jacket Man urges me to let him be. For you, soldier, the Fleadh is over.

Chapter six

DINGLE, MITCHUM, COOLEY & DOLPHIN MANIA

R iding along in my automobile. My baby beside me at the
wheel. Cruising and playing the radio. With no particular place
to go ...

Best toss for it then. Heads we do a right and make for Cork and
stop off at Castleisland (and try and make sense of Padraig O'Keeffe
and the Sliabh Luachra tradition), tails we bang on up to Clare and
attempt to find Tommy Peoples. It comes down tails. Clare it is then.
Put the kettle on, Tommy. Or shall we make it the best of three? But
then a song comes on the radio that changes everything ...

> 'Drinking all the day
> In old pubs where fiddlers love to play
> Saw one touch the bow
> He played a reel which seemed so grand and gay ...'

It's Mary Black performing 'Song For Ireland'. Dick Gaughan's
version is better but it's a lovely sunny day in Kerry and Mary hits a
peculiarly nostalgic nerve. Written by an Englishman, Phil Colclough,
'Song For Ireland' admirably expresses what so many of us think
about Ireland and the incomprehension we feel that such a tranquil
land can have such a bloody, tortured history ...

> 'I stood on Dingle beach and cast,
> In the wild foam for the Atlantic bass,
> When living on your Western shore,
> Saw summer sunsets, asked for more,
> I stood by your Atlantic sea,
> And I sang a song for Ireland ...'

One mention of Dingle and I turn the car right around. It's been, what, *16, 17, 18 years* since I was last in Dingle. Too long. Far too long. There's an old friend in Dingle I'd like to see again …

So the coin goes out of the window and we head for what claims to be the most westerly town in Europe. Back round Tralee Bay, past the Slieve Mish Mountains and down into Inch. I'm almost afraid to look as we make our descent and get our first view of Inch Strand. I well remember the short, sharp gasps all round when we got our first glimpse of it all those years ago. We swept round a bend from the mountains and there it was laid out beneath us like a huge white carpet. A massive lawn of white sand that stretched for miles and miles and miles. There wasn't a soul to be seen. Or any evidence of human life at all. No houses, amusement arcades, beach huts, tea bars or souvenir shops. Not even a pub. Just an awesome sense of solitude that seemed to last forever. I remember thinking this is what the world must look like when you die.

At the top of the road leading down to the strand an eccentric old building seemed to be the lord of all it beheld. It had the ambience of an ancient colonial house and seemed an entirely inappropriate image to dominate such a mesmerisingly stark landscape. It was an enrapturing scene and I stood there looking at it for several minutes, gulping in a stillness interrupted only by the distant lapping waves.

'Johnny Lennon lives up there, y'know …' I nearly jumped out of my skin. An old man in comedy shorts and woolly vest had silently materialised at my side. 'Johnny Lennon?' 'Yip. Him and the other feller.' 'The other feller?' 'Paul McCarthy. They bought it a couple of years ago.' 'You mean Paul McCartney?' 'That's him. Nice feller. He came round for tea once. Nice feller.' 'They bought that house?' 'Yip. They wanted somewhere they could come and get away from all that mad London crowd and write all their songs for that group, what d'ya call that group?' 'The Beatles?' 'That's them. They wrote all their songs here.' 'They did?' 'Oh yeah, *all* of them.' 'I didn't know that.' 'Well, you wouldn't. It's a secret, see. I never tell anyone they're here. They don't want to be bothered. So they just come over here when things get too much for them and write their songs. We often see 'em, Johnny and the other feller. They always wave. Nice fellers. They were up here together last weekend. We had a nice li'l chat. They said they were writing some new songs. Nice fellers.'

I hadn't the heart to tell him John Lennon was dead.

So we climbed the hill to discover that the mystery house was a hotel. Sort of. Tatty and tumbledown it looked like something out of a lost universe. The door creaked and wobbled off its hinges and an arcane bell jangled above us as we crossed the threshold. We stood at the window trying to make out the seals and otters out on the rocks below and waiting while a doddery elderly woman made a slow, painful journey to meet us. 'Two cups of tea, please.' 'Whaaaat?' 'Two cups of tea, please.' 'You'll have to speak up, I'm a little hard of hearing.' 'TWO CUPS OF TEA, PLEASE.' 'I can't understand you. You're not from round here, are you? I can't understand your accent.' She was getting quite grumpy about it all now so I pretended to be Austrian and started writing down the order on a serviette. 'It's no good, I don't have my reading glasses on,' she barked in the affronted manner of one who'd been asked for some under-the-counter porn.

In the end we mimed drinking two cups of tea and she disappeared for an hour or so while we fretted about what sort of hideous poison she was preparing for us. The magic of Inch Strand somehow seemed lost along the way, though you could see why they'd chosen to film *Playboy Of The Western World* here in 1962 and *Ryan's Daughter* in 1970. Eventually the old lady returned shakily with two cups of seaweed delivered in majestic gold china. Not that it mattered. Most of it was slopping in the saucers or seeping into the floorboards by the time it made the table. I thanked her profusely and asked her to say hello to Paul McCarthy.

Inch looks very different today. Johnny Lennon's house – the Strand Bar – is still there overlooking the beach but it seems a lot smaller now. It also has a chum along the front, an oddly flat creation called Sammy's Store & Café, which offers you accommodation as well as books, postcards, crafts and trinkets. Ask nicely and they'll even serve you tea, though alas not in a gold china cup. Its white wall is also emblazoned with an intriguing message. 'Dear Inch must I leave you, I have promises to keep. Perhaps miles to go to my last sleep.' Who wrote it? What does it mean? Why are we here? Don't ask me, guv, I'm only the driver.

There are cars parked on the beach now and we grumble a bit about that. A mirage of beauty now seems tarnished and, given a nudge might even verge on tacky. It's still a great beach and we sit in the sun for a while watching a bunch of Spaniards playing footie.

We eventually head on round the coast to Dingle ('host town to South Africa'), eager to renew acquaintance with the quaint sleepy rundown little fishing village we'd stumbled on all those years ago. We are in for a shock. We pull into the harbour and find … a throbbing *metropolis*. The place is full of *people*. That didn't happen before. I remember two pubs and a couple of fishing boats. Now there are boats of all shapes and sizes all over the harbour and where there once stood just a handful of tumbledown cottages, there are shops and restaurants and bureau de changes and B&Bs coming out of your ears.

My God, there's even a betting shop, a café advertising *espresso coffee* and a cinema. I park in the huge car park, march into the tourist office on the harbour front and say 'Excuse me, I was looking for Dingle.' 'This *is* Dingle.' 'It *is*? What happened?' 'What do you mean, sir?' 'Dingle has ... er ... *changed* a lot.' 'Yes, I believe so but I don't really know, I'm from Monaghan.' Then a 30-stone American waving a map calls 'Miss ... miss ... I need to know the fastest way to Tray-lee ...' and she's gone to field a more familiar line of questioning.

It's all my mate Fungie's fault. We'd come here that first time in search of petrol. Some hopes. 'Well now, it's petrol you want is it?' puzzled an old chap as if we'd asked for a rocket to the Moon. 'You might ask ol' Jack in the pub, he sometimes knows where to find petrol.' We had a wander round the harbour and noticed a scribbled note on a bit of cardboard stuck in front of one of the small boats. 'Trips To See The Dolphin'. I sensed a con and quizzed the captain mercilessly.

'Dolphin? What dolphin?'

'They call him Fungie,' said the captain.

'Why?'

'After the fisherman ...'

'What fisherman?'

'The fisherman who first started looking out for him. He had a beard.'

'The dolphin had a beard?'

'No, the fisherman had a beard so we called him Fungus. And we called the dolphin Fungus's dolphin ... and it got shortened to Fungie ...'

'This is a joke isn't it?'

'No, it's as true as I'm stood here.'

'So where is he?'

'The fisherman?'

'No, the dolphin.'

'Out there ... in the harbour.'

'Why?'

'I dunno ... he lives in the harbour. He just sort of appeared one day ... and stayed.'

'If we go out with you how can you be sure we'll see him?'

'Oh, you'll see him.'

'How do you know?'

'He always comes when he hears the boat.'

'What if he doesn't?'

'He'll come ...'

'But if he doesn't ...'

'Look, I won't collect your money until you see the dolphin, okay?'

'Okay.'

By the time we collected our punts together and clambered into the small open-top craft, a few more stragglers had been similarly attracted by the tatty sign, and had roughly the same conversation with the captain. And off we went into Dingle Bay in search of Fungie. Twenty minutes into the harbour and Fungie came to say hello, leaping in and out of the water and splashing alongside the boat, while we all ooh-ed and aah-ed and took photographs that would never come out. It seemed amazing then and it seems amazing now. 'He sometimes tosses fish into the boat,' said the captain and we all took a step back. 'It was the old lighthouse keeper Paddy Ferriter, he was the first one who spotted the dolphin, then he started following the boats. I don't know what brought him here but he seems to like it.'

A young American girl was in a frenzy of excitement every time Fungie approached the boat. 'Can I swim with him?' she asked the captain. 'Sure … brought your swimsuit?' 'Nope.' And with that she stripped down to her undies and dived in, shrieking with delight as the dolphin came to nuzzle and play. 'Why did she do that?' a little girl asked the captain. 'She's American,' said the captain. 'Oh, I see,' said the little girl, understanding all. The American dolphin swimmer was in the water for what seemed like hours while the rest of us shivered but she was eventually coaxed back on deck in a state of euphoria. 'Oh wow … that was just so … I mean … too much …' she kept saying, shivering and dripping. 'Hope you've got some dry clothes back in Dingle,' we said as we closed in on the harbour once more. Her face went pale as she squinted at the quay. 'Oh no …' she said, 'my coach has gone.' Coach? What coach? 'I'm on a coach tour from Killarney. We only stopped here for a cup of coffee. I just saw the sign about the dolphin and got on the boat. The rest of them are probably back in Killarney now.' The poor girl looked distraught and was suddenly asking the captain about guest houses where you didn't have to pay because she'd spent all her change going to see a dolphin and her traveller's cheques were back in Killarney. So she stayed overnight at a local pub, fell in love with the landlord's son and never went back to Killarney … or Kansas.

Okay, okay, that last bit *is* a complete lie. I'm sorry to say I've no idea what happened to the American girl who swam with the dolphin. Or her soggy undies.

We return to find that Fungie is now a major celebrity … and as his fame has grown, so has Dingle. The tourist office is festooned with pictures and newspaper cuttings about Fungie, while he also stars on numerous postcards, has two books and a video dedicated to him and has been featured in TV shows all over Europe. Now you can't move in Dingle Harbour for boat companies offering trips out to see him and they come from all over the world to see him. You even get the odd pilgrimage from ME and MS sufferers hoping Fungie will cure them. A couple of early TV documentaries was all it took to open the floodgates and they started arriving in their hordes armed with snorkels and wet suits to make chums with the dolphin in Dingle Bay. There were celebrations all over Kerry when Fungie was seen with a mate, but sadly it didn't work out and Mrs Fungie didn't hang around. It must be tough living in the shadow of a legend.

You can find plenty of amateur dolphin experts in the local pubs to tell you chapter and verse about dolphin behaviour. 'Fungie's changed you know,' one knowing armchair dolphin fancier told me. 'He used to be much more playful than he is now. He used to give kids rides on his back and everything, but I think it's all got a bit much for him, all the camera crews and everything. See, it's unusual for dolphins to live on their own like he does so he's a law unto himself. I mean, don't get me wrong, he still likes all the attention but he keeps his distance a bit more now. Loads of people still go out from Slaidin Beach to try and swim with him, but he's not so responsive any more.' Sounds like celebrity fatigue to me. The next day I decide to go and have a word with him.

At 10 euro a throw, Fungie trips go in and out of the harbour every few minutes and you can't blame him for feeling a bit bored with it all. I mean, I've no idea how old he is in dolphin years but he's no spring chicken and after 20 years or so, he's bound to feel a bit jaded. Still, he dutifully does his bit when the flotilla of boats move deep into Dingle Harbour, suddenly appearing among them and darting from one boat to another doing his tricks. We poodle around for a bit watching him and then off he spurts into the distance and the cry goes up 'Follow that fin!' and we're racing after him. Then he disappears for a few minutes and as we peer out at the water he suddenly leaps out of the sea behind us. The boy's a natural performer, he can't help it. He may be tired but one smell of the greasepaint and roar of the crowd and he's doing somersaults and darting from one boat to another, spreading his favours, making sure we all get a photo opportunity. Somehow it all seems a bit undignified.

Still, can't sit around talking about dolphins all day, we've got some music to hear. And in Dingle we are spoilt for choice. We adjourn to Murphy's. A new sign outside being painted a garish shade of purple is a bit worrying but we are coaxed in by a plaque proclaiming an Irish Pub Guide award-winner as Best Traditional Music Bar. In fact this seems to be a suspiciously ubiquitous plaque. Once you start foraging around Kerry, Clare and Galway, every other pub you meet seems to be sporting a plaque making similar claims about the quality of its musical content. I reckon the Irish Pub Guide people are a bunch of old softies who just can't say no. Unfortunately, another twenty cold and hungry boatloads of the Fungie Fan Club have just invaded Murphy's and the place is teeming. There won't be any sessions in here for a while, not with all those shepherd's pies to be cooked, so we explore the town further.

A stroll uphill into Green Street and the sound of music drags me into Dingle Record Shop opposite Dick Mack's pub where a woman with cascading red hair, an equally bright poncho and a deeply engaging smile is singing along with an unfamiliar record while nursing a babe in arms. I've never heard the song or the singer before but she knows every word and she sounds pretty good too. So good it sounds like she's deliberately harmonising with the singer on the record. 'That's lovely,' I tell her and ask whose record it is she's singing along with. 'It's *my* record,' she says proudly. 'I'm minding the baby for my daughter. I like to sing to her so she'll have the music with her. I talk to her in Irish too for the same reason. I think it's important, don't you?' I don't really have an opinion, but her happily gurgling grand-daughter would appear to concur.

I browse and she talks. Her name is Mazz O'Flaherty and her album is called *When The Day Is Done.* 'I'm selling four or five copies a day at the moment so I'm very happy,' she says. 'I could have just done the most popular songs of all the best-selling CDs here and it would have sold very well commercially,' she says, 'but I'm not doing it for that reason. Six and a half of the songs are written by myself and on the other tracks I deliberately chose tracks that aren't well-known.' I am drawn to the bold, colourful impressions of local scenes decorating the walls. Waves crashing over rocks, flowers bending in the wind, bleak wintry views of the village. 'Who … .?' 'They're mine,' she says. 'I've got my own studio gallery … we call the collection *Images Of Mazzland.*' So Mazz, you've recorded the records on sale, you've painted the pictures on the wall, did you build the shop as well?

I want to buy something but I think Fungie must have nicked my wallet so instead I ask Mazz if there is anywhere we might be able to see her perform live. Or maybe she knows of some good sessions in town. 'I do sing in public when I have the time,' she says. 'Usually in O'Flaherty's … it's my brother's pub.' And off we skip in search of O'Flaherty's. We don't make it that far. The ornate front and welcoming glow of An Droichead Beag – 'The Little Bridge' – is very diverting. Now here's a place that aims to keep the punters happy. Pool table, big screen for those essential sporting occasions, T-shirts for the tourists, a compilation CD for the real diehards and, get this, *internet access*. I'm still thinking two pubs and a fishing boat, and the idea of trawling through the web in a bar in Dingle is doing my head in. But tonight the big screen's wrapped up tight, the pool table is empty, the internet is silent and there's that tell-tale empty corner respectfully kept vacant by the drinkers. Definite session on the cards in this place. Sorry, O'Flaherty's will have to wait.

We don't even have to wait long before the action starts. Eoin, a skinny character with distinguished silvery features is disrobing a set of uillean pipes and in no time at all he's away on some intricate chanter work, while an avuncular guy gives him formidable support on the bodhran. Others swiftly join the party. A young American with long hair wanders in with a banjo on wheels and sits nervously on the edge of the growing semi-circle of musicians. The bodhran player, Finbarr, eyes his banjo with interest. 'I like your wheels,' he says. 'It makes life easier,' says the earnest young newcomer, who's called Darcey. 'Are you gonna play it then?' 'Oh, okay,' says Darcey, and the rest all shuffle up to make room for him. Instantly there's a rapport between the Eoin, the piper, and Darcey on the banjo and the others – now including Eoin's sister Muireann on concertina – draw inspiration from growing sparks of their improvisation. A couple more fiddle players arrive and then another young American, Larry, appears at the front of the throng trying to hide a flute behind his back. 'What's that you've got?' says Finbarr. 'A flute,' says Larry. 'Oh,' says Finbarr. 'I've been to the fleadh,' says Larry. 'Did you play at the fleadh?' says Finbarr. 'I did,' says Larry. 'Well, get your flute out and play with us,' says Finbarr. 'I don't want to muscle in on your gig,' says Larry. 'It's not a gig … it's a *session*,' says Finbarr.

As they step up a gear, the crowd tumbles in, captivated by the zest of their playing. You don't have to know the first thing about traditional Irish music to recognise the class of the primary musicians here and the instinctive understanding between them. Yep, there's a lot of tourists here but nobody's playing to the gallery and don't tell me this session would be any more sparky or emotional were it being conducted entirely for their own satisfaction in some back room away from the prying eyes of daft visitors demanding to experience the mysteries of the craic.

The plan had been to stay briefly, en route to Bridge Street and O'Flaherty's, but there's no leaving this place. We're wedged into an alcove watching the action from close quarters while a throng gathers ever deeper behind us. I glance out of the window and they are dancing in the street outside, faces pressed on the glass studying the faces of the musicians, taut with concentration, broken only by knowing glances and flickering smiles. Camera flashes light up the room as the Yanks make themselves at home and with one nod from Eoin a tray of drinks comes scurrying across the bar. The place is humming until Muireann gets up and sings an unaccompanied song in Irish and the whole pub listens in a suitably respectful hush. It is mightily impressive.

As it all finally subsides I want to talk to Darcey, the young long-haired American with the banjo on wheels who'd shyly sat watching at the side of the session until Finbarr had bullied him into joining in. His eyes didn't seem to leave Eoin's pipes the whole night and he matched him every step of the way, pausing only to sip ginger ale between tunes. Clearly an outsider, I am anxious to discover his take on this ol' craic thing. To find out what brought him here, what he thinks of it and has he made any CDs? But by the time I make it out of my alcove and through the packed masses at the bar he's disappeared. In the loo I bump into Eoin, the piper, but even though for the last three hours they've shared a rare musical bond, Eoin knows no more about him than I do. 'There's a spiritual being about him,' says Eoin profoundly. 'I'd say he wouldn't be a hard man. But a great banjo player.'

Eoin – pronounced Owen – Duignan is one of the mainstays of the Dingle scene. He was taught to play pipes by the great Leo Rowsome ('a very gentle man') who also made his pipes. He was in a reasonably successful band called The Wild Geese, who were big in Europe, and has won wide respect as a piper and composer, recording several CDs. He also composed for, played and appeared in the 1997 movie *Angela Mooney Dies Again* which involved the star Mia Farrow in several water scenes, an event that resulted in a section of Lough Corrib being heated for the occasion. Eoin Duignan came to Dingle for a weekend twenty years ago and decided to stay and set up a wholefood shop and restaurant. Twenty years ago, Eoin? The days of two pubs and a fishing boat when Fungie was still doing auditions for Dolphin Academy? A wholefood restaurant in Dingle must have caused a bit of a stir way back then, Eoin?

'The locals were a bit confused at first but they were very open to it and I think we came in at the right time. Now all the pubs are doing food but it wasn't like that then. But it's a great place. When the weather is good, there's no place to match it.'

I can't believe how much Dingle has changed since I was last here, Eoin ... 'It's changed mostly in the last two or three years, since the Celtic Tiger hit Ireland,' he says. 'In that time the change has been astronomical. In the first ten years the change was more of a gradual thing. When I first came the only place in town that had music was O'Flaherty's ... and it's the one place that hasn't changed at all.'

Eoin has been a lynchpin of the local music scene ever since and is proud of the reputation Dingle has acquired for the quality of its sessions and the visitors who've been thronging to the town in search of dolphins and music. Yet it's a pride tempered by criticism of those he feels exploited the musicians as the image of the craic enveloped the area. He tells of the 'abuse of musicians' by pubs happy to use the musicians who'd gather to play informally in their bars to pull in the visitors only to treat them like skivvies. 'They might give you a free drink if you were lucky.' The punters aren't always respectful either. 'I've walked out of sessions when people haven't been listening,' he admits. These days there's more of an order to it. A local musician will be invited to lead a session and be paid for the trouble and the amount and quality of those who spontaneously turn up to join in is more a measure of the respect in which that musician is held than the pub in which it takes place. I ask Eoin what is the best pub in Dingle. 'The best pub is the one where the best musicians are,' he replies. And where might that be? 'It can be any pub in town. There's a good few of them in Dingle now. It's the musicians who are important, not where they play.'

Still, I can't stay chatting in a pub toilet with uillean pipers all night – people will surely talk. So I thank Eoin for his time and bid him goodnight. 'We're putting on a concert in St James' Church tomorrow night, come along if you're not doing anything,' he says. I'm not. 'I'll put your name on the door.'

So the following night we are enjoying the fading early evening sunshine outside St James' Church. A gloom merchant I'd met in MacCarthy's earlier had insisted no one would come. 'Why would they pay to come to a concert when every pub in town has Irish music for free?' he'd said and I had visions of me and the priest clapping politely as Eoin and his chums entertained us. Happily the man in MacCarthy's is wrong and an impressive crowd has gathered outside the church. Mostly they are middle-aged Americans clutching huge cameras full of film of Fungie doing his party pieces. One man in a frankly ludicrous cowboy hat is attempting to play 'Amazing Grace' on his newly purchased tin whistle from the Dingle Music Shop. His friends whoop and give him a huge round of applause. The rest of us pull our fingers from our ears. This guy's gonna go back to Ohio or Minnesota or Connecticut or wherever the hell he's from and he'll bore them all rigid with his endless photies and his stories of quaint Kerry and the little people and then he'll get out his tin whistle and play 'Amazing Grace' badly and next thing you know a trillion of his mates are booking flights to go charging after Fungie and squeeze a little bit more character out of Dingle.

Inside St James' Church there is a slightly musty smell but a dramatic ambience as we perch in the pews staring at an illuminated harp occupying centre stage. An American called Steve plays something by Bach and a bloke next to me annoyingly hums along. There's a German guitarist in a strange green satin shirt who sings a song about Dracula and an assortment of fiddle music which rather loses its charm when a mobile phone starts ringing and the entire audience starts fishing guiltily in pockets. God bless the mobile phone, where *would* we be without it, eh?

I'm beginning to wonder about the fabled musical tradition of the area amid a succession of performers from overseas when Eilis Kennedy arrives. A local teacher, she's accompanied by a guitarist from New Jersey called William Coulter who plays a mean instrumental version of Neil Young's 'After The Goldrush' and she sings – beautifully – a mix of Irish language and more familiar folk songs. And then Eoin appears all blazing eyes and intense concentration, his silver hair and beard gleaming under the lights to add his consummate pipe playing to the equation.

Afterwards I congratulate Eilis Kennedy on her performance and she tells me more about the vibrant tradition of the area, which has made it such a mecca of music. In particular it's famed for the slides and polkas – brought international acclaim through the work of Seamus Begley and Michael Cooney – emerging from the set dancing fraternity.

Eilis was brought up in an Irish-speaking family at Feothanach, a village a few miles from Dingle. 'I grew up speaking Irish as a first language but in our house we were always encouraged to speak both languages. My dad was a teacher with a big repertoire of songs in English and Irish so it rubbed off, I suppose. But it's not unusual to be from a singing family, it's a way of life here. There's a lot of lovely Gaelic singers from my parish.'

So you always wanted to be a singer, Eilis? 'Oh, I always sang but my dad said, "Never make your living by singing, it will break your heart!" So I became a teacher for fifteen years.' All these years later she's decided to discount her dad's advice and, for the time being at least, has given up teaching to concentrate on singing and, formerly in the group Melting Pot with Mazz O'Flaherty, she has now made her first solo album *Time To Sail*. Hubby John is also deeply into the music, playing with – but not as a founder member – the local fife and drum band which first started parading through Dingle on St

Patrick's Day in 1900, in defiance of a ban on public assemblies between dawn and dusk. The ban doesn't exist any more but the fife and drum band tradition lives on.

Not that Eilis and John have got much chance to lounge around, not with three children and a busy pub – An Chonair – to run. But then the whole world is Irish now. Eilis has just come back from a tour of Taiwan to prove it. 'We did twelve concerts there singing in these huge concert halls without any microphones, it was fantastic. It's an amazing feeling singing an Irish song in the middle of Kaohsiung. You'd think they wouldn't want to listen but not only do they listen, they want to know what all the words mean. It was hot and humid and involved a lot of travelling but it was a great experience all right.'

It also gave her an insight in this weird tourist thing that has changed the face of Dingle. 'It's not just Dingle, it's the whole of Ireland. In Taiwan I was doing all the same silly things the tourists do here, taking pictures of road signs and all. Looking at it from a tourist point of view this is a pretty good place to go on holiday and I don't resent tourists at all.'

She doesn't even blame Fungie for the influx. She reckons it's all down to David Lean, John Mills, Sarah Miles and Robert Mitchum, who came shooting the dramatic epic *Ryan's Daughter* here in 1970. In Dublin everyone you meet claims to have been an extra in *The Commitments*, and in Dingle everyone over a certain age claims to have been an extra in *Ryan's Daughter*. There must have been loads of homeless people at the time, too, considering all those who claim they vacated their homes so Robert Mitchum could live there for the duration of the movie. So maybe the experts have got it all wrong all this time. Maybe Fungie wasn't lost when he turned up in Dingle Bay for the first time. Inspired by Flipper, he came to Kerry to be a film star, but was a bit late and by the time he arrived David Lean's cameras had gone home.

But come on, Eilis, don't tell me you don't get a tad irked when you are in the bar trying to sing some sensitive Gaelic ballad and somebody sticks a camera in your face or they all start chatting about tomorrow's coach outing to Tray-lee? Don't you secretly yearn for the days when you and some mates would just sit around and play for your own satisfaction? That's the real craic, is it not?

'Oh I remember magical nights in pubs with people like the Begleys and my uncle and dad and many, many singers and, as soon as you started singing, there was total silence. I grew up with that. It's more difficult to get it now but there's no point in getting into a struggle about it. I can't go around insisting people keep quiet 'cos you're taking away the atmosphere of the pub then. That's what people like about the pubs in Ireland, they are alive and vibrant, you don't have to sit down and behave yourself! So it's give and take really.

'Sometimes when it's *really* noisy the best thing to do is get up and sing the quietest song you know. See, if you have a microphone all that happens is the noise level goes up. Believe me, I've been in the middle of this for a long time and I don't think it works to close off the music in a separate room. It doesn't work to make it exclusive. You don't want the music to have barriers.'

From the tranquillity of St James' Church and the calm sense of Eilis Kennedy we walk along Main St to be lured by a wholly different vibe. Inside The Dingle Pub a father and son duo are belting out republican songs with cantankerous determination in the manner of the old-time ballad groups. Even the beaming Americans look a bit overwhelmed by their velocity and I wait for the inevitable 'Fields Of Athenry' and move swiftly on.

Next morning we decide it's time to leave Kerry. But not without undertaking the greatest drive in the history of the world ever. You head west around the Dingle Peninsula, up to Ventry and hey, yes the sun is just about over the yardarm, stop for a sharpener at Paidi O Se's pub in Ventry, where local legend has it that Dolly Parton and Tom Cruise are among its previously satisfied clientele. Good golly, Miss Molly, if it's good enough for Dolly, it's good enough for me. The journey continues amid raucous choruses of 'Jolene'.

We drive on past Fahan, eyes on stalks gulping in volatile waves mounting vicious assaults on unamused cliffs to one side and the extraordinary network of prehistoric Celtic ruins, ring forts, stone crosses and ancient beehive huts on the other. In one place you can stop and view the Famine Cottage and reflect on the extremes of chance that located the Kavanagh family in one of the most magnificent spots on God's earth and then contrived to starve them out of house and home and ultimately out of Ireland altogether. You want to weep but the sheep are staring in that plaintive way. They've seen it all before. 'You think it's beautiful but sad up here, right?' says one. 'You should come up here in the middle of January when the wind's howling and the rain's lashing down, it's not beautiful but sad then, mate, it's bloody tragic ...'

On to Slea Head in a surreal daze as the ever more narrow road makes you feel like you're tumbling off the ends of the earth before taking you on another surge of wild twists and turns, filling your head with weird metaphysical thoughts. I get this ridiculous urge to shut my eyes and put my foot down as I approach the next blind hairpin. I really shouldn't have had that pint at Paidi O Se's. Should I see a psychiatrist? Why bother? That Guinness lorry hurtling towards me round the corner will get me first. I always knew Guinness would be the death of me.

At the most extreme, most westerly, eeriest hairpin of all, a vision appears. Sea, cliffs, narrow road and white figures appearing in front of you. The huge crucifixion shrine right on the edge of Slea Head never fails to put the fear of God into me.

Keep going if you dare, gazing at the shipwreck embedded in the sand and we may let you take a breather at the cliffside overlooking Dunquin Pier. The imposing Blasket Islands are clearly visible in the distance and wouldn't you like a word with *them* at the dead of night? Never largely populated, the Blaskets nevertheless enjoyed a great reputation for producing good literature, good music and good potatoes. The few hardy souls who stoically remained on the Blaskets without electricity or any other modern conveniences finally abandoned the islands in 1953 after a child died when storms prevented medical aid reaching him in time. Weather permitting, Dunquin ferries will still take you the eight miles out to visit the Blaskets and the locals will tell you how they all starred in *Ryan's Daughter* and that Robert Mitchum, what a grand man he was.

Not us, though. We complete the loop back to Dingle for the Peninsula Drive is merely the warm-up to the main event ... laydeez and gennelmen, I give you ... the *Connor Pass*! Scenic drama at every turn ... mountains, sea, lakes, waterfalls, the sparkling surf hitting Brandon Head over the way, County Clare in the distance, mad sheep, the lot. Today, though ... can't see a thing. The mist is down, the eyes are shut and we glide over the highest pass in Ireland down into the village of Cloghane with a feeling of mild disappointment. Never mind, there's bound to be lots of people wandering around Clogher Round with anecdotes about how they starred with Tom Cruise and Nicole Kidman when they went there to shoot scenes for *Far & Away*. Alas, the place is deserted and they haven't even got around to building a pub called the Far & Away. Shoddy stuff. Need to get the heritage industry working on this one.

Anyway, where was I before the Rose of Tralee so rudely interrupted? Galway, of course. The pride of Connacht. No more messing around with dolphins and mountains, it's time to get serious here. This time we'll head straight for Galway and there'll be *no diversions*. Except maybe a quick break in Clare en route.

Ennis. Let's break the journey in Ennis. Ennis is a fine town. Ennis is Tommy Peoples country. A man can drown in great music in Ennis. A man can also get convicted of road rage in Ennis. At first we think the mounting traffic is a particularly horrendous overspill from the dreaded Limerick and then we think we've maybe hit the fall-out from a glut of landings at Shannon Airport. But as we crawl nearer we realise that yep, this *is* the queue to get into Ennis.

We inch forward into the outskirts of town noticing only 'Car park full' signs and unprepossessing B&Bs with their shutters closed. A car emerges from a designated parking spot and while I'm wondering if I might be able to negotiate the 38-point turn required to slot into the hole, five angry vehicles suddenly appear in front of me to contest the spot in a volley of horns and one-fingered gestures. I am thinking I could maybe be a bit sly about this and park on a verge when a car launches itself broadside in front of me. All the mellow kindness engendered by the rolling calm of Kerry evaporates in an instant and a torrent of words I never even knew I knew come hurtling out of my mouth in the direction of the figure emerging from the car that has just parked in front of me. I suck them right back in when I realise I am addressing a man of God. 'Ya forking eejit' is miraculously transformed into 'Good day to you Father, that's a smart bit of parking you've done there.' 'Aye, you have to take your opportunities where you can find them in this town,' he says with a beatific beam. 'Is Ennis always this busy, Father?' 'No, only when it's this busy ...'

I'm still trying to work this one out when we flee Ennis. Tommy Peoples, I know you're in there. I will return. In the meantime, the amended plan is no sleep 'til Galway. Keep right on to the end of the road and no distractions allowed. It works a treat. Until we get to Gort. To be honest, Gort is the sort of place you don't look at twice. The sort of place you just drive through and casually say 'What town's this, then?' and by the time Mrs Colin has got the map up straight it's been and gone and you're into the next round of identifying cars' county of origin by their number plates. MN ... it's got to be Monaghan. D ... easy, that's Dublin. WW ... hmmm ... tricky, but *Wicklow*. KY ... Kerry? Or is it Kilkenny? See, not as easy as you think.

But on this one occasion as we pass through anonymous blink-or-you'll-miss-it Gort, a poster in a shop window catches my eye ... COOLEY COLLINS TRADITIONAL MUSIC FESTIVAL. It seems rude not to stop. In truth Gort looks a little bedraggled around the edges. There was a violent storm last night and the bunting is on its knees, but a few Guinness flags flutter defiantly in the wind as we follow the sign pointing to FESTIVAL OFFICE. We find ourselves inside a church with a service about to begin. 'Sorry, Father,' I say, not for the first time and make my excuses and leave. The festival office is eventually located in an antiques shop. A *shut* antiques shop. A note in the window re-directs enquiries to O'Sullivan's pub. Which seems a particularly sneaky way of driving a man to drink.

So O'Sullivan's pub it is, where enquiries are referred to a poster on the wall which tells you about a storytelling competition at the library, a golf tournament and a ceili, which presumably isn't in the library. Unless it's in the mobile one parked up the street. Could be quite exciting ... a herd of dancers clumping up and down to the *Bridge Of Athlone*, while a strict librarian in high heels, horn-rimmed spectacles and blonde hair in a bun goes 'SHHHHHH ...' Or is that just *my* fantasy?

Still, now we're here ... we squeeze past the musicians who seem to be reproducing before our eyes. When we start the journey to the bar there's a couple of fiddles, an accordion and a flute. By the time we've get there and order the pints they've been joined by a flotilla of concertinas, whistles and bodhrans and any newcomers with a thirst are left on the outskirts of the pub gazing longingly at the bar. You don't find many pubs where the drinkers play second fiddle to the, er, *first fiddle*.

The music's good but a bloke at the bar engages me in surreal conversation. 'D'ya know yer man Ricky Gervais?' 'Well, not personally but ...' 'He's very funny that feller, isn't he?' Yes he is. 'He makes me die that feller ...' You get that series *The Office* over here then, do you? 'No, but we see Manchester United.' Pardon? 'Man U ... they are some team, aren't they?' They are certainly a team, yeah. 'Yer man Giggs can play, can't he?' Did I miss something? Has Ricky Gervais signed for Man U since I've been gone? I ask him if he knows anything about Tommy Peoples. 'Tommy Peoples, you say?' he says, furrowing his brow. 'Y'now somethin'?' No. 'I haven't heard anything of Tommy Peoples in a good while.' No, me neither. I was wondering what may have happened to him. 'Mmm, me too,' he muses. 'Y'know what ... now I come to think of it ... he hasn't played in a good while ... I'd say he'd be out with one of them, waddya call 'em?' Fiddle elbow? 'No. Cruciate ligaments ...'

The tin whistle player comes to the bar for a cup of coffee. 'Hiya, grand day,' he greets me perkily. Actually it's pissing down, but no matter. 'Last night, eh ...' he beams, raising his eyebrows to the roof. 'Oh yeah, last night ...' I raise my eyebrows in sympathy without a clue what he's talking about. It turns out he's from Caherlistrane in Galway. I get excited at the mention of Caherlistrane, home of the great singing family, the Keanes. I tell him I'm on my way there. 'I'm related to the Keanes. My aunt is the mother of Dolores' aunts ...' Sarah and Rita? 'Yes, Sarah and Rita.' How are they? 'They're grand.' Can I get you another coffee? 'No thanks,' he says, 'I have to keep a clear head for the playing.' And he rejoins the circle of musicians which has now expanded to include a couple of bouzoukis, another dozen fiddle players, a bunch of tubas, the odd sousaphone and the Dagenham Girl Pipers.

Can't stay, we say, we've got to get to Galway, but hey, this pub looks quite good and look, there's a pint with my name on it! So we enter John Walsh's bar and find a crowd grouped around a studiously distinguished-looking fiddle player. He is superb. He has an unusually individual style, controlled and unhurried but with verve too and throwing in the odd trick to keep the punters happy. He looks and sounds vaguely familiar and for a second from the back of a crowded bar I just glimpse the grey hair and the flowing bow and my heart spins ... surely it's not Tommy Peoples? 'That fiddle player ...' I whisper to the guy next to me ... 'Jim McKillop,' he says. No wonder he sounds good. From Cushendall in Antrim, Jim was in his early 20s, working as a ship's engineer when he fell in love with the fiddle after hearing Sean Maguire. He threw himself into the instrument to such an extent that within four years he was an all-Ireland Fleadh champion and is now not only one of the country's most renowned fiddle players, but fiddle-makers too. The pub is silent throughout Jim's set, erupting joyously at the end of each tune and I gaze on in wonder that you can wander unannounced into an otherwise anonymous town in Galway and chance upon one of the best musicians in Ireland.

This festival is held annually in Gort in honour of two of its most revered musical sons, whistle player Kieran Collins and button accordion legend Joe Cooley, who made his last public appearance in Kelly's Bar here thirty years ago. Joe was born in Peterswell, just up the road from Gort, in 1924. Both his parents played the melodeon and music filled the family home, where informal dances were held on an almost nightly basis. House and 'crossroads' parish dances had been a regular feature of life in rural Ireland at the time until the Black and Tans and then the clergy became suspicious of the perceived immorality and intemperance they fretted was going on behind closed doors. The church condemned unsupervised, unlicensed dancing and used its considerable influence to stop it. The Public Dance Halls Act of 1935 outlawed unlicensed events, resulting in the emergence of ceili dances, where the dancers tended to keep their hands to themselves and the priests could keep an eye on them.

A labourer and bricklayer, Joe was one of life's inveterate wanderers, moving initially to Clare where he played with the fiddle player Joe Leary and joined the Tulla Ceili Band. He famously travelled to gigs on a big old motor cycle with a fiddle on his back and his accordion strapped to the fuel tank.

He moved around Ireland to play at fairs with the legendary trav-

Beware of impersonators:
the real Christy Moore

Tipp's finest, Shane MacGowan

Liam Clancy and friend

The greatest band of all time. Probably. Planxty (l-r: Donal Lunny, Andy Irvine, Liam Og O'Flynn, Christy Moore)

Ah, bless, Sinead O'Connor

Who are you calling bankers? The early Chieftains (back l-r: Paddy Moloney, Peadar Mercier, Martin Fay, the late Derek Bell (front l-r: Sean Potts, Michael Tubridy, Sean Keane)

'The Rose of Tralee', Tamara Gervasoni waves at the author at Tralee Races

Kerry's greatest superstar, Fungie the Dingle Dolphin

They were big on fashion in Donegal in the 1970s. Early Clannad, with Maire Brennan and Enya at the front

Mary Coughlan taking no prisoners

Never off the turntable at Leo's Tavern, Enya

Is that a pair of spoons in your pocket or are you just pleased to see me? Frankie Gavin, a fierce fiddler

Sarah, Rita & Dolores Keane at home in Caherlistrane, Co. Galway

Ireland's most legendary piper, traveller Johnny Doran

The pride of O'Donoghue's: early Dubliners (l-r: Cairan Bourke, Barney McKenna, Luke Kelly, John Sheahan, Ronnie Drew)

"Tommy Peoples, I presume…"
The lad himself at Matt Molloy's,
Westport, Co.Mayo

Like father like daughter…
Siobhan Peoples in a pub
in Ennis, Co.Clare

"A lot of people don't like my
opinions…" The controversial
Seamus Tansey at home

Friends reunited. Matt Molloy (flute) and Tommy Peoples (fiddle) relive their youth at Matt's pub in Westport

"Does that sign say what I think it says?"

Tommy Peoples
Alph Duggan

fiddle and guitar

At **Molloy's**,
Westport

Monday,
28th October
Doors Open
9.30 p.m.

Admission:

"Is it a pint or a song you're after?" Jim O'The Mill in the pub that only opens on Thursday nights

elling pipers Johnny Doran and his brother Felix and settled in Dublin for a while before moving to London. When he emigrated to America in 1954 his friends and fellow musicians clubbed together to buy him a new accordion, which he solemnly named 'The Box' and which subsequently became almost as famous as Joe himself. Originally settling in New York he frequently moved around the States too, living variously in New York, Boston, Chicago and San Francisco, and played in various ceili bands with his brother Seamus, a flute player. He was frequently featured on the radio and, eventually settling in San Francisco, taught accordion, played regularly with Kevin Keegan and Joe Murtagh, and established a massive reputation with an inspirational, evocative style rooted in East Galway.

In 1973 he went home to Ireland. He was 49 and dying of cancer, yet the magic of his playing remained undimmed and on a wet Thursday night in November he roused himself for one last hurrah at a packed Lahiff's Bar in Peterswell. His brother Jack played bodhran and Des Mulkere played banjo and one of his students, Tony MacMahon, who was given his first accordion by the great man, recorded the occasion for posterity. Three weeks later Joe Cooley was dead.

But that last session at Lahiff's contributed most of the material on Joe's one and only album, *Cooley*, which was released by Gael Linn in 1975 and which came to inspire and influence a whole new generation of musicians. 'Here was a man,' wrote Tony MacMahon in his original sleeve notes for *Cooley*, 'who for 25 years moved people by his music and his followers stretched from Peterswell to the hippy communes of San Francisco ... his strong, lonely sound is a heartbeat of the past.' MacMahon went on to wax lyrical about Cooley's style. 'There was a total unity in every part of Cooley's body with the instrument as he played. Especially his face – his eyes, his mouth – and his fingers always seemed to move in slow motion over the keys. He was a person to whom music was something altogether other than a series of notes.'

Many famous tunes were associated with Cooley, not least 'Last Night's Fun', 'Boys Of The Lough', 'The Boyne Hunt', 'The Bucks Of Oranmore' and 'My Love She's In America', learned from Johnny Doran. 'He has the same wild and haunted call in it that Johnny Doran had in his piping of that tune,' wrote MacMahon. 'Whether or not this music was made in the black famine times of death and the living death of emigration, nobody knows, but in the beautiful notes is the lonesome cry of our people. Cooley had that soul in his music.' Glorious stuff. With sleeve notes like that, who needs the album?

If I had a Joe Cooley tape in the car I'd play it now, but I don't.

And attempts to find Joe's grave at Peterswell also fail miserably, so there's nowt else to do but hit that N18, whack on The Fugees and it's no sleep 'til Galway. It's … what … an hour from here? A main road. A straight drive. Nothing's gonna stop us now. *Nothing*. No more distractions. No more diversions. No more whims. Galway here we come.

We nearly make it, too.

And then I see the sign for Athenry …

Chapter seven

CONNEMARA: PLANES, HOT TODDIES & UNICYCLES

'By a lonely prison wall I heard a young girl calling … *Michael they are taking you away …*'

Like Kennedy being shot, the Berlin wall coming down and that Louis Armstrong geezer landing on the Moon, everyone remembers the first time they heard 'The Fields Of Athenry'.

I was staying at O'Shea's Hotel in Dublin in the mid-1980s and got back late after a night on the town. Knackered, I retired to my room but the sound of a band playing loudly downstairs and, more importantly, the whoops and the hollers they were inciting dragged me down to the bar to find out what all the fuss was about. I never could stand the thought of a party to which I hadn't been invited.

I'd no idea who the band was then and I've even less idea now. They were playing routine bar fodder for a routinely bladdered Friday night crowd … the Christy Moore Song Book, 'Dirty Old Town', 'Black Is The Colour', 'The Holy Ground', 'From Clare To Here'. Their audience was too pissed to care one way or t'other, erupting with the recognition of every song they played. And then they went into 'Fields Of Athenry'. That's when the bar crowd *really* erupted.

I heard the song again on the radio a day later and then I saw it on the track list of some dodgy compilation album of 'Favourite Irish Songs' and then I saw some busker doing it in O'Connell Street. It took a while to register, but there is something about the chorus that really just won't go away and, as seemingly corny and melodramatic as they are, it's hard not to be touched in some way by the forlorn dignity of the lyrics. A woman trying to be brave as she tries to talk to her husband on the other side of a prison wall and watching from the harbour as the ship takes him off with the other convicts to Botany Bay and she knows she'll never see him again. His crime? Stealing some corn so his kids can eat during the famine.

If that doesn't get you sobbing into your beer, just wait for Michael's valiantly defiant reply from the other side: 'Nothing matters, Mary, when you are free/Against the famine and the crown/I rebelled, they ran me down/Now you must raise our child with dignity ...' Heartwrenching stuff. And once you hit the big 'low lie the fields of Athenry' chorus, the eyes well up, the heart swells, we link arms and by God we have an anthem. And now, the alternative Irish national anthem. It gets sung spontaneously by the crowd at Ireland international football, rugby and – I shouldn't wonder – Oz rules internationals too. It's been No 1 in the Irish karaoke charts for over a decade, it's sung by every busker you meet, has been covered by everyone from James Galway to the Dropkick Murphys, is estimated to have cumulatively sold over four million and, as I'm rapidly discovering, you can barely enter a pub in Ireland without hearing it in some shape or form.

Music pubs are defined by whether or not you're likely to hear 'Fields Of Athenry' inside and you can usually tell the minute you cross the threshold. In fact you can almost tell just by looking at them. Just by how big the lettering is in the window. Or whether they have one of those Irish Pub Guide plaques. Familiarity breeds contempt and the sentimental overkill makes it hard to take the song seriously as a song and not merely an icon, like the shamrock or the little people or the stout. And yet, I've developed a love-hate relationship with 'Fields Of Athenry'. I mean, so many pubs, so much sentiment, so many cheesy singers battering the daylights out of it. And yet to hear a football crowd singing 'Fields Of Athenry', complete with harmonies, is a deeply moving experience. I apply the Shane MacGowan litmus test and I reckon Shane's not averse to a chorus of 'Athenry' in the bath. Not that this happens too often if we are to believe Victoria Clarke's biography of Shane.

'Athenry' seems to fulfil every musical sentiment the Irish hold dear. It encompasses the national tragedy of the famine, the heartbreak of enforced emigration, the outrage of legal injustice, the preciousness of the family and a deep, enduring, harrowing, emotional love story to boot. Ultimately, the spirit of rebellion, defiance, independence and hope hits a chord that runs deep into the very bowels of the Irish psyche.

'For she lived to hope and pray for her love in Botany Bay/It's so lonely round the fields of Athenry ...'

The song is set around 1846 and supposedly based on a true story from the potato famine when Tory Prime Minister Robert Peel imported large quantities of corn from India in an attempt to alleviate the human disaster. The man given the task of administrating the crisis was an apparently unsympathetic Lord Trevelyan, who decreed that the Indian corn was too hard to be milled and was therefore useless. In desperation some men broke into the stores to steal the corn and those caught and arrested – including our hero from Athenry – were deported to Australia.

Who originally put the story into verse is long lost in the mists of time, although there is evidence that is was first published in a broadsheet in the 1880s. But it was a Dubliner, Pete St John, who adapted the verses, wrote a new tune and effectively created the monster we see before us now. Originally an electrician, he emigrated to Canada and has also lived in Alaska, Washington, Central America and the West Indies, with a variety of jobs from truck driver to PR man to author. He's also been actively involved in the Peace and International Civil Rights movements.

He returned to Dublin in the late 1970s and started writing songs inspired by an Ireland that had changed dramatically from the one he'd left behind, perhaps best reflected by his poignant, nostalgic song about the Dublin of his youth, 'Rare Ould Times'. He put together 'Fields Of Athenry' in 1979, describing it as 'a song about poor innocents being caught up in disaster', but it was another Dubliner, ballad singer Paddy Reilly, who took it to the top of the Irish charts. It then took on a life of its own and St John has merely been a bystander watching the song's remorseless rise in public consciousness. Yet its progress to the footie terraces hasn't been entirely free of controversy. When Celtic fans started singing it at matches and Pete St John was personally invited to perform it at Parkhead, there were fierce objections on the grounds that the song was emotively political and would inflame old sectarian divisions between Rangers and Celtic. Pete pointed to his long-term involvement with the peace movement, and told them not to be so stupid.

'Fields Of Athenry' has now become part of the furniture in Ireland. Probably a sofa to be precise. One that's full of Guinness stains and with the lining all torn and with a goldmine of loose change and old pens in the bottom, and the springs pop up and dig you in the arse at regular intervals … but it's still kinda cosy and familiar and you love it really.

So when I see a sign for the town of Athenry I really can't help myself.

Athenry is just 15 miles east of Galway city and the first thing to be said about it is that, while I search frantically, I find no fields here. In fact I find not very much at all. Some medieval monuments, a thirteenth-century priory, the remnants of an ancient castle, a couple of walls around the town and a gift shop called – wouldn't you know it – the Fields Of Athenry. I'm not sure what I was hoping for here. Monuments to the tragic couple who inspired the song maybe ... gangs of schoolchildren skipping along the road singing 'Low lie' ... genuine Trevelyan corn being flogged to American tourists ... street theatre re-enacting the sorry tale ... an Athenry theme park featuring rides around Lord Trevelyan's estate ... a life-size model of the prison walls ... and a statue of Pete St John. If he'd written 'Fields Of Ballybunnion' they'd have had a statue of him knocked up in the town square before he'd finished the second verse.

We are in East Galway. The area is littered with names of legends who are frequently mentioned but whose music is seldom heard. Dinny Delaney was a blind uilleann piper, born in Ballinasloe in 1819, and in time-honoured fashion travelled around the area playing at house sessions, fairs, crossroads ceilis, weddings and for the rich folk in the big houses. He gained the epithet 'The Rebel Piper' after being arrested for playing 'seditious tunes' at a fair and his name is on one of the earliest surviving cylinder recordings.

Pipes were once a major feature of East Galway life. One of the most famous pipers of them all, the left-handed maestro Patsy Touhey, was born near Loughrea in 1865 although the family moved to Boston when he was a kid. Both his father and grandfather were noted pipers and Patsy followed in their footsteps with some relish after wandering into a Bowery music hall in his late teens and meeting 'the white piper of Galway', John Eagan. Inspired and tutored by Eagan, he developed not only a distinctively tight 'close fingered' piping style but a flair for showmanship that eventually took him into vaudeville. He teamed up with Charlie Burke to develop an act full of comedy sketches, slapstick humour and Irish nostalgia and invariably climaxed with a demon-stration of uilleann pipes while his wife Mary danced.

It proved to be a hugely popular act, though not everyone was impressed. The Irish tenor John McCormack, for one, is said to have been disgusted and embarrassed by Touhey's vaudeville show, though others suggest it may have been Patsy's friendship with McCormack's wife that upset him most. Touhey also had a sharp commercial eye and, after an appearance at the World's Fair in Chicago had alerted him to the potential of cylinder recordings, he advertised himself in *The Irish World* as 'The best Irish piper in America' and flogged his cylinder recordings by mail order at a dollar each. This was significant in itself – Patsy was at the vanguard of a flood of Irish music that circulated to expatriates in America and eventually filtered its way back home to re-ignite the flame there too.

In this area, though, the name of the Ballinakill Ceili Band looms largest of all. They were formed in the late 1920s by Father Tom Larkin, a fiddle player who tried to offset the popularity of the immoral 'jazz dancing' going on behind closed doors by encouraging local musicians to play at public ceilis where the dancers didn't tend to rub up against each other in *that way* and which were considered much healthier all round. Even Father Larkin couldn't have imagined the effect they'd have.

It's a story that was told to me by Martin and Bridie Fahy. Bridie's father Tommy Whyte and sister Aggie were original members of the Ballinakill Ceili Band and the name of the late Aggie Whyte is still revered as one of Ireland's greatest ever fiddle players. 'The music survived down the years and people would have set dances in their kitchens,' says Martin Fahy. Then they'd have dances on the flagstones at the crossroads. On Sunday evenings the boys and girls would get together and the musicians would come along and they'd dance the night away.'

To be a member of the Ballinakill Ceili Band then, said Martin, was to be akin to royalty. It didn't make you rich but it made you a lot of friends. 'To be a musician in those days was very important. You got the best seat in the house, you got nearest the chimney corner, you got everything that was going. There was no wage from it but you were treated like a gentleman.'

Ballinakill's fame attracted visits from collectors and broadcasters and the band appeared all over Ireland. On St Patrick's Day in 1931 they went to London to appear at the Royal Albert Hall and, after recording for Parlophone, their slow, measured style was aped by other bands springing up in their wake. And this little corner of East Galway garnered a fame several trillion miles beyond the sum of the parts of one tiny parish.

'The music,' Martin Fahy told me solemnly, 'was handed down from father to son.' Or indeed daughter. The Ballinakill tradition has been continued in some style by the young generation of Fahys who between them have won various all-Ireland titles and further went on to make their mark with the excellent young band Reeltime.

Galway is such an eloquent county. It lends itself to song. 'In Oranmore, in the County Galway/One pleasant evening in the month of May/I spied a damsel, she was young and handsome/Her beauty fairly took my breath away ...' Ah yes, we're back to Margaret Barry singing 'Galway Shawl'. Hang on, let's try this one ... 'If you ever go across the sea to Ireland/Then maybe at the closing of your day/You will sit and watch the Moon rise over Claddagh/And the sun go down on Galway Bay.' That'll be Josef Locke then. Or Bing Crosby. Nah, too many Clancy parodies there for comfort. I'd love to have heard Josef Locke singing 'From Galway To Graceland', Richard Thompson's mighty tale of a confused woman's pilgrimage to Memphis, and one day it could happen. Forget Elvis, they say Josef's dead but I swear I saw him working at the check-out desk at Sainsbury's.

Galway itself is a bonnie city. As soon as you hit Oranmore and try to remember the tune to 'Bucks Of Oranmore,' you see the bay sweeping out in front of you, then the posh hotels start, then there's the roundabouts and before you know it you're having a pint in The Crane. A university town, Galway has arts festivals coming out its ears and a young, vibrant feel born of young, vibrant bars that seem to swarm with serious drinkers whatever time you come calling. There's a distinctly international feel about it as high fashion and go-getting modernism blends easily with penniless students, artful dodgers and serial bohemians. The streets are narrow and the bars full of interesting nooks and crannies while the Spanish Arch and The Claddagh keep the tourists' cameras clicking as they come to pay their respects to Lough Corrib. Stand in the middle of Eyre Square for a moment and absorb the mix of cultures and lifestyles ... backpackers, students, conventional tourists, city dwellers and business people ... but don't absorb it for too long or you'll get mown down.

There is also music in Galway city. Lots of it. It's a modern city with modern sounds and whatever gets your kettle boiling – throbbing clubs with dense beats and groovy DJs, dreamy jazzers with rolling eyes and yellow teeth or slam-dunk pubs shaking to the migraine-inducing thrash of hot metal – you'll find it somewhere in the city. And there's a good smattering of sessions at colourful old bars like The Crane, King's Head, Taafe's, The Quays Bar, An Pucan, Winkles and Roisin Dubh for those of a more traditional persuasion. Tigh Neachtain in Cross St, with its grocery shop at one end and its bar at the other, has played an important role in the growth of Galway's reputation as a music city. Not too long ago it was the only haunt in town that provided music of any kind and was integral to the seventies explosion of traditional music in the area when the likes of De Dannan regularly frequented it. In 1989 Gael Linn even recorded a live album of musicians who played there.

A somewhat newer place, The Roisin Dubh in Dominick St, also has a few stories to tell with posters boasting the patronage of everyone from Donovan to Midge Ure. They even persuaded Steve Earle to serve behind the bar once. Was that really a good idea? You fancy there were tequilas on the house all night.

The Roisin Dubh, where Mary Coughlan recorded her deeply emotional *Live In Galway* album, has also become a favourite haunt for album launches. Well, I came here for a Sharon Shannon album launch once. Ah, dear, dear Sharon Shannon ... what a night of revelation that was ...

See, when people ask how I pay for my supper I usually pretend I'm a quantity surveyor or a chartered accountant or an estate agent or a traffic warden. Guaranteed conversation stopper. But if the words 'music journalist' somehow involuntarily escape, an instant barrage of questions inevitably follow: a) Who's the most famous person you've interviewed? b) What's Elton John really like? c) Ever met Madonna? d) Is Van Morrison as stroppy as everyone says? e) Got any more Andrea Corr pictures? f) Westlife – *why*? g) What's the scandal on Kylie? h) Are all rock stars gay drug addicts who never play on their records and aren't even kind to dumb animals? i) Who's going to be the next big thing? j) Is it true Josef Locke is alive and well and working at a supermarket check-out desk?

I fend these off as best I can: a) Pele b) Ask David Furnish c) Only in my dreams d) You may think that but I couldn't possibly comment e) Get out of here you dirty geek f) Oh sweet mystery of life ... and Louis Walsh g) She has a nice bottom ... allegedly h) Only the good ones i) If I knew that would I really be talking to you? j) So you've seen him too?

And then they ask the big one: who's the most difficult person you've had to interview?

As it happens, I've given this some thought. Enoch Powell, for one. Scariest man I ever met in my life, all piercing eyes and darkly threatening monotone voice. And there was Tim Hardin, a uniquely gifted creator of startlingly poignant songs like 'The Lady Came From Baltimore', 'Reason To Believe', 'If I Were A Carpenter', 'Black Sheep Boy' and 'Red Balloon'. In some awe, I asked him one innocuous question about his new album. Inexplicably it provoked an outraged stream of consciousness which led him into ripping off his shirt, verbally assaulting me for 35 minutes and challenging me to find any track marks on his body as he ranted on about how sick he was of people accusing him of being a junkie. He died of a drug overdose not too long afterwards.

And, of course, there was the incident of Peter Tosh and the unicycle. Tosh was one of The Wailers, and indeed widely perceived to be Bob Marley's right-hand man. Shortly after Marley's death from cancer in 1981, Tosh came to London to promote his own solo album. I was despatched to a hotel in the West End to interview him but on arrival I was informed Mr Tosh had left the building, his whereabouts unknown. I decided to wait. And wait. And wait. Suddenly twelve big dreadlocked Rastas materialised in the hotel lobby and marched straight to the lift, ignoring my rather pathetic cries of 'Pete … Pete … I'm …'. As the lift doors closed, I leapt in with them – which was a pretty radical thing to do because it was a '12 Persons Only' lift. I continued to try and engage Pete in conversation without, in all honesty, knowing which was Pete.

Pete and his posse remained silent during the ascendancy and when we landed on the third floor, they marched purposefully to their suite without a glance in my direction. Again I dived in behind them at the very moment they slammed the door – and the world – shut behind them. Within seconds a spliff the size of Montego Bay was being passed around and every time I tried to introduce myself the spliff passed over my head and they engaged each other in vigorous patois. The gift of invisibility isn't all it's cracked up to be. One of the Rastas picked up an acoustic guitar and started strumming and I decided this must be Peter Tosh and sat next to him. Instantly he put the guitar down, got up, and started riding round the room on a unicycle that seemed to have been produced out of thin air. I laughed and applauded and said things like 'Good on ya Pete, mate, you're a man of many talents, where d'ya learn a trick like that then, Pete ol' son?' He ignored me and glared at the floor.

Bored with the unicycle he took another drag from the spliff, picked up the guitar again, took it to a different part of the room to continue his strumming, while his chums talked among themselves. I kept talking but not one of them answered or even acknowledged my presence. Even a juicy round of expletives deleted would have been better than this.

By now, though, it had become a matter of honour and, cassette machine defiantly primed to 'Record', I sat next to the artist formerly known as Bob Marley's best mate, firing questions at him. 'Tell me about the new album, Pete. Have you spent much time in London before, Pete? Are you going to be touring, Pete? What do you listen to on the road, Pete? Who's the biggest influence on your career, Pete? What's Kingston like, Pete? 'No Woman, No Cry', eh Pete? Don't suppose you've bumped into Tommy Peoples in your travels, Pete? Josef Locke working in a supermarket, what do you reckon, Pete?'

Not a flicker. He just sang softly to himself, the torrent of questions sucked into the wacky backy mists now visibly enshrouding him. The ritual humiliation of the journo was nearly complete and my resolve was weakening. 'I guess Bob's passing must have hit you hard, Pete, him being the king of reggae and all …'

He stopped singing. He stopped strumming. And he LOOKED AT ME! Suddenly he was wagging his finger at me. Talking to me in angry, urgent, gushing tones. 'Let me tell you … Bob Marley was no king of reggae, *I'm* the king of reggae, I always was, Bob Marley stole my glory, Bob Marley stole my songs, Bob Marley stole ...' At one point I thought he was going to say 'Bob Marley ate my hamster' as he continued to rubbish Marley for ten minutes without pausing for breath. And then, as suddenly as he'd started, he stopped abruptly and returned to the guitar and unicycle and ignored me again. I hung around for a few minutes, but an ice wall again materialised around the Rastas and I was totally ignored again. I let myself out.

But in the realms of difficult interviews, the name Sharon Shannon features prominently, albeit for very different reasons. Originally from Corofin, Co. Clare, Sharon started playing whistle at six, but soon graduated to accordion and fiddle and, under the tuition of Frank Custy, was swiftly acclaimed as one of the most exciting and innovative young traditional musicians of her generation. She spent a short time with Arcady and then, in 1989, met up with Scotsman Mike Scott, who'd relocated to Galway, inspiring him to re-shape The Waterboys into a born-again Irish band. The result was that Sharon, accustomed only to playing in bar sessions in Clare and Galway, joined The Waterboys, who were by now being tipped to replicate the breakthrough of U2 and Simple Minds as international stadium bands. Sharon's first gig as a Waterboy was in front of the great unwashed at Glastonbury and she went on to spend 18 months weaving her magic with them as they toured the world and lived out Scott's vision of a contemporary rock band fuelled by the Irish tradition on the *Room To Roam* album.

So when she left The Waterboys to launch her solo career in the early nineties there was plenty to talk about and I looked forward to meeting her. Round One was at The Mean Fiddler in Harlesden, West London, where she was playing a solo gig in front of a rampant Irish audience. I spoke to her before and after the gig and tried to talk about Clare and Galway and The Waterboys and the accordion and Tommy Peoples and the weather and the price of coal and the state of the loos and everything. But, agonisingly shy, Sharon just shuffled nervously, stared at her shoes and mumbled unintelligibly. I attempted to interview her again with similarly painful results when her *Out The Gap* album was released in 1994. It was hard to equate the Sharon on stage with the Sharon off it. On stage she was confident and vibrant, seemingly lapping up the applause and acclaim justifiably accorded her virtuoso playing and the innovative way she used it. She dared to take breathtaking liberties with the music, collaborating extensively with reggae kingpin Dennis Bovell on *Out The Gap* and continued to break barriers in 1997 with *Each Little Thing*, an album left field enough to include a Fleetwood Mac cover, a South American tune and a Kirsty MacColl guest appearance singing on 'Libertango', a song once performed by Grace Jones.

Each Little Thing was the album launched at the Roisin Dubh and after a wonderfully animated set from Sharon and her band The Woodchoppers the assembled hacks who'd been deputed to interview her began to wince in anticipation. 'Do you think she will actually *say* anything this time?' said one veteran victim of her averted eyes, embarrassed giggles and indecipherable murmurs. Frankly, we doubted it, and hit the bar in an attempt to numb the awkwardness of what lay in store. Sharon, bless her, seemed to have had the same thought. It was around 2.30am when I was steered in, kicking and screaming, to face my punishment. I was a gibbering wreck and Sharon was on her way. Shy? This girl could talk for Ireland. Jokes, anecdotes, insight, history, musical analysis, confidence, laughter … she'd turned into the dream interviewee. Shame I was too pissed to take it all in. At the end I hugged her a bit too tightly and told her how terrified the hacks had been of that embarrassing wall of silence that always materialised when a cassette machine appeared in front of her. 'Really?' she said in genuine shock. 'Was I that bad? I had no idea.' She looked mortified now. 'I'm so sorry … I didn't mean to … I wasn't being … you know, *difficult* … I'd no idea I was as bad as that …' Oh Sharon, you were just a tad shy, you weren't *that* bad … 'Are you sure?' 'I'm sure.' 'Oh, that's grand.' We hugged again. Top woman, Sharon Shannon. Peter Tosh never hugged me.

It's a hot day – incredibly that's the second of this trip – so we drive a couple of miles west from Galway city and sit on the beach at Salt Hill. Not the greatest beach in the world but it does the job and there's a formidable funfair lurking in the background to prove that, yes, this *is* the seaside – official. Salt Hill's greatest attractions, however, are the gleaming new space-age toilets that have mysteriously landed on the promenade. A group of quizzical people have gathered round to gaze in awe and wonder at the silver-chromed miracle, milling around admiring the craftsmanship, dazzled by the flashing red and green lights, eager to sample the pleasures inside. Just 20 cents for a unique lavatory experience. It's a bargain, my friend, a bargain.

The Salt Hill lav goes on to provide endless entertainment as its growing queue of customers grapple with the baffling intricacies of the engineering. It is cleaned internally after each visit amid a volley of flashing lights worthy of a disco in a small town in Norfolk and a loud elongated swooshing noise that makes you wonder exactly *what* the embarrassed rapidly fleeing last resident has been doing in there. Lord alone knows what happens if you don't make it out of there *before* The Big Flush … every time the doors open you expect to see some poor drenched wretch crawling from the wreckage, clean but sodden. The automatic doors seem to have a mind of their own. They're like stage curtains, at one point opening to reveal a man looking like a character from a saucy seaside postcard, desperately trying to retrieve his trousers from his ankles before he comes into full view of the audience. At another point they won't open at all, leaving an unfortunate trapped inside yelling for help while the posse outside shout back a mixture of helpful advice and genial abuse. 'Press the buttons in there?' 'I *am* pressing the buttons!' 'Press them harder!' 'Oh jayzus, will y'just do the business and get the feck out of there, I can feel me insides about to burst here!' 'I've done the business, I'm *trying* to get out!' 'Well, press the buttons!' 'I *am* pressing the buttons!' 'PRESS THEM HARDER!' By the time he gets out the other guy is ready to deck him. Except he's bursting.

Salt Hill seems full of signs to Clifden, goading me on. 'Come on, English tourist,' they are saying, 'come to Connemara, you know you *want* to.' And they're right. I *do* want to. 'If you want to hide,' Donal Lunny told me once, 'go to Connemara. Nobody will ever find you there. If you don't want to be found people will swear blind they haven't seen you … even if they're standing next to you.' And before I know it we're driving further west. A quick drink in Spiddal, perhaps?

It's the gateway to Connemara and everything changes at Spiddal. We are entering Gaeltacht Irish-speaking territory, where all the signs are in Irish only and the landscape becomes dramatically morose and mystical. The roads narrow and seem to lead nowhere, loughs appear out of the blue, habitation is random, steep hills emerge on either side and the roads get craggier. No wonder Donal Lunny says a man can get lost forever in Connemara.

But first you have to deal with Spiddal. It was but a quiet village in 1974 when it was immortalised in Irish folklore as the birthplace of one of the most important Irish groups of them all, De Dannan. Frankie Gavin and Alec Finn got together playing sessions at the Cellar Bay in Galway and formalised the partnership with Charlie Piggott and Ringo McDonagh at Hughes's pub in Spiddal. I'd met them there on my first visit to the west of Ireland … about a thousand years ago. Frankie Gavin was an ebullient teenager then with wide eyes and a deep thirst, drinking in the excitement of De Dannan's thrilling potential and his own snowballing reputation as the finest young fiddle player of his generation.

We'd talked in Hughes's until that bit when they say 'Have you no homes to go to?' and then surreptitious calls were made, whispered conversations conducted, instruments gathered and we were whisked off deep into Connemara to some pub that popped out of the undergrowth, had a quick look to make sure we weren't being followed and urgently beckoned us in. The lights were off and all seemed silent … you could indeed get lost in Connemara. We were ushered into a back room and as the door opened it was like one of those dreaded surprise parties. Lights, drinks, action, music. De Dannan got the drinks in, immersed themselves among the motley assortment of old and young limbering up with their fiddles and flutes and melodeons, engaged in some gentle banter and enquiries about the health of their companions and started to play.

As an initiation into the ways of the *seisun* it was pretty spectacular. The night was long and dawn was breaking when we finally left and I have little memory of it beyond a bizarre conversation with an old farmworker in a flat cap who talked my ears off about Manchester United and an impossibly fruity barmaid who ruffled my hair and called me Colm. And I remember laughing like a drain at jokes that weren't even funny. And I remember Frankie's running commentary on the women he wished to pleasure. And I remember drinking Smithwicks with some unspeakable spirit chaser. And I remember endless tunes flowing through the bar with seamless ease and spontaneity, while the musicians cackled and howled and spilled drinks and playfully insulted one another as the craic grew mightier the closer we got to dawn.

Spiddal these days is a slightly different beast. It's still small but it has talked up its beach, scenery and views of Lough Corrib as well as the celebrated company it has been known to keep and is now a regular haunt for visitors. And they tend to be German. They sit on walls writing postcards and poring over maps and with the size of the maps these days, Spiddal is soon full to bursting.

The Waterboys might also be held to account for Spiddal's modern iconic status. The band's charismatic founder and driving force Mike Scott first came here in 1988. Hitting a blank while working on the *Fisherman's Blues* album, he decided to take a few days off in the west of Ireland to recharge his batteries and find new inspiration. He wound up in Galway city and got involved in a session at Tigh Neachtain and became friendly with a fiddle player called Sean Lennon, the son of the celebrated fiddler, pianist and composer Charlie Lennon, who was living in Spiddal. The next day Scott was coaxed out to Spiddal and ended up joining Charlie Lennon at a session at Hughes's. Instantly smitten, Scott found it impossible to leave Hughes's … or Spiddal. He immersed himself in the local scene, wrote a whole load of new material and summoned the rest of The Waterboys to join him there to complete the recording of *Fisherman's Blues*.

Its successor *Room To Roam* was directly inspired by the west of

Ireland in general and Spiddal in particular. Shy Sharon Shannon had by then been inducted into the band to link her magic accordion to Steve Wickham's belting fiddle and The Waterboys' adoption of and by Irish music was complete. Some of the hardcore fans and most of the critics were mystified by why and how the future of rock had taken such a strange turn to wind up playing in a tiny bar in Spiddal when they should have been inspiring baying kids to light matches in their honour at some faceless aerodrome in Phoenix, Arizona, but the Irish loved them for it. Scott repaid the village he'd come to call home with a new song in its honour, 'Spring Comes To Spiddal'. It was only a loopy, fall-about little ragtime song, but it painted a cute picture and it immortalised the village. Waterboys fans have been coming to pay homage ever since.

Mike Scott doesn't live in Ireland any more but he says 'I still think of Spiddal as home' and looks back on his Irish years with acute affection. On his occasional returns he is still prevailed upon to join a late night session at Hughes's, ruefully admitting the odd *faux pas* in his early days on the session scene. 'What you *can't* do is go in thinking you're a star,' he tells me. 'It doesn't matter who you are, in a session it doesn't matter and they really don't care. There's a protocol and I remember breaking it once when I heard a session going on in a pub and I thought I'd be really cool and I walked through the door playing my guitar. That didn't impress them one bit.'

Now we've dipped our toe in we might as well go all the way and Connemara is a constant source of wonder and confusion. No journey here is ever the same and I love this place to bits for its sheer unpredictability – the unpredictability of the terrain, of the weather, of the state of the roads, of the state of the road signs. And for its rugged, ragged beauty … dark, untamed and dangerous to know. And the underlying sense of melancholia offset by the warmth of the welcome for strangers. And the untold secrets you sense lie round every corner and the devil in its soul. And the eccentric signs that seduce you off the beaten track and lure you to God knows where. And the dark bogs and tall mountains and the array of wildlife and plants. And the startling views of the ocean and the evocative lunar landscapes that fire the imagination and lift the heart. And the absence of traffic wardens and burger bars and themed pubs and the fact that nothing is written in English.

I love the glorious smell of peat too, but I feel guilty about that. I mean, out there in the west of Ireland you can't beat being curled up in front of a peat fire with a glass of something that probably isn't very good for you. The smell of the peat bog is an integral ingredient of the deal when you find room to roam over here. But once you stop sniffing and start looking you see the ecological carnage of bogs with the peat ripped out of them it puts a different slant on it. The lobby to curtail turf farming to preserve the bogs seems to strike at the very heart of one of the essential romantic Irish images of the peat fire and the sweet aroma, but they do have a point.

As we're up this way it would be rude not to call in at Roundstone. It's mad, undisciplined country up here and on a cold wet day in February it can seem impossibly bleak, but those romantics who like their Ireland free of clichéd charm and souvenir shop cutesiness will find great reward in the hardy free-spirited landscapes. Here is one of the oldest fishing communities in the country with a lively harbour, some decent beaches, seals and dolphins frolicking in the Atlantic and a plethora of wild flowers. The village of 'Ballinagra' featured in the 1997 film *The Matchmaker* – a daft romantic comedy about an American senator and his spin doctor in search of Irish roots – was actually Roundstone.

There's also a striking sixteenth-century Franciscan monastery here which looks like ... well, it looks like a sixteenth-century Franciscan monastery. Not that I'm an expert. But this is no ordinary sixteenth-century Franciscan monastery. It's the home of Roundstone Musical Instruments, bodhran centre of Ireland. The official bodhran supplier for *Riverdance,* they make something like 10,000 bodhrans a year in the workshop here, meeting orders from all over the world with customised designs and individual heraldry. Celebrity customers include Bono, Keith Richard and Bill Clinton, but it's more fun not being a celeb and making the trek out to Roundstone and choosing one of the dazzling array of bodhrans on display off the peg.

Malachy Kearns, a relative of the great Sligo fiddle god Michael Coleman, was eight when he first encountered the bodhran at a wake in Donegal. The doyen of all Donegal fiddle players Johnny Doherty was there paying his respects with a few tunes when a traveller also there whipped out a bodhran and thumped along. The young Malachy was mesmerised.

He was even more mesmerised when he heard the bodhran again some time afterwards, this time played by Seamus Tansey . A blind flute player Josie McDermott was also present and, sensing the young boy's awe, urged him to touch the skin of the bodhran. When he did, Josie leaned over and whispered in his ear: "You can hear the oul' goat's heart, can't you boy?" Malachy could... and he sold his soul to King Puck there and then.

After learning his trade from the old school bodhran makers in Kerry, Malachy set up his own business in Roundstone in 1976. He's since supplied most of the bodhran greats along the way and has become a legend in his own goat skin. He's featured on Irish stamps (but only the 32p ones) and has written his own book Wallop! talking with spiritual fervour about goat skins and all who beat them. He describes the day the goatskins are delivered to as 'a day of pagan resurrection' and is particularly eloquent in his vision of the bodhran sound as a rebirth of the goat's soul. 'When you strike the skin with your fingers you can hear the pitter patter of the old puck's wild soul coming alive again,' he says, 'like the sound of his hard hooves against the rocks in the high places where nobody else lives but hawks...it's an elemental pulse.. wild and pagan and maybe essentially Celtic.'

You may very well wonder what they put in the water in Roundstone but he means it, talking with equal ardour about the processes involved in making a bodhran. Once the goat skins are delivered they are soaked in baths of hydrated lime and then immersed in a sulphide solution to make the skins supple. They are then stretched in a heat chamber before being glued and tacked to rims usually made of beechwood, varnished, artwork applied and voila! Except that Malachy has always used a secret ingredient with which to soak his bodhrans and give them that distinctive Roundstone je ne sais quoi. People have plied him with drink, begged on hands and knees and threatened his goldfish, but Malachy's secret ingredient has never been revealed. Naturally I wouldn't dream of revealing it either – mainly because I have absolutely no idea what it is – but suffice to say it was well-known practise for the bodhran makers of old to add a certain spice to the sound of their bodhrans by splashing them with the contents of their chamber pots...

It takes an age to drive through Connemara. Mostly because I am constantly lost and following the path of deadbeat tracks that lead to nowhere purely on the basis that they look mysterious and interesting. Even the historic landmarks are baffling. In 1907 the first Marconi transatlantic telegraph station was built around here somewhere, just a few miles south of Clifden. And close by in 1919 Alcock and Brown landed a Vickers Vimy plane after an epic 16-hour, 1,900-mile journey from Newfoundland to make history with the first transatlantic flight. You'd think it would be monument city, right? Erm, *wrong*. The Marconi building was burned down in 1921 and, while there's an Alcock and Brown Hotel in Clifden, there is a disarming lack of singing and dancing to direct you to the site of the landing itself.

Alcock and Brown may have been making aviation history but it was a less than glitzy arrival. They certainly hadn't planned to pitch down in the middle of nowhere in Connemara but after grappling with the likelihood of a watery grave as their plane dipped and dived all the way across the Atlantic, decided to dump the plane at the first sight of land and get the hell out. So when they glimpsed a nice juicy green meadow from the air they got the plane down quick. Unfortunately, their green meadow turned out to be the hostile swamp lands of Derrygimlagh Moor. Terra firma turned out to be terra infirma and their historic journey ended in the humiliation of mud-drenched boots and a sinking plane.

In their dreams they'd have been welcomed by cheering crowds, glasses of champagne, and the world's press taking photies of them draped round a bevy of scantily clad nymphets. In fact they landed shortly after 6am, cold, wet and miserable, and the only person who came to greet them after landing was some bloke who probably sounded like an Irish Kenneth Williams saying 'Who are you then?' You can imagine Captain Alcock replying 'Me? Oh, nobody special. I'm only the bloke who's just flown across the Atlantic' in a Tony Hancock voice, obviously. And Kenneth Williams would say: 'Oh go on, stop messin' about!'

The least we can do is make a small pilgrimage to the site that marked the end of the Alcock and Brown adventure all those years ago. A few quiet moments reverie in the bog, remembering. I mean, we'll have a drink to them in their hotel in Clifden later but it's not the same, is it? So a trip to the Alcock and Brown monument it is then. If we ever find it. The expedition to the memorial probably takes longer than the original flight. We are talking rugged terrain. Tracks that go on for miles but lead nowhere, gradually narrowing into a trickle and then vanishing into thin air. Flying 16 hours from Newfoundland must have been easy meat for Alcock and Brown compared with this little lot.

And then we see a small sign directing us to what looks like a precarious rocky path full of puddles and branches. There's also a gate barring the entrance but hey, gates can be opened and this one does. We follow the track half expecting to be gobbled up by the mud or at least set upon by a crazed sect of worshippers descended from superstitious country folk who'd seen the Alcock and Brown plane land, imagined they were aliens from outer space and had subsequently sworn eternal allegiance to the sacred bogs that had been their first point of contact.

In fact we see no one and nothing. Just a couple of sheep who stare suspiciously across the stark, unwelcoming moor.

Eventually finding our way back to a road big enough to hint that we may yet avoid spending the rest of our lives on these moors and then we see another sign: 'ALCOCK AND BROWN MONUMENT'. It's like a treasure hunt this and I'm beginning to wonder if whoever's in charge of sticking up signs hasn't any more idea than me where Captain Alcock landed his bloody plane. I reckon he's just erected a lot of different signs at various different tracks into the undergrowth in the hope that one of them will stick. Still, only one way to find out and another detour it is. Another track, another long view of oblivion. Keep walking. You know, *just in case.*

Eventually we arrive at a most peculiar sight. A long pointy thing sticking out of the ground. It's like one of the Pyramids with anorexia. But this is it all right. The official Alcock and Brown monument. But what the hell is it? 'It's a fin,' says One Who Knows in the Alcock and Brown Hotel later. A *whaaat?* 'A fin.' I thought they arrived in a plane, not on the back of a frigging shark. I hope Fungie gets more than a fin dedicated to him when they eventually get around to building a statue to him in Dingle. 'No, the fin of an aircraft. It's pointing to the spot where the plane landed.' Oh it is, is it? Why didn't they put it where the plane ended then? ''Cos it would've feckin' sunk in the feckin' swamp like the feckin' plane did, that's why?' Monuments eh, who needs 'em?

Besides, we're too busy staring at a woman in a smock painting in a field across the way. Her bike is carelessly strewn on the ground while she pores over her easel, paintbrush in hand. It's a bemusing sight. Of all the beautiful landscapes in this part of Ireland why would she haul her bike to this one? Nothing but moorland, hillocks and scruffy lanes. It can't have been easy cycling all the way over there through barbed wire fences and Alcock and Brown monuments either. And it's damp and cold, hardly the weather to be sitting in random fields sketching the scenery. We look harder, trying to garner clues from the painting on her canvas but she's too far away. We stare at her for 45 minutes waiting for some sign, for *anything* to indicate who she is or what she's doing here. Nothing. Nothing at all.

Whatever she's doing she's concentrating hard for she's barely moved in all the time we've been watching her. At one point I become worried she may have died in that chair for there are no signs of movement. She could have been dead for days and no one has noticed. I call out but if she hears she makes no acknowledgement. I start to clamber through the undergrowth for a closer look but the barbed wire and the swamp get angry and I turn back.

Back in the Alcock and Brown Hotel I report the worrying experience to a quizzical barman. 'I mean, she might be dead for all I know,' I tell him, 'I really think we should get someone to go out there and see if she's all right.' The barman looks at me hard. 'Near the monument, you say …' 'Yes … a woman in a smock.' 'And you say she has a bike with her?' 'Yep, there's an old bike alongside her.' His face breaks into a smile. 'That'll be Mary.' Mary? 'Yeah, you fell for it.' I did?

'It's a scarecrow.' *Never*! But the *bike* ... 'Oh, the kids round the farm like to play games with the tourists, they move her chair and her bike into different positions to confuse everyone. They were probably watching you and having a right good laugh.' I drink up and leave in a hurry.

The first time I came to Clifden was for a Waterboys concert in a marquee in the early nineties. On holiday in County Mayo, I'd driven to Westport and undertaken the magnificent drive across the spectacular Partry Mountains. These mountains go on forever and you barely see man nor beast for the duration. It's so desolate and remote and as the mists descend you feel you're the only person left on earth. Up here that's not such a bad feeling. And then you start the descent and that's thrilling too. Down into the impossibly gorgeous village of Leenane nestling cosily at the foot of the mountains and the tall trees and swinging its toes into the vast still waters of Killary Harbour.

There's a cup of coffee and a camera with your name on it at Leenane, but don't use up all your film because a few bendy corners later you'll hit Kylemore Abbey. Across Kylemore Lough, protected by the green come-over-here-if-you-think-you're-hard-enough slopes of the Twelve Bens, is the stunning sight of the Abbey. First time I saw it I screeched to a halt and gawped and gawped. It's like something out of a Disney fairytale, a romantic, gothic dream. And, of course, next time you visit you have to take a closer look just to confirm it wasn't all part of some immaculate fantasy about Connemara.

It was built in the nineteenth century by a Manchester surgeon called Mitchell Henry – later MP for Galway – as a present to his wife Margaret after visiting Connemara on honeymoon in 1850. Now that is some present. It makes the chocolates and flowers I usually give Mrs Colin seem a bit paltry. But when Margaret died, Mitchell Henry sold it and it eventually became a refuge for Benedictine nuns fleeing from Ypres in the First World War. The nuns liked it so much they stayed – and who wouldn't? – and now run the Abbey as a girls' boarding school, making a few bob on the side flogging coffee and knick-knacks to gobsmacked tourists.

It's all so peacefully idyllic you continue the journey in a loved-up haze with a beatific smile on your face. And then you cross the bridge and hit Clifden. After the stark solitude of the Partry Mountains and the quiet contemplation of Leenane and Kylemore Lough, the sheer noise in Clifden knocked me sideways when I came to see The Waterboys here all those years ago. They were hanging out of the pubs, dancing in the streets and jabbering at each other in a variety of languages. The place was a madhouse, creaking under the invasion of trenchant Waterboys fans, in addition to the usual motley assortment of international backpackers with their interesting haircuts and their discovery of the delights of alcohol. I made my way to the huge marquee to see The Waterboys, intrigued to witness the reaction of a local audience in their adopted home to the Irish roots they'd spectacularly acquired. I was especially looking forward to seeing the Irish contingent of Steve Wickham on fiddle and Sharon Shannon on accordion.

But there had been a change of plan. Wickham and Shannon had left the band and The Waterboys had suddenly reinvented themselves again as a straight-ahead rock'n'roll band. They were good at it too, but it wasn't The Waterboys that I, or most of the rest of the audience, had come to see, judging by the ecstatic ovation accorded Sharon Shannon when she joined them to play just a couple of numbers. When it was all over I set off back for Mayo at the dead of night and found the Partry Mountains a rather more intimidating proposition than the gentle giant that had nursed me south earlier in the day. It was pitch black and misty and without cat's eyes it was impossible to know exactly how close I was to the edge of the mountains on either side. When offshoot roads started to appear I was firmly of the conviction I'd taken a wrong turn and would end up being devoured by the evil beasties of Partry or at least kidnapped by a gang of poitin makers.

That's when it appeared. A small furry black and white thing suddenly materialised in the centre of the road, its head and back clearly illuminated in my headlights as it scurried along in front of me. I'm no David Bellamy but after imagining all sorts of scenarios about leprechauns and little people I decided it was a badger. Belter the Badger, as I came to call him. I put all my faith in Belter that night and I've got to tell you, that badger never wavered. He maintained a straight line in the centre of the road and without even a glance in my direction he guided me every mile of the way across those mountains right down into Mayo. And then, with Westport in sight, he just sort of … *disappeared*. So I never got to thank him and every time I've crossed that Partry pass ever since I've looked in vain for him. So if you're out there Belter, thanks. You were my guiding light that night. Badgers are fab, okay?

Clifden itself is one of Ireland's new towns. Well, if you call nearly 200 years old *new*. It's one of only a few planned towns in Ireland and it was founded by a High Sheriff, John D'Arcy, in an attempt to bring some sense of prosperity and law and order to the poverty-stricken bandit lands of Connemara. It was a thankless task and despite the growing industries of fishing, wool and marble, D'Arcy's family ultimately went bankrupt in the attempt. Yet his vision of a civilised outpost and trading centre did eventually bear fruit. Clifden is now a bustling summer haunt for visitors, its small roads shuddering under the weight of it all and its bars rocking and rolling with plenty of live music and serious drinking. It's not quite as much fun in the winter when the icy winds howl off the Atlantic and the economy goes into free-fall, but Clifden still has a likeable spirit of independence.

Then there's the Mexican connection. After the famine and resultant mass emigrations to America, a lot of expatriated Irish found themselves drafted into the American army when it invaded Mexico following battles over disputed land in Texas. There were grave misgivings even in America about the justification of the war – Abraham Lincoln and Ulysses Grant were among those who spoke out against it – and the Irish immigrants, already angered by bigotry and the discrimination they'd encountered in the US Army, wondered why they were now being asked to kill fellow Catholics. A lot of them simply decided they liked the Mexicans more than they liked the Americans and crossed the Rio Grande to fight for the other side.

One of the ringleaders of the mutiny was a Clifden man, John Reilly, who ended up commanding the *San Patricios*, a battalion of largely Irish troops who fought under a green banner decorated with the joint emblems of St Patrick and the Mexican eagle. News of their valour in battle spread throughout Mexico and their legend intensified after the disastrous Battle of Churubsco when their ranks were decimated. Fifty of the *San Patricios* were hanged – after being forced to stand on the scaffold for hours with nooses round their necks while the Americans waited for the Mexicans to surrender – and many others were flogged and branded on their cheeks with the letter D for desertion.

Strong links between Clifden and Mexico have remained ever since, giving the town a faintly surreal Latino flavour. The town was even granted special tax status for a Mexican-related industrial development at Market Hill and there's a plaque somewhere explaining it all. And now Clifden holds an annual commemoration of those tragic events across the Atlantic in 1846. So if you're ever in Clifden on September 12, get yourself down the Alcock and Brown Hotel, order a glass of tequila and drink to the *San Patricios*.

Driving out of Clifden I listen to the earthy, soulful voice of Dolores Keane. 'She's the best singer ever to come out of Ireland,' Tommy Makem told me once and if you want to argue with Tommy Makem fair enough, but I'm not going to. As with the great fiddle, flute, pipe and accordion players, Dolores' voice is at one with the environment you see around you. The character of the people, the nature of the land, the whole history of the country seems to be enveloped in her voice, even when she sings – as she has on occasions – material that simply isn't worthy of her. She's a modern evocation of Irish traditional song … instinctively revealing its heart and soul.

But then it's in her blood. The Keane family from Caherlistrane, close to Lough Corrib, have long been a treasured part of the Irish tradition and the pride of Galway. The early song collectors would beat a path to the door of sisters Sarah and Rita Keane, a central focus for the song-swapping and informal sessions that were such a prominent feature of the rural farming community. People knew that if you came from Caherlistrane and your name was Keane, you could sing and play, it was as simple as that and any traditional musician or singer passing through Galway would invariably take a detour out to meet them. Dolores' brothers, Matt, Pat, Sean and Noel, all have the music, as do her two sisters Teresa and Christina, but it's Dolores – and to some extent Sean too – who took their musical legacy to new heights. Initially she did it as a singer/flute player within the family ceili band, but more famously in a duet with first husband John Faulkner, in the all-conquering De Dannan and ultimately with her own Dolores Keane Band.

A couple of years ago I went to Caherlistrane to meet Dolores with her aunts Sarah and Rita Keane in the big thatched house surrounded by endless green fields in which they raised her. The front door was open – the front door is *always* open. They'd lived there all their lives and, come rain or shine, winter or summer, the first thing they did when they got up in the morning was to open the door, closing it only at dusk. A lively fire lit up the hearth and Sarah and Rita welcomed the new arrivals with large hot toddy that didn't spare the whisky. My companion, a teetotal radio producer, slyly nudged his hot toddy in my direction and I was feeling no pain as Sarah and Rita talked quietly and shyly about the family farm and the musical traditions it embraced.

Their father Matt Keane was a fluent Irish speaker who played jew's harp, and their mother May Costello was well-known locally as a fine singer. 'She was a beautiful singer,' Rita told me. 'She had a very haunting, melodious voice … she was a real traditional singer, a sad type of singer. We could never be anything like her. There was just something about her, such great feeling in her songs.' At this point they mentioned their mother's favourite song was 'Ayr On The Rhine' and, quite spontaneously, began to sing it together. It may have been something to do with the bottom of the second glass of hot toddy, but listening to these two sisters in their seventies singing with such cherish and tenderness a song their mother had sung in the same kitchen half a century earlier brought a tear to my eye.

The music, they said, was as natural to them as walking and talking.

Sarah played the fiddle and Rita the melodeon, though it was their unusual unison singing – initially in the Irish language – which made them famous. 'We got all our songs from our mother,' Rita told me, 'but we had no tape recorder at the time and a lot of the songs went with her, God rest her soul. There was no television in those days, of course, so it was our entertainment.'

They did have a gramophone, though, and breaking news about the arrival of a brand-new 78 recording would spread around the parish like wildfire. Relatives who'd emigrated to America would send Irish records home from the States – to the great excitement not just of their immediate family, but the whole village. Once word got out that a new 78 had arrived, everyone else would make a bee-line for the farmhouse to hear it. And there were weekly shopping trips into Tuam, too, with May Keane spending 2/6d on a new gramophone record every Saturday. 'We'd get it home and play it over and over, even all night on the gramophone until we'd learned how to play it. Once we knew how to play it we waited for the next one.'

In the summer they'd travel to the Fleadh Cheoils, often returning with half the festival in tow. They'd all turn up in cars and caravans and mobile homes and the fields outside would be full of the aroma of rashers on primus stoves. Then they'd all assemble in the Keane kitchen and the music would start. It would go on well into the night until someone said 'Jeez, let's go to the pub' and they'd all troop off to Tuam and the session would go on there.

It was an extraordinary musical environment which the young Dolores Keane absorbed and fully appreciated. 'People would call in just to say hello and they'd end up staying four days and by the time they left I knew all their songs,' said Dolores. 'So many people came to this house from all over Ireland, from England, America, Australia … you didn't have to travel because you got the music all here. Records were made in this house, films were made here, *everything*. It all happened and Sarah and Rita wouldn't be bothered by any of it.'

Dolores even began to get emotional as she recalled growing up in Caherlistrane and reflected, not just on the great musical life, but on the hard times that invariably afflicted all the farming families – and the community spirit that pulled them through. 'It wasn't just a cup of sugar you shared with the neighbours,' she said, 'it was *everything*. You always helped each other out. When you had the old traditional thing of killing the pig, the meat went round the whole village …'

Does that kind of spirit still exist? 'No, not in the same way,' said Rita. 'No, those people are gone and they will never be replaced,' said Sarah. And Dolores reflected on what it actually meant being raised on a rural farm in North East Galway. 'If you're brought up living off the land you are at one with the land,' she said. 'You know the seasons, you know the wild flowers, you know when the birds start to nest, you know when the Canadian geese come in. It's a smell in the air that you instantly recognise. People have lost that. It's not taught in the schools.'

Dolores' moment of revelation occurred while she was having her breakfast at the kitchen table during a period of retreat at Sarah and Rita's house after a particularly gruelling foreign tour. 'It was where I'd always had me breakfast as a kid and then twenty years later I was sitting there at springtime and I suddenly jumped up and said "Sarah and Rita, the snowdrops are out!" The smell of the flowers had come through the door and I ran outside and there were two little snowdrops poking up their heads. That's when I thought "This is what life is about. It's not the fast lane, it's *this* … "'

Tears welled in her eyes and there was a long silence broken only by the loud tick-tock of the clock and the sound of birds singing outside. Suddenly the emotional impact of Dolores' nostalgic reverie was rudely shattered by the jarring sound of the phone ringing. That was a shock in itself. A phone in a thatched cottage? 'If it's a gig, Reet, TAKE IT!' shouted Dolores after her. Rita talked briefly. 'UP THE MONEY, REET!' yelled Dolores. When she returned there was another shock. 'Do you mind,' she said politely, 'if we take a break now and watch *Emmerdale* on the television?' Phones, cigarettes and *Emmerdale* … the essential weapons of the traditional singer. 'Would you like another glass?' said Sarah, before settling in front of the telly. 'Er, no thanks,' I said, still a bit wobbly from the last lot. 'We really should be going.' As we bid our goodbyes she scurried back into the kitchen and returned with a loaf of home-made bread. 'We baked it for you,' she said. 'You're very welcome.'

It was the finest bread I'd ever tasted.

The drive across Connemara to Caherlistrane is another thrillingly bleak adventure through Joyce Country (nothing to do with James Joyce, it comes from a Welsh family who settled in the mountains between Lough Mask and Lough Corrib in the twelfth century). You pass between the loughs from Maam, hitting the other side at Cong, where they filmed John Wayne in the Oscar-winning John Ford movie *The Quiet Man* in 1952 (and boy, do they still go on about it!), I acquired a copy of *The Quiet Man* just to wax lyrical about it here but the truth is the sight of John Wayne sitting on a bale of hay wearing a chequered flat cap and the words 'a rollicking piece of Irish blarney' on the video cover prevented me from feeding it to the video machine.

We check in at the Corrib B&B in the centre of the small town of Headford and visit friends John and Imelda for tea. 'Would there be any music here tonight?' I ask tentatively. John's immediately on the phone and breathless discussions follow. Eventually he returns in triumph. 'I think we might find some music at Campbells tonight,' he says. He's not wrong. At Campbells there is indeed music. A dark-haired girl called Yvonne is wearing red trousers and playing fiddle to die for with earthy vibrancy, but she's in good company, vying with an old-school accordion stylist as the session rapidly expands. A young lad joins the fray on fiddle, there's an English flute player here on his holidays and the bush telegraph is obviously in overdrive as more fiddles, flutes and accordions arrive by the minute. Oh yes, and the odd bodhran too.

As the session heats up I become fascinated by real or imagined session etiquette. I could be imagining it but there seems to be a musical power struggle going on between the old hand on the accordion and the brilliant young fiddle player. The accordionist is initiating most of the tunes and most of the others look to him for their lead, but Yvonne's growing fervour threatens to steal the show. When he takes a break to sip his drink she launches into a tune and I sense the session initiative shifting. She's raised the stakes in power, volume and speed and the younger players go with her, while the older ones attempt to restrain her with a more tempered rhythm.

It's fascinating, fiery stuff this and, three pints on, the conspiracy theories are raging in my head. Is there such a thing as session rage? It's getting pretty intense in that corner and I am imagining the night climaxing in an epic musical face-off between the old accordion gunslinger and the new kid in town on the fiddle. This is bigger than Duelling Banjos. Bigger than the rap head-to-heads. Eat your heart out, Eminem. You think you've got problems with all that hissing and dissing with Snoop Dogg and Ol' Dirty Bastard, you should come out to Campbells in Headford and see what's going on here, mate.

Then again, never let it be said a great session is about musical analysis, conflict and body language. When you talk of *a great craic* you don't mean music alone. You are talking complete social occasion – people, conversation, drinks – and this occasion is *very* social. I find myself locked in a fantastic debate about the new 'ponderosa' society of Ireland with a woman who I think tells me her daughter has been representing Galway at the Rose of Tralee. Then there's the guy from Leeds with a flute in his pocket – but don't tell anyone.

I also get to shake hands with Dolores Keane's brother Pat; I slag off George Bush with an American woman who thinks he'll end up bombing every country in the entire world until they all agree to be American; debate the current state of hurling with a local farmer who used to play for Galway and seems to know what he's talking about;

discuss the new Irish experience of immigration and the influx of professional Africans – which has thrilled the liberals in Clifden – with an earnest young man from Ballinrobe; and ask a baffled barmaid if we're likely to see Tommy Peoples in the house tonight. I also have a lovely chat with Barbara, who is 70 years old and recently acted as 'sweeper-up' at a marathon, jogging along at the back of the field picking up the fallen and making sure there were no unaccounted-for competitors heaving their guts up in a hedge or taking refuge in a pub. Barbara tells me she used to live in the East End of London but has had more exciting adventures since then. She recently raised a load of money so a poor community in South America could have a water supply. Escorted by a priest she smuggled the illicit money into the country in her bra. The craic is indeed mighty this night.

They're amazed when we check out of the Corrib B&B next morning. 'We have no record of you.' Oh but we definitely booked in. 'And you stayed the night here, did you?' Yes. 'Are you sure now?' Well, I'd had a drink, but … yes. 'That's strange, we didn't know you were there.' Oh. 'You could have just slipped away and we'd never have known.' Fancy that. 'Did we give you breakfast as well?' You did. 'Well, wouldn't you know, we have no record of that either.' Amazing. 'Isn't it just? Did you have a good night then?' We did. 'Where did you go?' Campbells … there was a session there. 'Oh that's grand. It was good, was it?' Yes, it was great. 'That's grand. You'll have to come and see us again. We'll check you in next time!' Irish B&Bs are wonderful.

We take a peek at Tuam, a city of two cathedrals, which seems a bit greedy considering what a small place it is. The very name reminds me of a holiday in the early nineties when every time you turned on the radio you could guarantee that one song would come booming out. It was one of those really irritating songs you couldn't get out of your head, yet couldn't help singing along with. I always listened with grudging admiration, partly due to the mind-numbingly catchy chorus and partly due to an extraordinarily lyric about lustful thoughts during mass. Not only did it feature the word 'ostentatious' – not a word you find in pop music too often – it also used the word 'ass' in a rumpish context. The clergy wasn't best pleased and Ireland lost a generation of priests to coronaries due to the regularity with which it was played on the radio.

The song – 'I Useta Love Her' by the Saw Doctors – went on to top the Irish charts for nine weeks, becoming the biggest-selling Irish single in history at that point. If anybody had any doubts from where they'd emanated, the title of their second album, *All The Way From Tuam*, eradicated them. They continued to flaunt their locality with tracks like 'N17' – which was kept off the No 1 spot by Zig & Zag

(!) – and then organised a big concert in Tuam under the banner 'The West's Awake'. They were given the freedom of Tuam, but in 1993 they lost their Welsh keyboard and accordion player Tony Lambert after he won a million in the Lottery.

Before leaving Galway I want to meet Frankie Gavin, who in three decades with De Dannan has proved himself not only a monumental fiddle player but a richly entertaining raconteur, too. If there's a man who knows where the action is it has to be Frankie. He's played the world's concert halls but while you can take the Galway fiddle player out of a pub session, you can't take the pub session out of the Galway fiddle player. Or something. And if you're going to have a drink in Galway – and in Galway it's hard *not* to have a drink – there's no one better to share it than Frankie Gavin. But Frankie, cherub-faced ball of confusion that he is, also proves elusive.

Eventually, after a series of near misses, we arrange to meet in a bar in the village of Oughterard where he now lives on the banks of Lough Corrib. So off we go again over the bridges, past the posh hotels and country clubs and thatched cottages and pony trekkers and golfers and anglers to find Frankie's favourite pub cowering behind a frankly unnecessary conglomerate of craft shops. I get the drinks in and wait. After finishing both our drinks I call him. He's breathless, apologetic and breathlessly apologetic. 'Had a situation … problems … be there in five minutes.' I get some more drinks in and wait. I'm halfway through the second when he arrives, red-faced, presenting me with a copy of his new CD amid a torrent of apologies and involved explanations about a catalogue of domestic problems.

He downs his pint in a matter of seconds. 'The thing is I can't stop now …' he says, tumbling out his apologies again … got to take his family to the airport … America … going to join them there later … so much to do … so little time … nightmare of a day … so many problems … but hey, it's great to see you again. No time to talk now but are you doing anything tomorrow?' Nothing that can't be obliterated from the diary, Frankie. 'I've got a gig in Doolin tomorrow night, do you fancy coming down to Clare to see it?'

Now, apart from the free curled-up cheese and pickle sandwich the barman has pushed in my direction, that's the best offer I've had all day. Frankie ol' son, you're on. 'Grand … that's grand …' he says, still flustered, 'I'll see you in Doolin then.' And in a puff of smoke he's gone. I nibble a stale cheese and pickle sandwich, order another pint, and study the route to Doolin.

Chapter eight

CLARE: CLIFFS, FARMERS' WIVES, DE DANNAN & DOOLIN

'It's a long, long way from Clare to here … it's a long, long way and it gets further by the day, it's a long, long way from Clare to here …'

And after the shock of Kerry and discovering that while my back was turned Dingle had become a throbbing metropolis with Fungie the dolphin as lord mayor, I approach Doolin with trepidation. A couple of decades ago when was I last here Doolin barely even qualified as village … just a couple of pubs, a harbour wall and a sign for a ferry boat to take you to the Aran Islands. No boat, mind, just a sign.

Yet even then Doolin's fame as a secret hotbed of great music was growing fast and the pubs were wall-to-wall with Germans sporting comedy beards and mandolins slung over their backs looking for the local music hero Micho Russell. They didn't usually have to look far either. Micho would invariably be found in the middle with a wink and story for all-comers.

I couldn't imagine what Doolin would be like all these years later. Will it have Micho Russell theme parks? Road signs in German? A fancy bridge and motorway to take you to the Aran Islands? Aussie rules football pitches on the seafront? Ibiza soundtracks booming out of art deco bars full of posters announcing 'NO FIDDLES, MANDOLINS, FLUTES OR TRADITIONAL INSTRUMENTS ALLOWED UNDER ANY CIRCUMSTANCES ON THE PREMISES BY ORDER OF THE MANAGEMENT'.

But first we have to get there and the journey from Galway hasn't started well. It's raining and as I pop out of the car to get a paper I am struck in the face by an unlicensed umbrella. I spend the rest of the journey composing my list of things to put in Room 101. Umbrellas are at the top.

Hats! What's bloody wrong with *hats*, people?

We take refuge in The Burren. You can't imagine people worrying about umbrellas in The Burren. Here you find perfect desolation. Grey skies, flat limestone rocks as far as the eye can see, miles and miles of emptiness and a stillness that makes you think you've slipped into some sinister black void. Oliver Cromwell's surveyor came here in the 1640s and reported back to his boss that The Burren is 'a savage land, yielding neither water enough to drown a man, nor tree to hang him, nor soil enough to bury'. That's a relief then. When aliens abduct you and dump you in the middle of The Burren you won't drown and if the bogey men get you they won't be able to hang you. And even if they find some other means of killing you they won't be able to bury the body. This sheer barren wilderness will probably drive you bonkers long before that happens anyway.

If you dare investigate The Burren on foot there's all manner of wonders to be found within the jagged limestone. A bundle of prehistoric monuments, for one. There's also a load of stone arrangements that tourists always get excited about, fondly imagining them to have been the work of Celts thousands of years ago. And to be fair some of them are. Mostly, though, they were knocked up a couple of years ago by some architecture students.

In the 1940s a local farmer was out with his sheepdog when the dog suddenly just *disappeared* before his very eyes. One minute he was romping along terrorising the sheep and the next he vanished into thin air, just like that. Help was summoned, searches were made, digging begun and eventually a cave was uncovered. And there, deep in the bowels of the earth the farmer found Fido grappling with an old bone. When the bone was analysed it was discovered to have belonged to a brown bear. The spooky thing is brown bears have been extinct in Ireland for thousands of years. The caves – named Aillwee – were found to stretch for miles right into the heart of a surrounding mountain and now at the dead of night the locals often pop down there for a game of Aussie Rules footie and maybe the odd sly card school.

We hit the coast road at the fishing village of Ballyvaughan and travel a path of breathtaking beauty. Past the bleak rocky outpost of Black Head, continue down the coast to Murroogh and onward alongside the imposing mountain of Slieve Elva into Roadford before starting the descent into Doolin – host town to the Ukraine. A fleet of scooters appears in the road as it narrows and seem to be escorting us. What's this then? A mods convention? Has the village been bought by Vespa? Is Paul Weller the Lord Mayor? Or am I witnessing the arrival of the Ukrainian Special Olympics team?

Doolin is buzzing. Ominously the first thing we see is a German coach party, and the harbour is crawling with people. Backpackers sit on the walls writing postcards; families are queuing to get into O'Connors for a pie and a pint; lads in mackintoshes are making purposeful strides towards the sea armed with fishing rods and boxes of wriggly things; others are busily erecting tents in one of the farmyards; and lads in parkas roam around looking naked without their scooters.

It's not as I remember it, but it's not the abomination I'd feared either. For sure there are too many people – *far* too many people – but the pubs retain an unassuming charm, the tourists aren't overly indulged and while you do wonder if the old bicycle propped outside the quaint little music shop has been planted there purely as a photo opportunity, Doolin has hung on to its identity. It seems even better once we've checked into Cullinan's guest house, which is tucked discreetly up the road away from the harbour frenzy. Even better still when we've found elbow space in Gus O'Connor's pub.

It's 8pm when I call Frankie Gavin on his mobile, imagining we can sneak in a couple of cheeky pints before his gig. I can hear the sound of traffic. 'I'm on my way now,' he says. 'Where are you, Frankie?' 'Galway.' 'Galway? *Galway*? You're meant to be in Doolin! What time's the gig?' 'Midnight.' 'Oh …' 'See you later then.'

Doolin's status as a nerve centre of traditional music probably dates back to the 1970s, though it did attract the bohemian set years earlier after being discovered by the likes of George Bernard Shaw, Dylan Thomas, JM Synge and Oliver St John Gogarty, who were often found enjoying a pie and a pint at O'Connors. Yet, paradoxically, Doolin and surrounding enclaves have constantly battled poverty and hardship and while George Bernard Shaw and Dylan Thomas were drinking the bar dry and holding brilliant conversations, chances are people around them were wondering where the next pennies were coming from.

Reliant on farming and fishing, this rarefied outpost of Clare has known more than its fair share of bad times and, while it's unquestionably beautiful, the winters can be particularly cruel. For a lot of people growing up in the area, their main ambition was to get the hell out. That was certainly the case in the 1960s and 1970s when most of the young population saw no future except one away from Doolin. The one thing they did have was music. And the pub. And the two were often intertwined within the regular informal, spontaneous sessions at Gus O'Connor's pub in Fisherstreet. Invariably, those sessions would be driven by members of the Russell family from Doonagore.

But elsewhere great things were happening in Irish music. Traditional music had remained a constant in the pubs in many rural areas of the west but it scarcely disturbed the national consciousness and there had been little since the big ballad groups of the 1960s, like the Clancy Brothers and The Dubliners, to give Ireland any outward sense of musical being. Gradually that changed as a new self-aware generation searched for a cultural identity not driven from Britain or the States.

The underground fostered by the work of the collectors manifested itself on radio programmes and specialist concerts and, after The Chieftains released their landmark debut album in 1963, something stirred. Other young musicians raised on the pop culture of the day actively investigated and sought inspiration from the old music and tentatively injected an Irish feel into their folk rockery.

The Johnstons introduced two young musicians who were to go on to make a big mark in the future – Paul Brady and Mick Moloney – joining two sisters Lucy and Adrienne Johnston from Slane, County Meath, in an Irish riposte to Mamas & Papas. Meanwhile Joe Dolan, Andy Irvine and Johnny Moynihan were having some success introducing a daring Irishness to a style that originally owed most to old-time American music in their band Sweeney's Man. They even had a hit of sorts with an Irish song 'Old Maid In The Garrett'. After Terry Woods – later to be a Pogue – replaced Dolan, Sweeney's Men went on to lay much of the groundwork for the explosion in Irish music that was just around the corner.

There were others. The Ludlows, featuring Jim McCann, had some early commercial success; Emmet Spiceland introduced a young Donal Lunny and had an Irish hit with 'Mary From Dungloe'; and Skara Brae were formed by Maighread Ni Dhomhnaill with her brother and sister Micheal and Triona (later together in the Bothy Band) and Daithi Sproule (later in Altan) pioneering a mix of English and Irish language material.

In 1973 Thin Lizzy crashed into the charts with a rock version of the old folk perennial 'Whiskey In The Jar' and, novelty or not, the notion of an Irish band playing Irish music didn't seem quite as absurd. Horslips were another rock band intent on adding their own national heritage to the mix. At the same time as Phil Lynott and his chums went over the Cork and Kerry mountains and met Captain Farrell counting all his money and going whack-for-the-paddy-o (never did understand that bit), Horslips were putting the final touches to *The Tain*, a Celtic concept album based on Irish mythology. Finbar & Eddie Furey were taking the music abroad – and enjoying remarkable success in Germany in particular – while Christy Moore was doing his stuff in England and the scene was set for the floodgates to open and the likes of Planxty, Clannad and De Dannan to come gushing out.

Visitors began to arrive in Ireland, exploring the west coast in search of the roots and spirit of the music that was starting to establish a firm following in Europe and beyond. And it eventually brought them to Doolin. They liked what they found there. Habitually ensconced at O'Connors, Micho Russell and his brothers Pakie and Gussie were not only superb traditional musicians, representing the very essence of authentic Irish roots the visitors had come to find, they were convivial hosts too, relishing Doolin's unexpected new status as a tourist haunt. In an age of soul-searching, self-discovery and back-to-nature idealism, more and more Europeans, Americans and even Australians renounced their hectic, capitalism-driven lifestyles and came to the west of Ireland. Many of them stayed. And a lot of them stayed in Doolin.

In an ironic shift in population gravity, the young locals marching out of Doolin in search of prosperity, self-respect and quality of life collided head-on with hordes of hippies, bohemians and adventurers moving in the opposite direction in pursuit of inner peace, old-fashioned values and the lessons of the land.

Tonight, O'Connors is a league of nations. It's baking hot and it's packed to the rafters and you reel beneath the rumble of excited conversation in a myriad of different tongues. The pub has altered radically since the days when European hippies first started descending here. Or indeed when *I* first descended here. I remember O'Connors as a barn of a bar in which everyone in the place seemed to have an instrument. Micho Russell was here then, too, a lovely, ruddy-cheeked man with a mischievous grin and a ready wit who entertained the adoring visitors with flowing anecdotes and reminiscences ... then whipped out his tin whistle and knocked them dead with a few tunes.

There are a couple of other pubs in Doolin, of course. McGann's and McDermott's both look enticing – and equally busy – but it seems only right to spend the evening in the company of the wonderful old posters and newspaper cuttings that adorn the walls of O'Connors and celebrate the memory of Micho Russell. There have been three extensions added since I was last here so the pub now goes off on a long horseshoe bend round the elongated bar. Wherever you go it's frantically busy, the young bar staff coping admirably with food orders flying at them from all directions in a variety of accents but still taking time out to accommodate a constant flow of requests for the black stuff, with pints poured in the time-honoured fashion.

Musicians gather at the back of the bar but such is the vastness of the place there will be many on either side that will have no idea they've been here. Even those in close proximity find it hard to hear as the Guinness sinks ever faster and the chatter gets more raucous. That's a shame because the music – supplied by some of Clare's finest young musicians, the Ceili Bandits – is top quality. A dedicated group stand at the bar in front of them getting into it, swapping banter and roaring them on, but it's a battle of wills against the din of the rest of the bar. It's a conundrum, all right. The popularity of Doolin – and O'Connors – is largely built on music, the very same music you can barely hear now because of all the noise of the people who've come to hear it. The music now seems to be treated as a glorified jukebox in the corner. It's a far cry from the days when the Russells would sit in the bar chatting and playing and the whole pub would be gripped listening to them.

The music of the Russells has been closely associated with this area for as long as anyone can remember. Micho's father Austin was a well-known *sean-nos* singer, his mother Annie played the concertina and single-row melodeon, his uncle was a mean step dancer and his aunt was one of Clare's most celebrated concertina players. Micho initially taught himself to play tin whistle and flute when he was 11, absorbing the various family influences to develop a uniquely individual style of playing. He left school at 14 to work on the farm – he remained a farmer for the rest of his life – but his passion for music never wavered. He and his brothers Pakie and Gussie, who played concertina and flute respectively, initially built their reputations playing at the regular house dances and then became central figures in the music sessions at the Doolin pubs. That's when Micho became adored not merely as a subtly innovative whistle player, but also as a singer and storyteller. He didn't just play tunes, he told you chapter and verse about how he'd come by them, with colourful tales about the musicians who'd first played them.

Micho himself later said that one of his biggest influences was the travelling piper Johnny Doran, whom he met playing at a fair at Ennistymon in 1935. 'When Johnny Doran started playing everything from making a deal, to crying children, nagging wives and animals left unattended was forgotten about, so enchanting was his music,' said Micho. Doran was to become a regular visitor to Doolin and, along with the local fiddle player Paddy Murphy, was integral to the village's early appetite for sessions music. There was much interaction, too, with the music of the fishermen from Inish Thiar, the smallest of the Aran Islands, who'd regularly row the four miles to Doolin Quay to sell their lobsters.

In the 1960s and 1970s, the Russells were discovered by the world at large and became revered by the new young folk-revival fraternity. The always sociable Micho was tickled pink, revelling in his new role as both an iconic mascot of Doolin and a father figure of Irish music. He was generous with the numerous researchers, collectors and tourists who frequently came calling and happily gave the benefit of his experience to any young musician who passed his way, Paddy Moloney among them. He toured with the likes of the Fureys and Clannad and he appeared at fleadhs, concerts and festivals all over Ireland and Europe.

Perhaps the best record of the family, *The Russell Family Of Doolin, Co. Clare*, was recorded at O'Connors, but Pakie died in 1977, soon after it was made. Micho, too, was lost in a car crash in 1994 at the age of 79. Gussie, the shyest of the three brothers, still lives in Doolin, regularly cycling down to the quay to quietly absorb the craic in O'Connors, but he doesn't play any more and simply sits in the pub largely unrecognised and ignored.

As the Ceili Bandits pack up to go home I start to wander back to the B&B and notice a large queue forming outside the restaurant a few doors along. I didn't get where I am today without joining a queue when I see one, and then I remember Frankie Gavin. That's it. Frankie Gavin. The midnight concert. Right here, right now.

It's a full house, which is one in the eye for the doom merchant at O'Connors who'd insisted nobody in their right mind would pay to see Frankie Gavin at midnight when they could see the Ceili Bandits for nowt at a reasonable hour.

The Gavin gig is part of a series of experimental late-night concerts put on for serious lovers of traditional music by Peter Pandula. A tall man with floppy hair, an engaging Eastern European accent and – today at least – black leather trousers, Peter is a fascinating character in his own right. Originally from the Czech Republic, he went to see Finbar Furey playing in Germany in the 1970s and decided he wanted to be a professional uilleann piper.

His quest naturally brought him to Ireland – and to Doolin. And who was the first person he met? *Micho Russell.* I begin to think he's pulling my plonker. 'It's true!' says Peter, pouring me a lifesaving glass of red wine. 'I was walking up the cliff road in the fields and we had a nice chat and I told him why I'd come and he invited me to stay on his farm with his brothers.'

Peter ended up staying with the Russells for the whole summer, cutting the turf, working the hay and feeding the donkeys in between learning the pipes. He spent the next five summers with the Russells, working on the farm and getting piping lessons at the Willie Clancy summer school in Milltown Malbay. In time he joined a couple of Celtic rock bands but maintained his links with Doolin, setting up his own agency when he discovered that friends of his, the young Irish band Oisin, were having problems with a German tour. That agency expanded and now Peter Pandula proudly runs not only the attractive Lodestone Restaurant in Doolin's main street, but also Magnetic Music which stands next door claiming to be 'Co. Clare's first trad record company'.

He has seen the Doolin tourist industry boom out of sight and is the first to recognise the economic and other benefits this has had on the area and its people. It has, after all, helped give him a living for many years. Yet he's not immune, either, to the negatives Doolin's soaraway success has had on its grass roots music. 'The music was very spontaneous in the old bar but then the crowds got bigger and to a certain extent you had to mic it. A lot of people started coming in for the craic and the booze, not just music lovers, and they didn't really care if the music was there or not,' he says regretfully.

That's why he's started running midnight concerts for real music lovers to hear quality traditional music in Doolin without the background din and overcrowding that blights the pub sessions. Not, he hastens to add, that he's slagging off the pubs. 'The pubs bring in the people and we couldn't do what we do without them. But a lot of people who come to Doolin for the craic aren't too happy in the pubs because they are often too full and too hot. But it's up to us, the people who live here, to preserve the music and present it in a way where the music comes first. We offer an unplugged concert in a cosy non-smoking atmosphere and a lot of people who come to Doolin have the opportunity to hear music in this way.'

I find a spare seat at a side table next to an oldish bloke who gives me a wink and eyes my glass of wine mischievously. It's all very quiet and orderly. I'd somehow imagined the audience would be full of people who'd just been poured out of O'Connors and fallen in here because they fancied another drink. Like me, I guess. Or they'd simply seen a queue and joined it. Like me, I guess. But no, they seem like real students of the music, sipping their red wine with aficianado-esque anticipation while awaiting Frankie Gavin's arrival.

Well, that's what I *was* thinking until an American with narrow eyes and a pencil moustache leans over to me and says: 'Say, do you know who's playing here?' Yes, I tell him haughtily, always eager to be the smart-ass, it's Mr Frankie Gavin. 'Oh, right ...' says the American doubtfully. 'Is he any good?' Oh, say I, he's the *best*. 'Oh good. I'm only here because I thought it was the queue for the bathroom. I thought it was strange when they took 15 euros off me. I thought "It's expensive to have a piss in this country!"' The old boy on the other side of me starts falling about laughing ... a little too loudly for comfort.

I'm just thinking about giving Frankie Gavin a call on his mobile to see if he's left Galway yet, when he suddenly appears in garish shirt and sheepish grin, followed on stage by keyboard player Brian McGrath. The old feller next to me is on his feet clapping and cheering while my American friend pokes me in the back and says 'Is that him?' 'Yes, that's him.' 'Which one?' 'The short one with curly hair and the fiddle and the dodgy shirt.' 'What's his name again?' I open my mouth but the old guy the other side gets there first. 'Frankie Gavin ... that's the great Frankie Gavin ... my friend Frankie.' He cackles manically and alarm bells ring in my head.

Frankie starts to play and the room is instantly enthralled. I am transported back to that night of the illicit drinking den in the wilds of Connemara. A cheeky young pup then, he'd flounced into the bar all cocky circumstance and the ol' boys were debating which one of them would clip him round the ear first when he started playing. Lights flashed, bells rang, dancing belles appeared doing the can-can and champagne corks popped ... nobody could have been in any doubt they were in the presence of a master fiddle player in the making. Thirty years a virtuoso in De Dannan and the master has landed.

Don't get me wrong, I'm a huge fan of De Dannan, but it's great to hear Frankie showcased in this way and, as he ebbs and flows his way through a rich array of traditional tunes, Peter Pandula's elitist policy is fully vindicated. In De Dannan you didn't often get to hear him playing with such purity and clarity; they were a band not averse to roughing up the folk police with elaborate novelties such as their 'traditional' arrangements of 'Hey Jude' and 'Bohemian Rhapsody', while their fondness for thematic mix'n'match albums also dropped the odd stinker. Their Irish-gospel album *Half-Set In Harlem* was a particular worry.

Frankie could always play a lot of different tunes in a lot of different ways, but tonight is pure, classic Gavin. At one point he plays a slow air of such pain it almost cuts through you. 'My late father used to play a lot of slow airs,' he says. 'I never used to be able to play them because I'd start crying.'

But you can't please all of the people all of the time ... as the noisy departure of the American ('he's very good but it's a bit late for me, going to Killarney tomorrow so it's an early start, no offence') and a running commentary from the old chap on my right confirms. 'Ah, that's a grand old tune,' says Frankie at one point as he completes 'Star Of Munster'. Instantly, the old boy comes back at him: 'Aye, it is that and it's a difficult one too if you play it properly ...'

Halfway into the set, yer man pulls a couple of spoons from his pocket and starts to snap out the rhythm on them. He's good too, as he's not slow to tell me. 'I'm the best spoons player in Ireland,' he whispers loudly in my ear. 'Really?' Doubts suddenly appear and an unexpected burst of modesty springs forth. 'Well, maybe not the *best* spoons player in *all Ireland*, but definitely in *Clare*.' I ask his name. 'Johnny Spoons,' he cackles, 'but you can call me Johnny.'

Johnny Spoons continues as Frankie Gavin's unofficial backing band but there are frowns from the management. Peter Pandula arrives to whisper sternly in his ear and he puts the spoons reluctantly in his pocket. But as soon as Frankie ups the tempo the spoons are out again, Johnny's head rocking back and forth erratically as he taps out the beat. It sounds good to me but Peter's wife is over like a shot and the spoons are confiscated. Johnny's not too bothered. He's got a spare pair in his other pocket. Halfway into the next set of tunes they're confiscated too. Johnny looks inconsolable, but as Frankie moves up the gears again, I suddenly notice a young guy crawling on his hands and knees under the table in front of us. His head bobs up in front of my crotch and I fear the worst, but he's tapping Johnny Spoons on the shoulder. Johnny peers down at him and the guy surreptitiously passes him a substitute pair of spoons ... and then disappears, undetected, into the nether regions of the restaurant. It's just like an episode of *'Allo 'Allo*.

Johnny caresses the new spoons lovingly under the table as Frankie plays flute. But his new discretion doesn't stretch as far as refraining from comment on Frankie's flute skills. 'That's bloody awful, he should stick to playing fiddle,' he tells me loudly before darting under the table to retrieve a lost spoon. Frankie, meanwhile, has heard the remark, and, with no sign of Johnny in his line of vision, identifies me as the heckler and glares at me hard. I smile weakly and wave back at him.

As the concert continues Johnny discreetly plays the spoons on his knees under the table. The management antennae instantly alerts code red and a management search party is launched. But by the time they're circling our table he's secreted the offending items down his trousers and is gazing innocently into space. As the dobermans are hauled off, he whips the spoons out again, starts playing along and the whole ritual is repeated. By now Johnny has a network of willing accomplices on standby ready to hide the spoons should it come to a strip search but Johnny's making a stand for spoon players of the world and decides this is a battle he must fight on his own, gazing beatifically back at the spoon police every time they come calling. Me? I'm dying to say 'Is that a spoon in your pants or are you just pleased to see me?'

But while butter won't melt in his mouth, spoons burn a hole in his pants and when Frankie starts to play 'The Mason's Apron' as a personal tribute to Micho Russell, Johnny Spoons exposes himself. In a manner of speaking. With a defiant yell of 'Micho will never be dead', Johnny decides to go out with a bang. The spoons are dancing on the table at a volume that threatens to drown Frankie's fiddle and may even rouse Micho Russell from his grave. The inevitable spoon swoop isn't long coming and Johnny is relieved of his weapons of mass distraction amid much finger wagging and showing of yellow cards. He decides to play one desperate final card. 'Frankie …' he cries. 'Frankie … they won't let me play the spoons!' 'I don't blame them,' shouts Frankie back at him without blinking, 'I wouldn't let you play the spoons either.' 'Why not?' returns Johnny Spoons, 'are you a *prima donna* all of a sudden?' Frankie laughs and plays another tune. The spoon wars are over.

Morning has broken at Cullinan's Guest House and I've just tasted the finest tomatoes in the history of the world … ever. The poor old tomato never gets much of a look-in. Okay, it has a walk-on part in salads; it's the stooge in cheese, ham and tomato sarnies; it has an unglamorous workmanlike role in pizza; and its only real starring role is in soup, the Conference League of dining.

At breakfast this morning in Doolin, though, the humble tomato takes centre stage with a vengeance. Herb tomatoes baked overnight … a culinary experience that won't be forgotten in a hurry and in Clare at least tomatoes will walk tall forever more, never to be dissed by cheese, mushrooms, cucumber or ham ever again. I look across at the German campers cooking their rashers on primus stoves in the rain on the farm across the stream and wave my baked tomato at them. Eat your hearts out, losers!

Reinvigorated, I decide to jog to the Cliffs of Moher. Ten minutes later I'm a gasping mess and crawl back to get the car. I blame the tomatoes. Just a few miles up the coast from Doolin, the Cliffs of Moher are one of Ireland's most spectacular sights and the coaches lined up in the car park are proof enough of their starting grid position on the tourist trail.

An awesome concertina of sheer, jagged rock faces, the Cliffs have attracted animated argument around these parts lately as the local authority debates turning the Cliffs into an all-singing, all-dancing heritage centre. God forbid. Are they planning to emulate the scandal of Land's End and flog tickets so guides can escort you to the cliff edge to describe what you can see for yourself? You can still jump off the edge whether you've got a ticket or not. Or do they just want to usher you into a cinema and show you a film about the cliffs and flog you a video afterwards so you can tell your mates you've been there?

Besides, there's free enterprise to spare at the Cliffs today. Barely out of the car and some hideous Irish muzak blasts out from the direction of the Cliffs. 'VISIONS OF IRELAND – 16 ENCHANTING INSTRUMENTALS' reads the sign on a caravan which is not only responsible for subjecting us to this nonsense, it's adding insult to injury by attempting to persuade us to buy it too. If I hadn't had those tomatoes I'd be torching it now.

Climb the path to the cliff top and any number of buskers are there to entertain you. Johnny Teran, for one, a pan piper from Ecuador, fresh from the Ballybunion Busking Festival. There's an old guy with a penny whistle who plays three notes and then spends 15 minutes trying to chat up a group of teenage girls from Denmark. And there's a girl playing the harp. I vaguely wonder if it's the same harp that caused a gridlock while it was being pushed along the middle of the road just outside Limerick and have half a mind to give her a lecture on road manners, but she's otherwise engaged with a Japanese coach party.

The genteel sound of the harp scarcely suits the aggressive back-drop of cliffs, hills and ocean, but the girl looks good against the skyline and the crowd around her multiplies. Today's winner of the Cliffs of Moher busking competition by a mile. The Japanese politely queue to take it in turns to take exactly the same photograph of her in front of the hills. 'All Irish music is about sex or death,' I hear her telling the shocked Japanese photographers. Which is a nice line, if not entirely true. Whatever happened to emigration, religion, drinking and *horse racing*?

On the cliff itself there's a sign saying 'DANGER! DO NOT PASS THIS POINT!'. Obviously nobody takes a blind bit of notice. Masses of people clamber past it and venture to the very edge of 200-metre-high cliffs with a sheer drop into the Atlantic Ocean without a care in the world. A couple of hardy/sick souls are actually perched on the cliff's very edge, dangling their legs over the side. I start feeling queasy and seek refuge on the safer slopes with Johnny, my pan piper from Ecuador, consoling him over having his basking ass whupped by a harpist who can't stop talking about sex and murder.

As we're in North Clare, there is one town that *has* to be revisited. I came to Clare for the first time in 1979 to visit Lisdoonvarna Festival. I've met people since who know only Christy Moore's classic song 'Lisdoonvarna'. They bellow out the chorus, slap each other on the backs and cheer as they get to the bit about the German looking for Liam Og O'Flynn and chortle like divvies at the line about Shergar being ridden by Lord Lucan. Yet lots of them don't even know Lisdoonvarna is a real place and that Christy is singing about a real event. In fact he more or less made up the song on the Lisdoonvarna stage as he went along in true talking-blues style, scat singing about the events unfolding over that bizarre festival weekend.

'A 747 for Jackson Browne/They built a special runway just to get him down/

Before the Chieftains could start to play / Seven creamy pints came out on a tray ...'

I'm listening to the song now as I drive into Lisdoonvarna wondering if I'll recognise it with its pants on ...

'There's The Burren and the Cliffs of Moher and the Tulla and the Kilfenora /

Micho Russell, Dr Bill, Willie Clancy and Noel Hill ...'

Jecz, even the 'Welcome To Lisdoonvarna: Traditional Spa Town and Gateway To The Burren' sign is making me tingle ...

'Mighty craic, loads of frolics, pioneers and alcoholics ...'

Lisdoonvarna, host town to Ukraine. Lisdoonvarna and Doolin, *both* hosting Ukraine? Exactly how many Ukrainians *are* there?

'I like the music and the open air, so every summer I go to Clare /

'Cos Woodstock, Knock, nor the Feast of Cana /

Can hold a candle to Lisdoonvarna ...'

I don't recognise this town at all ...

I've been to a few extraordinary events since – remind me to tell you about the shenanigans at Nyon Festival in Switzerland some time – but nothing ever quite matched Lisdoonvarna. I came to the festival here in both 1979 and 1980 and I still imagine I was hallucinating at both. The bus out here from Ennis was an entertainment in itself as people perched in luggage compartments, unwrapped sleeping bags to lie on the floor, passed cans of beer round to all the passengers and throughout the journey maintained a formidable chorus of 'Do You Want Your Oul' Lobby Washed Down, Con Shine?' of which Ralph Reader's boy scout Gang Show would have been proud.

The two years blur into one now but certain memories will never fade. The freezing cold rain that bucketed down leaving icicles on my nose. Maire Brennan of Clannad with her hair permed. Emmylou Harris in a big white stetson singing 'Save The Last Dance For Me' and telling the pissed-up lads in the audience who kept inviting her back to their tents so they could do unspeakable things to her that they were 'beautiful'. De Dannan being dynamite. Seamus Ennis being magical. Paul Brady being emotional. Mick Hanly being political. Ralph McTell playing his classic song 'From Clare To Here' while admitting this was the first time he'd set foot in Clare in his life. Vin Garbutt being rounded on by feminists angry about his anti-abortion song 'Little Innocents'. Louisiana's wonderful Rockin' Dopsie & the Cajun Twisters making their caravan open house to all and sundry. Sean Cannon doing the backstage cooking. People dancing in the mud. People swimming in the mud. People *fornicating* in the mud. And Christy inventing 'Lisdoonvarna'.

But mostly I remember the scenes of carnage back in the town.

The streets were swimming with cans and bottles and wherever you looked there was human wreckage as people collapsed in an ocean of alcohol. Others sought shelter in doorways because their tents had been washed away and some were just too exhausted to take another step. But that was only the half of it. Getting back into my hotel in the early hours was a major exercise. The hotel – like *all* the hotels in town – was wall-to-wall with broken bodies and people willing to sell their own grannies for a drink. At this time of night the hotels were the only places serving drink and everybody wanted one. Except the hotels were only allowed to serve drink to residents. I was a resident and I couldn't even get *inside* the hotel, it was so full, let alone get to the bar for a drink.

When I eventually made it up to my room on the second floor I still had to wade in over a family of bikers sleeping in the corridor. Careful not to tread on them I gingerly put the key in my lock. The door sprang open and three Hells Angels fell into my room snoring soundly. They didn't wake and it seemed prudent not to disturb them. They were still there snoring when I left the next morning.

Another night I took the precaution of dining in the restaurant early before setting off for the night's events at the festival, which was being held about a mile away up the hill out of town. Early, but not early enough, obviously. I'd barely touched the baked herb tomatoes when the window flew open and five huge skinheads climbed in, and one by one planted size ten boots on my table, paused for a second to admire the view, and leaped off towards the bar. The last one looked back at the mountain of mud that mysteriously materialised on my dinner and, with just the glimmer of an apology, said: 'It's okay, we only want a drink.' 'Radical idea but … ever thought of using the front door?' I asked him. 'Quicker this way,' he said. 'Besides, the bouncer won't let us in.' I couldn't imagine why.

However, Lisdoonvarna's fame isn't entirely due to Christy Moore and bad behaviour at a music festival. It has been a tourist target since the middle of the eighteenth century when a Limerick surgeon announced that the town's natural mineral waters had healing qualities. They've been coming here ever since to drink the water and if that doesn't do the trick they drink whatever else is on offer. You know, just in case that Limerick guy had got it wrong and when he said 'water', he really meant beer and whiskey.

The regular influx of people sampling the spring water – and their propensity to party – had an interesting side effect. Ladies and gentlemen habitually got acquainted in the worst possible way – and how often have we heard that after a night on the mineral water? Lisdoonvarna subsequently earned itself a reputation for getting people together. It's said the original matchmakers were dealers at street fairs who, because of their occupation, got to know all the sons and the daughters around the country who were ripe for plucking – as it were – and invited the farmers to Lisdoonvarna in September so that they could be, well, *plucked*. If any of them made it down the aisle it resulted in a nice little earner for the dealer concerned. It still happens, apparently.

You'd imagine that whole match-making tradition would be out the window by now. I mean, you can't open a paper or turn on the computer without being offered mail-order brides from Russia or Thailand or Basingstoke, but every August and September Lisdoonvarna still hosts its match-making festival. The tourist office insists that yes, people do still pour into the town in the belief that their perfect partner is at a tea-dance at the Royal Spa Hotel awaiting introduction.

I don't buy this for a second. Clearly, it's just an elaborate excuse for a beano. All this talk of polite dances in genteel hotels with well-mannered men in dark suits approaching coy dark-haired lasses in sensible frocks saying, 'Miss, I was wondering if you would do me the very great honour of accompanying me round the dance floor when this very fine band play another waltz,' is pure cobblers. Look, I've been to festivals in Lisdoonvarna. I *know* how it ends! At the end of the night the guys are completely ratted, on the tables doing *The Full Monty* to 'Fields Of Athenry' and the dainty ladies are lurching around taking slugs from bottles of cider and making lewd comments about boy's bums. And when all's said and done there's only one question that needs answering: 'Do you fancy a shag?'

Still, you've got to keep up appearances and during match-making month there's all manner of events to keep the customer satisfied. It takes a leaf out of Tralee's book with a Mr Lisdoonvarna and Queen Of The Burren 'talent contest', while you also get a 'country and western' music weekend (hold me back) and, this whole charade's one salvation, an amateur horse and sulki-racing meeting. Curiously, there's also a barbecue festival. *Barbecues*? In Ireland? In *this* weather? Just because they beat the Aussies at Oz Rules footie, they seem to think they can take the Australians on at their national sport of barbe-cuing now. If you ask me it's a charcoaled grill too far.

There's no evidence of barbecues, sulki racing, Queens of the Burren, guys in stetsons, or *anything* today. The place still looks shell-shocked from that folk festival in 1980 ... or maybe it is just cowering after hearing the news that it is being revived. Lisdoonvarna's long main street is soggy and uninviting. I look around searching for signs. There's the Hydro Hotel ... was it there that the little blonde girl threw up over my new leather jacket or was that at the Imperial? Walking further along the street I come across 'The Irish Bar'. Which is a bit odd. I mean, we're in Ireland … they're *all* Irish bars here, aren't they?

The town is stuffed with B&Bs and they all look empty. We walk up and down the town three times trying to decide which of the cheeky little places should benefit from our custom tonight. A word about the current state of Irish B&Bs: they are brilliant. No, *really*. Coffee and muffins in the front room when you arrive followed by a detailed history of the landlady's life, personal history and immediate family. They show you to nice clean rooms, furnish you with towels and biscuits ('just in case you feel a bit peckish'), shower you with guide books, provide a detailed analysis of the personal habits of the local barmen (in case you are considering taking refreshment later), pass comment on the latest world events ('what do you think of all these wars then? I don't like them, meself'), share insights into telly culture ('it's not the same without Gay Byrne on the television, I used to love Gay Byrne, so I did …'), and pack you off into the night with a smile and a wink and a last call of 'you did say breakfast at *10.30am*, did you?'.

In the morning they fire a million questions at you about what you'd got up to the night before ('Ah, sure you woke us up when you got in but it's no matter, them are very thin walls …'). They then produce a mountainous Irish breakfast containing black *and* white pudding (but rarely overnight baked tomatoes) that will keep you going for a month – though it could be the last month of your life. They laugh nervously and look confused when you ask if they've ever heard of Tommy Peoples, apologetically relieve you of a bunch of euros, tell you it was an absolute delight having you stay and wave you off with warm smiles as you waddle off to the car. That's my experience anyway. Except in Lisdoonvarna.

We inspect the inviting selection of B&Bs but there's just too many to choose one, so we eventually opt for a small hotel that lies off the road and looks unassumingly cute. Bad move. I ring the bell and wait for ten minutes before a Ukrainian shot-putter comes to the desk, an elderly cigarette dripping ash down her chin and a scowl the size of Galway Bay. 'I think we have one room left,' she says confrontationally. Which is a blatant lie. No cars in the car park, keys all dangling on their pegs, no sign of any other human life … clearly the place is totally empty. Huffing and puffing, she rummages through a pile of old magazines, cheese rolls, bowls of buttons, telephone directories, bottles of water and half-empty cold coffee mugs piled up on the reception desk as she searches for the registration book that presumably lurks somewhere beneath the rubble. She yelps and spits out a torrent of oaths as she puts her hand on a stray drawing pin, wraps a dirty hankie round the wound, demands payment up front, tosses a couple of keys at me and stomps away. It's not the Lisdoonvarna welcome I've come to expect.

The room itself is tiny and nothing works. There's no lights, no hot water, the bathroom door won't open properly, the cold tap sounds like the QE2 docking as it slowly rouses itself into a painful trickle, wallpaper peels off the walls in wads, and there's a pair of old boots in the corner that look like they were abandoned here in 1980. It does have a telly but that's safely out of arm's reach on a shaky looking plinth high against the ceiling and a remote control welded into a large block of wood for security reasons gave up the will to live long ago. Of all the crummy joints in all the world, we have to book in at this one.

We flee into the streets of Lisdoonvarna looking for the action. This takes a good long while. So long in fact we abandon ship and drive a few miles up the road to the village of Kilfenora. Kilfenora is a name long etched into the very fabric of traditional music culture having given birth to one of the world's oldest groups, the Kilfenora Ceili Band. Its roots can be traced back to 1909 when Canon Cassidy organised a dance in the school house to raise funds for church renovations and the band came together from the ashes of the old fife and drum and brass bands of the area. They played at parties, village events and local dances, but Canon Cassidy ruled them with a rod of iron and insisted the music was painfully sedate, lest it encouraged untoward excitement or lascivious behaviour. In time they loosened up and, with the advent of radio, their fame spread and during the 1930s they played regularly for ceilis at the Queen's Hotel in Ennis.

They went into hibernation for much of the 1940s but, inspired by the advent of the fleadhs, PJ Lynch — whose father John Joe had been prominent in the band's early days — prodded the sleeping giant back to life. Through the 1950s the Kilfenora were regular a fixture at fleadhs, winning various all-Ireland titles and in 1958 were recorded commercially for the first time.

There are many stories of hardship and sacrifice involved in keeping the band going. One time flute and piccolo player Jimmy Ward was told by a doctor that if he continued to play wind instruments he'd kill himself, but instead of giving up the band, he acquired a banjo — then rarely seen in the area — and went to Limerick every weekend to take lessons from a traveller. Thirty years later he was still playing banjo with them when they recorded the 1974 Mick Moloney-produced self-titled album that spread their name way outside Ireland. At a point when ceili bands had been dismissed by

Sean O'Riada as 'the buzzing of a bluebottle in an upturned jam jar', set dancing had shifted into the pubs and a deluge of young bands with fresh ideas and new attitudes threatened to blow their old-fashioned style clean away, Kilfenora did well just to hang on in there.

There was always a traditional osmosis with the band, too, with fathers handing on the tunes and the skills to sons and daughters who subsequently took their places in the band. John Joe Lynch's niece Kitty Linnane, a pianist and fiddle player, assumed the running of the band from PJ Lynch and when she relinquished the stewardship due to ill health in 1991, the baton passed to PJ's son, John Lynch. The Kilfenora dynasty now continues with a new young generation of local musicians maintaining the ideals of an ancient tradition, playing the same style of dance music and upholding the band's great sartorial history with their suit and ties and smart waistcoats. They even entered the twenty-first century with a brand new album, *Live In Lisdoonvarna*, recorded at the Royal Spa Hotel and produced by Kieran Hanrahan.

The musicians involved in the band down the years haven't all been from Kilfenora, but they have all been from Clare. Except for one lone fiddle player from Donegal. Tommy Peoples. But then Tommy was an adopted son after marrying Marie Linnane – daughter of Kilfenora legend Kitty Linnane – in 1969. Back in Doolin I'd asked Peter Pandula if he'd come across Tommy Peoples at all. 'Ah Tommy,' he'd said with furrowed brow. 'Yes, I've seen him lots.' Was he playing? 'Yes, Tommy *was* playing.' Where was Tommy playing?' 'At Kilfenora …' *Where* in Kilfenora? 'At Linnane's pub …'

I'm looking at it now, an inviting red and white bar that reposes nonchalantly at the back of the village square. There's a sign outside promising traditional sessions on a Wednesday night, which isn't a whole lot of help on a Tuesday, and inside there's a stone floor and enough references to 'Kitty's Corner' to leave no doubt of its connections to Kitty Linnane. But there's no sign of Tommy Peoples. 'He lives in Ennis, doesn't he?' says one. 'He's in London now, I think,' says another. 'He moved to America,' says a third.

We check out Vaughan's, Kilfenora's other main traditional music pub with its impressive frontage and a 250-year-old bar. It offers set dancing and ceilis at the weekend but, like Linnane's, gives little hope of much sport tonight. At this point I make a tactical error. I should have stayed and made more enquiries. Tommy Peoples doesn't live here any more but the scent is surely still fresh and vital clues are to be gleaned of his whereabouts. But then it starts raining. I remember we are stuck at the hotel from hell in Lisdoonvarna and abandon Kilfenora.

Back in Lisdoonvarna there are no more signs of life than there were when we escaped a couple of hours earlier. We slide into the vast ballroom of the Rathbawn Hotel, where a well-scrubbed young group are playing – perfectly satisfactorily – a selection of populist pop folk songs. Hang around long enough and they're bound to play 'Fields Of Athenry' at some point but frankly the ambience of the place is already sending me to the funny farm. It's like that awkward time at a wedding reception before anyone gets pissed and the two sets of relatives stare at each other across the great divide while the band battle on with false bonhomie and pretend everyone is having a good time.

Instead, we buy tickets – 10 euro each – to see Susan McKeown perform at the Royal Spa Hotel. I sit next to a Dutch girl. 'Here for the match-making?' I ask pleasantly. 'I don't understand,' she says. 'Are you here on your holidays then?' 'No, I live here.' 'Where?' 'Fanore ...' I am instantly jealous but graciously congratulate her anyway. Fanore is one of Clare's most sumptuous spots: ocean on one side, mountains on the other and you feel all your senses being massaged as you allow it to float all over you. 'Yes, I am very lucky,' she says. 'I can watch the sunset from my living room every night, it is a great experience.' 'So what brought you here?' 'It's a long story.' 'It must involve a man, then.' 'Not at all,' she says, 'it involves *Ireland*.'

I pause, waiting to hear the story. Normally, when you want someone to tell you something, you just to have to bite your tongue and stay silent and eventually they'll feel awkward and start spilling the beans just to fill the void because they can't handle the silence. But the Dutch are clearly made of sterner stuff. 'Go on then,' I say, 'tell me.' 'It's a long story ...' she repeats. 'Don't worry, I have all the time in the world,' I lie. Before either of us gets the chance to say another word, the curtains open and Susan McKeown walks on stage.

A Dubliner now domiciled in New York, Susan McKeown arrives and puts on a decent enough show with a good family mix of old and new songs, but it's not quite the night I had in mind when we arrived. I look around to see if there's any mischief to be had, this being Lisdoonvarna and all and me not wanting to go back to spend the night at Fawlty Towers, but it's no go. Outside Lisdoonvarna's lights are switched off and there's definitely no one home.

Christy Moore's song is a million light years away and somehow seems defiled. You know what they say ... *never go back*.

Chapter nine

SLIGO: COLEMAN, DERVISH AND THE BOYS OF BALLISODARE

'I don't understand these Americans ... they only ever come to Sligo as a stopping-off point on their way to Donegal and they don't realise what we have here. It's such a shame, it makes me want to cry ... some of the places here are beautiful, just *beautiful*, y'know? So much to see but nobody knows it's here. It makes me want to cry. The Americans come and all they ever want to know is which way to Donegal? I tell them to stay in Sligo and see what we've got here, but they never listen. They only stop in Sligo because they are tired. They arrive here and go to their beds, then they're up at the crack of dawn for their breakfast and then they're off away to the north, it's not fair, I'm telling you, it's *just not fair* ...'

Pat has an axe to grind and don't we know it. I'm thinking we must have wandered into the front-line of the Sligo Tourist Board but we're just checking in at our B&B on the outskirts of the town. We've barely crossed the threshold and she's quizzing us to find out if our intentions are honourable. 'Is it just the one night you're staying then? I hope you'll not be rushing off to Donegal first thing in the morning like them Americans ... we have some lovely sights in Sligo, so we have ...'

I like Pat. She tells it like it is. And her basic argument is that Sligo beats Donegal into a cocked hat, but it gets a bad press – or more, accurately, *no press* – and those silly Americans, they don't even stop to unpack. 'They think Donegal's more glamorous, see, because it's got the mountains and all.' And what with September 11 and foot and mouth and the recession and the Iraq war and terrorism and all, tourism is having a rough time, even in bloody Donegal. 'What we need is a big campaign,' continues Pat loudly, 'we need to *sell Sligo* ... shout it from the rooftops to get people to come here. It's hard enough making a living running a B&B at the best of times, sure it is, it's hard work all right. What time will you be wanting breakfast in the morning?'

Oh late, I say, *very* late. It's not like I'm going to Donegal or anything. So we'll get up late and well rested so we can have a good long, slow exploration of the wonders of Sligo ...

Pat beams and the whole house lights up.

We've had a gentle meander up here to Sligo, involving a leisurely detour around the hills and dales of East Clare. We'd made another attempt to infiltrate Ennis to find out if Tommy Peoples really was in residence there, but again the traffic had provided an impenetrable barrier and we'd moved on.

We'd arrived first at Tulla, a delightful tiny village nestling on a hill whose name is writ large in Irish folklore courtesy of its local ceili band. In fact there is some rivalry between Tulla and Kilfenora about whose band is the oldest. Claiming a 1909 birth Kilfenora would appear to win hands down, but Tulla – whose official starting point was 1946 – point to Kilfenora's wilderness years and claim Tulla has the world's longest *unbroken* run as an active band.

Partly inspired by the Ballinakill Ceili Band from Galway, they were formed at Minogue's pub in Tulla by Bert McNulty – a fiddle-playing garda based at Ballinakill – and pianist Teresa Tubridy specifically to play at a *Feile Luimni* competition. With a celebrated line-up that included the great Joe Cooley on accordion and top fiddle players Aggie Whyte, Paddy Canny, Sean Reid and PJ Hayes, they won the competition with ease. With the great Milltown Malbay piper Willie Clancy also occasionally co-opted into the ranks they cleaned up at various other competitions in the area and went on to win a clutch of all-Ireland titles.

Tulla's most famous son, though, was the tall, correct PJ Hayes, whose name will forever be closely identified with East Clare's distinctively precise fiddle style. His mother played concertina and PJ picked up the fiddle when he was about 10, encouraged and assisted by his friend, future brother-in-law and fellow Tulla Ceili Band founder Paddy Canny. Irish American 78 records had a big impact on PJ, as he later recalled in an interview with *Irish Music* mag in which he entertainingly described the arrival in Tulla of the first gramophone from America. 'It was a huge big box-like coffin. My aunt sent it over when I was about nine. My father put it on and the first thing he would put on was a speech by De Valera, which suited him greatly. The speech was halfway through when the spring broke in the gramophone and he had to go to Limerick the next morning to get a new spring for it.'

The young PJ subsequently learned much of his early repertoire from the Irish records coming over from America by the likes of Michael Coleman, Paddy Killoran and the Flanagan Brothers. 'The gramophone had a little key on it and by turning it you could slow it down a bit. If it was tough to get a few nice notes down you could slow it down, but the trouble was if you slowed it down too much you distorted it. We learned a lot of tunes off the gramophone.'

In 1959 PJ and Paddy Canny recorded *All Ireland Champions* with Peader O'Loughlin and Bridie Lafferty, one of the first LPs of Irish music ever made in Ireland. It was a landmark recording that, in the days before music sessions became a feature of pubs, inspired and influenced a generation. The record soon became a rarity, thus adding to its legend, although it has since been reissued on CD. Not that either PJ or Paddy Canny ever exploited their fame. Both shy, reserved, modest men of good farming stock, they kept their heads down and put all their musical energies in the Tulla Ceili Band.

PJ remained the Tulla's public face and spiritual leader right up to his death a couple of years ago, but he was still around long enough to celebrate the band's fiftieth anniversary with an American tour and a brand new album. I only met him once, at a Green Linnet Irish festival in the Catskill Mountains. Well into his 70s by then, he looked frail, but happily soaked up and played a full part in the celebratory atmosphere in the Catskills that weekend. He stole the show, too, when, as the oldest musician on the bill, he was called on stage late one night to play a duet with the youngest on the bill, a gifted 13-year-old from New York. There was not a dry eye in the house.

In true hereditary fashion, PJ's celebrated son Martin Hayes, born and raised a few miles up the road from here at Maghera, near Feakle, cut his teeth in the Tulla, after getting his first fiddle as a Christmas present when he was seven. Odd to imagine the tousle-haired, happily eccentric, free-spirited Martin Hayes as a young short-haired teenager in shirt and tie, conforming to the strict tempo disciplines of the ceili band, but the old pictures don't lie and Martin played with the Tulla for seven years.

Far from rejecting its old values, Martin says he was in awe of the older musicians around him and insists that, while he happily goes off on musical tangents, the soul of his playing is deeply rooted in the style and values of the Tulla. At that critical point in his life in his late 20s when he was living the life of Reilly in Chicago and his partying and musical promiscuity threatened to push him right over the edge, Martin's response was to toss it all out of the window and go right back to basics to the music and life values that had fuelled him in the first place back in East Clare. He hasn't looked back since.

He may be one of the last in a dying breed as regional styles disappear in the global burger generation. As MTV bids for world domination, we all talk American and even the Keane sisters are hooked on *Emmerdale*, it's hard to imagine the survival of fiddle-playing techniques that are exclusive to one corner of Clare. In one sense those regional styles began to disappear the day the first Michael Coleman gramophone record arrived from America, investing Irish traditional music with a universal Sligo style. But the Hayes family continue to do their bit for the East Clare tradition. They help organise the annual Feakle music festival – one of the most prestigious events in the Irish calendar – and though he now lives in Seattle and tours all over the world, Martin Hayes always makes sure he's home in time for it.

We pause at Feakle, birthplace of another great fiddle player, Vincent Griffin. Shortt's Bar ('Oh, you mean Lena's' – bloke in the paper shop) attracts the eye with its symbolic harp and fiddle and its 'Traditional Irish Music' sign boldly displayed above the door. A big poster in the window raises the spirits. 'TONIGHT,' it announces breathlessly, and we get all excited, 'ALL STAR KARAOKE!' Yer *wot*? Is it a traditional music karaoke? Get ratted in the bar, then find your (ex) mates are pushing you to the front where a red-faced character in a blue waistcoat and pencil moustache presents you with a fiddle and points out a screen displaying a load of notes and asks which of the Tulla Ceili Band's greatest hits you wish to play.

Maybe we'd do better coming back next week when the hurling club is holding a quiz night. Who won the all-Ireland in 1899? 'That's easy. It's Horse & Jockey!' I'll shout triumphantly while the rest of the team tell me to 'shhhh ...'. 'It's not the answer on the card,' says yer man Bamber in the blue waistcoat. 'See ... while you are correct in saying Horse & Jockey were the victorious team in 1899 they were actually representing *Tipperary* and that's the answer I was wanting. You lose ten points. Very bad luck, sir!' My team mates show me the red card and I am never welcome in Feakle again.

I take refuge in the radio. Dear old Clare FM, with its cows in the road and lost budgies and parish priests, won't let me down. But what's this? Gareth Gates? On *Clare FM*? Surely some mistake. The world is indeed coming off its hinges. I remember reading something in the *Clare Champion* about Clare FM changing its programming in an article full of baffling phrases like 'increasing market share', 'modernising sound' and 'upgrading efficiency' and feared the worst. I'm listening to a radio appeal from a local resident who's lost his favourite pair of glasses and relax. That's the Clare FM I know and love all right. And then Gareth Gates comes on bleating his wretched cover of 'Unchained Melody' ... what's all *that* about?

I blame Simon Cowell. In fact, not just Simon Cowell – though he is a particularly odious manifestation – but the entire British record industry that doesn't have an original idea in its head. The mainstream record companies are clueless, *clueless*. Aided and abetted by the equally mindless national radio stations, they haven't an ounce of wit between them, perpetuating an environment that simply recycles the past in ever-decreasing circles. All they're doing is feeding a conveyor belt that clones the sound, image, marketing and style of whatever hapless pop idol passed five minutes earlier without a thought for the longer-term health of either the transient pop star concerned or the industry as a whole.

When the whole reality TV pop phenomenon started with *Popstars*, they had a real chance to break the mould. That original series was great TV and given all the exposure they had a guaranteed hit band at the end of it, whoever they were, whatever they looked like. The whole sorry nature of pop music driven by damaging images of pouting anorexic girls delivering sexuality out of a packet and athletic, nubile lads swinging their hips and spinning on their heads could have been laid to rest forever. So what did those muppets on the judging panel do? The big shot TV producer, the man from Polydor with no personality and the banal ingratiating blonde woman simply rejected every blemished square peg that crossed their path and ended up choosing a band that reflected every tired pop cliché that had got the industry into such a mess in the first place.

Pop was always manufactured to a point and there have forever been puppeteers behind the scenes. But there was still an innocence, an element of chance, an *unpredictability* about it all which made it so exciting. Now Simon Cowell and his chums have cynically moved the goal posts and, with the compliance of TV and radio and accountants, marketing departments pencil in their No 1s months ahead of release. And do they care that they have turned the music industry into a sad farce which will ultimately destroy it sooner rather than later? I doubt it, Oscar, I doubt it.

I switch off Gareth Gates and drive on.

Pat is right. Co. Sligo *is* very beautiful. Just not today. God's throwing a few wobblers, ambushing us with angry bouts of torrential rain, thunder and lightning. It's not the best introduction to Coleman Country. Yep, such is the legend of the great fiddle player Michael Coleman that this area of Ireland – around south Sligo, north Roscommon and north east Mayo – appears on the maps as Coleman Country.

We plough through the sleet to Killavill, where Coleman was born and raised on a small farm at the end of the nineteenth century. A replica house was built here a few years ago close to his original home at Knockraine, but somehow it eludes me. I drive on but the road gets narrower and the weather more threatening. We don't see anyone else for miles and, on a road not known to any map, things start to look bleak. Such is the violence of the rain, I can scarcely see more than a yard in front and I am beginning to wonder if I've driven off the end of the world.

I stop the car to try and get my bearings and notice a huge rock by the side of the road. I brave the storm for a closer look. A fiddle, flute and bodhran are engraved on the stone above the inscription 'TO THE MEMORY OF THE MUSICIANS OF DOOCASTLE'. Then it lists nearly 50 names: Michael Gorman ... Tom Killoran ... Sarah Kellegher ... Dennis McCoy ... Pake Spellman ... Patsy Hunt ... Mick Maye ...'

It's a nice thing to find in the middle of nowhere when the skies are crashing down on you. I gaze at the memorial for a few minutes getting soaked and wishing I'd heard all these musicians thus honoured. Reinvigorated, I get back in the car and miraculously find the road to Gurteen.

If there is a centrepiece to the Michael Coleman industry you'll find it in the village of Gurteen, home of the Coleman Irish Centre. We splash through the downpour to find the very modern redbrick tower fronting the Coleman centre on the corner of Gurteen's main street. It looks shut, it *feels* shut, but we push the door open and go in. 'Come in, come into the dry,' says a kindly lady at the reception desk. 'Now, would you like a nice cup of coffee to warm you up?'

The films, music, old photographs, documentation, instruments and other memorabilia at the centre tell a thorough story about Coleman and the Sligo fiddle legacy he has bequeathed. It tells you he was the youngest of seven children, the son of a flute-playing farmer. That he'd walk miles to play at house dances and sessions and was recognised early on as an exceptionally talented fiddle player with a voracious appetite for mastering new tunes and different styles.

It also tells you that he liked to travel and moved first to England and, in November 1914, to America. That he played fiddle on the liner and one of the other passengers happened to be a theatrical agent who said he'd help him. That in America he stayed first with an aunt near Boston and then moved to New York, augmenting his low wages at a shipping company by busking. He joined a vaudeville travelling show as a dancing fiddle player and built a following in New York playing in saloons and dance halls. When Columbia saw the potentially huge market for 78 rpm records among Irish immigrants thirsting for a taste of home in 1921, Coleman was one of the first to be recorded ... and his legend began.

'He was to Irish traditional music what Elvis Presley became to rock'n'roll,' is how Seamus Tansey describes the massive impact Coleman's records had, not just on the Irish immigrants in America but on Ireland itself when they started trickling back across the Atlantic. His fast, smooth, rhythmic, decorative style thrilled the expatriates who flocked to see him, listen on the radio and buy his records in America ... and re-ignited the traditional music flame back home.

His fame also invested Sligo with its reputation as Ireland's richest county for traditional music. Not that Coleman did it alone. His Sligo contemporary, childhood friend and fellow fiddle player James Morrison – reputed to be so brainy he was nicknamed 'The Professor' – followed him to America where he, too, enjoyed spectacular success, making a vast collection of recordings that had similarly influential results back home. They never recorded together and some self-appointed historians like to build a rivalry and enmity between them but in Sligo the consensus is that while they never duetted in public Coleman and Morrison did play informally together and remained firm friends throughout their lives. Their fortunes were certainly intrinsically linked. Both suffered badly during the depression that followed the Wall St crash in 1929. Both spent all their adult lives in America. Both suffered marriage break-ups. Both died at the age of 54. Both are buried at the same New York cemetery. And both are now revered all over Ireland in general – and Sligo in particular – and credited by many as saving living traditional Irish music from extinction.

The incorrigible Seamus Tansey tells a colourful story about James Morrison's wife Teresa, who'd lived next door to Morrison when he first arrived in New York. Apparently she didn't share his passion for the fiddle and, infuriated that he was devoting more time to the instrument than he was to her, vented her frustrations by one day taking a red hot poker to it. Unfortunately, James happened to be playing it at the time. His right bowing hand was permanently damaged as a result. But the resilient Professor is said to have simply shrugged off the potentially career-threatening injury and learned to bow with his left hand instead.

In his wonderfully passionate Michael Flatley-sponsored book about Sligo music, *The Bardic Apostles Of Innisfree*, Seamus Tansey also tells a spooky story about the death of Michael Coleman. He writes that at the very moment that a brain haemorrhage claimed Coleman's life in a New York hospital, the old fiddle he'd learned to play on as a child fell off the wall in the kitchen at his old family home in

Knockraine. 'The fiddle,' says Seamus, 'is still in the possession of Coleman's niece, who can verify this happening.'

Our genial hostess back at the Coleman Centre – herself a relative of the family – has some more insights to share over coffee. 'They *say*,' she says conspiratorially, 'that Michael Coleman's brother Jim was actually a better fiddle player than Michael.' Really? 'But because he stayed living here while Michael was going off to America and making all the records, nobody ever heard him.' I ask Irish music expert Harry Bradshaw about this theory and he laughs. 'Well, that's just one of those things you get in this country … you know … Michael Coleman was a good player all right, but you *should have heard his brother!*'

It's good to be back in Sligo. The first time I came here was in 1979. A festival was being held in a field several miles away in the village of Ballisodare on the banks of the River Oisin. They called it 'The Boys Of Ballisodare' festival because it was organised by the Flynn brothers from Ballisodare, who were boys. There's also a popular tune called 'The Boys Of Ballisodare'.

I was never much cop with tents (if you've got an hour or so to spare I'll tell you about how I met Mrs Colin when she saved my life when I burnt my tent down at the Cambridge Folk Festival) and B&Bs weren't invented in Ballisodare then, so I checked into a nice little hotel in Sligo town. I caught the train to Collooney and trekked a couple of miles in driving rain across the farms with the usual battalion of hippies.

Ballisodare turned out to be a lovely, if very wet festival, with the Bothy Band at the very peak of their ferocious power playing in a marquee that just wasn't big enough for the both of us. 'You know the biggest problem with Ireland?' one of the Flynn brothers had asked me rhetorically. 'In this country you just can't get a marquee *big enough*.' I did think that in 1979 Ireland had one or two other pressing problems that would run The Marquee Problem close, but I let it lie. Planxty were on the comeback trail that weekend, while the festival also marked Paul Brady's transition from inventive interpreter of traditional music to *bona fide* singer-songwriter. The only problem for Paul was that he needed a piano for some of his new songs. He'd gone into Sligo to hire one, but they told him they didn't *do* hiring, so he had to buy a piano. It looked very nice and I was especially looking forward to seeing how he'd get it back across all those soggy fields and then try and squeeze it on the train at Collooney.

The other thing I remember about Ballisodare was Christy Moore's sister Eilish, who was one of the compères. The band Stockton's Wing played a particularly inspirational set and the audience – who'd had a drink – were on the feet baying for more. The festival was hideously overrunning – now *there's* a surprise – and the boys of Ballisodare pushed poor Eilish on stage to impart the bad news to the seething hordes.

'MORE! MORE! MORE!'

'I'm sorry y'can't have any more…'

'WE WANT MORE! WE WANT MORE!'

'Youse spoilt!'

'GET OFF!'

'I will not…'

'*!@* OFF!'

'I will not !@* off, I have an urgent message…there's a blue Cortina on fire in the car park…will the owner move it please?'

'*!@* OFF YOU *!@!*!@!* *!@*!*'

'And mass will be head in the church up the road at ten tomorrow…'

I hitched a ride and got back to Sligo about 3am thanking heaven I wasn't spending the night in a drenched tent like all the other poor buggers. I got to my room, put the key in the door and opened it. I leaned on the edge of the bed pulling off my shirt, ready to sink into that pillow…and that's when it happened. A slight movement in the bed. Another movement. I took a closer look. There was a shape under the sheets. And I could hear breathing. That at least ruled out the horse's head scene from The Godfather.

I stood in the darkness staring at the shape beneath the sheets. It moved again. It was a person. And probably a human one too. Scooping up my clothes I crept from the room and checked the room number. Definitely my room. I tip-toed back inside, staring at the silhoutte under the sheets. The body had shifted its position and I could make out the shape of breasts. This suggested the person was of a female flavour.

I tip-toed closer…and stubbed my toe on the bag I'd carelessly flung on the floor when I'd checked into the hotel many hours earlier, and tripped on to the bed. I yelped… and a slim dark-haired girl sat bolt upright and screamed. I panicked and fled out of the room, running along the corridor in my undies dropping a trail of shoes and socks in my wake. I hid in a toilet . I shivered there for about 20 minutes, then tentatively retraced my steps to have another look. It was definitely MY room. The number, the key…it even had my bloody bag in it!

As I stood outside the door shivering, still in my undies, a million questions raced round my brain. Had the hotel simply forgotten I'd checked in earlier that day and booked the room out again? So how did she explain my luggage strewn everywhere? Is room share common practice in Sligo hotels? Did they think we'd both be too wasted to notice there was another person in the bed? Or had she broken in?

And then another darker theory presented itself. Could she possibly be a...ahem...a...gift? I kept thinking about this bloke who used to write for the NME. He'd told me a weird story about being offered an interview with Elvis Presley when The King was on the comeback trail. He'd flown to Memphis, checked into a plush hotel and told to await further instructions. On the fourth night there he was in the hotel bar having a drink when an attractive woman invited herself to join him.

They ended up having dinner together, sank a bit of wine and then returned to the bar for a night cap. At just the right moment he suggested she might like to come up to his room to see his etchings. She said she had to go and meet her daughter first but if he went to his room she'd meet him there later. So he went to his room and waited...thinking there was more chance of Elvis knocking on his door than this gorgeous woman. He was still pondering this when there was a knock. At the door was the woman. With a bottle of champagne. And her very sexy looking teenage daughter.

You can probably guess the rest.

The next day he got a message from Team Presley to say they were very sorry, but Elvis had left the building. They booked him on a flight back to London that night and apologised for his wasted journey, but hoped he'd had an enjoyable stay in Memphis anyway. 'What do you think?' he asked me, years later. 'Do you think that mother and her daughter were hookers sent by Elvis to apologise for changing his mind about the interview or did I just get lucky?' I looked him up and down. Brad Pitt, he wasn't. 'Do you know?' I said. "I really can't decide...'

That night in Sligo I 'slept' in a communal hotel bath. Forced to vacate it at some unearthly hour of the morning by a big fat ugly naked guy hell bent on some serious soaping, I spent several hours padding up and down outside my real room waiting for my sleeping beauty to rouse herself. When she finally slipped out for breakfast I let myself in, scooped up my gear and got the hell out. And that's the end of the story. I never discovered who she was or why or how she was in my bed. But Sligo town has always held an element of intrigue for me ever since.

We spend tonight at Furey's. This is a real music pub. As it should be ... after all, it *is* run by one of Ireland's top bands, Dervish. A product of the Sligo session scene, Dervish originated at the turn of the nineties and made an instant impression with the easy, instinctive flow of their instrumentals and the sheer natural joy in their playing. They were freely compared with the very finest Irish bands; the drive, passion, instrumental virtuosity and spirit of the session had numpties like me trawling out the names of De Dannan and the Bothy Band as reference points.

Dervish said thank you very much, they were flattered to be mentioned in such exalted company and if you *have* to be compared with someone you may as well be compared with the best. But the truth is that from the outset Dervish were very much their own band. They were from Sligo, after all, which made a difference and they had their own repertoire, their own style, their own attitude, their own agenda. The only real similarity with those old bands was the spirit they represented, the spirit of the informal pub session. They also had an ace card in the form of a truly exceptional singer/bodhran player Cathy Jordan. Guitarist/mandolin player Brian McDonagh, previously with Oisin, was the band's original singer, closing his eyes to sing 'The Broom Of The Cowdenknowes' at one famous early gig in Donegal. When he opened his eyes at the end of the song, the audience had all gone home. That's when they decided they needed a proper singer.

They went to Longford, found a charismatic pastry chef called Cathy Jordan and they haven't looked back since.

Dervish weren't fools. Mindful that those great Irish bands with whom they were so often compared had been stung worryingly often by the big bad record industry, they formed their own label Whirling Discs at an early stage, managed themselves and generally set themselves up as a self-contained unit.

And now, to complete a fantasy harboured by every traditional musician, they have their own pub.

'I was born in this pub,' the band's accordion player Shane Mitchell tells me as the pints start to flow and the session in the corner rumbles into action. 'It was always a music pub then. My father was a fiddle player and my mother was a dance teacher, so there was always music here. My father told me that some of the greats played here in the old days.' Wow, do you remember seeing any of them? 'No, they sold the pub when I was three.'

Furey's was in a sorry state when Dervish acquired it five years ago. 'It was just a shell,' Shane tells me. But they wanted a music pub and a music pub they got, committing themselves to get it knocked into shape and opened in time for the Sligo Arts Festival. 'It was mad,' remembers Shane, 'maaaddd! The place was in such a mess but we had this deadline for the arts festival so we worked all the hours to get it done in time. I tell you, it was just like *Challenge Anneka* …'

More musicians wander in to join the semi-circle at the window and Furey's heats up. Dervish are up at the crack of dawn tomorrow for yet another glamorous tour in an exotic clime (Belgium, I think) but the various band members are all in tonight meeting and greeting, sitting in on the session, serving the odd drink and, yes I'll say it, having a good *craic*.

The full title of Furey's pub is Furey's Sheela-na-gig. 'Do you know what a sheela-na-gig is?' asks Cathy Jordan. Nope, I don't, but I do have this strange feeling I'm about to find out. 'Wait here,' says Cathy, disappearing into the crowd but returning with a strange-looking map. It's hard to see exactly what's going on with the weird picture on the front of the map, but in this light it looks like a drawing of a female doing rude things with her naughty bits. Cathy is beside herself with glee. 'Yeah, that's *exactly* what it is, isn't *that* great?' Yes, but what is it, and *why*? 'See, sheela-na-gigs are carvings of naked females displaying the vulva. They were sacred religious symbols and they were put on churches in medieval times for good luck. They got rid of a lot of them because people thought they were filthy but there's a few of them left.'

And this map is what exactly? 'It shows all the sheela-na-gigs in Ireland. They've got them in England too. Isn't it great? Have you met John The Map? Come and meet John The Map ...'

I meet John The Map. Who's incredibly tall. And looks like he should be tossing the caber in the Highland Games. But when he's not propping up the bar at Fureys he gets his jollies in a very different way. Apparently John The Map's thing is to take off on his BMX bike with some sort of devilishly clever measuring instrument on the back, cycling somewhere remote and interesting, so that he can come home and draw a map of it. One of his greatest triumphs was a little jaunt round the wilds of Afghanistan in 2001. He'd barely got home when the Twin Towers were hit and his maps suddenly became vital references as the Osama hunt got underway. On another occasion John The Map was thrown out of China because they thought he must be a spy ... but I probably shouldn't mention that.

More and more musicians stumble in out of the rain to join the session. There's a Swiss banjo player, a fiddle player from Finland and a Japanese woman going mad on the tin whistle. She's studying Irish in Sligo apparently. And Irish studies don't get any more educational than this. People are dancing. Taking photographs. Drinking. Talking. Kissing. And that's just the ones peering curiously in the window from the street outside.

There's also a back room at Furey's where they hold formalised concerts and have had some memorable nights. 'Jeezus, we had that

Dick Gaughan here,' says Brian McDonagh, 'how good is that man? I mean, how good *is* he?' He's good, Brian. 'Ah, he is that, he is that. And we had yer man before he died ...' Which man? 'Y'know ... yer man ... yer man who died.' Erm. Freddie Mercury? Adam Faith? Lonnie Donegan? Elvis Presley? *Josef Locke*? 'Josef Locke's not dead,' says Mrs Colin, 'he's working in a supermarket.' None of these apparently. Brian calls to Shane, hammering away on the accordion in the middle of the session, 'Who was yer man?' 'What man, Brian?' 'Y'know, yer man, who played here ... and died.' 'He died *here*?' 'No, he died later ... Rose or sum'tin.' 'Tim Rose?' 'Aye, that's yer man.'

He turns back to me. 'Yer man Tim Rose, he played here.' Was he good? 'God almighty, he was full of himself all right ...' Was he? 'Oh, he thought he was sum'tin' special all right. A real prima donna, he was. He had a chip on *both* shoulders. It's such a shame to get to that stage of your life and feel so bitter. It was sad that he died though ...'

The night ends with much whooping and hugging and exchanging of mobile numbers and snogging and stubbing out ciggies and hurling instruments into cases, putting coats on and crying and laughing and ... all of a sudden Cathy Jordan starts singing. There, in the middle of a crowded, noisy room, without any fanfare. Unannounced, unaccompanied, she just sings. Instantly – as if somebody has just flicked a switch – the pub is deathly silent. By doing nothing other than sing a couple of notes Cathy has the rapt attention of the whole pub. We watch and listen, transfixed. A friend is moving away and Cathy is singing her a farewell song. It's a stunning moment. She sings quietly but her lilting, emotional voice cuts through the smoke and alcohol and people and lifts you to a different plane.

There are no words afterwards. Just a few silent hugs of unspoken thanks. Then we disappear into the Sligo night.

Chapter ten

DONEGAL: LEO'S AND MOLLY'S

'The time has come for me to go and bid you all adieu. For the open highway calls me back to do these things I do. But when I'm travelling far away, your friendship I'll recall. And please God I'll soon return unto ... the homes of Donegal.'

Pat the landlady implores us to spend more time in Sligo. 'There's so much to see here, so much. You haven't scraped the surface yet ... you must stay longer.'

'We will ...' I assure her while I'm grappling with a black pudding mountain '*next time!*'

She's not happy. What's wrong with *this time*?

'We have ... erm ... things to do.'

She doesn't let me off the hook that easily 'What things? You're going to Donegal, aren't you? I can tell ... they all go to Donegal. Why do they all go to Donegal?'

We dive into the car vaguely wondering what terrible experience she'd had in Donegal and why it made her hate the place so much and wave our goodbyes. 'So where are we going now?' says Mrs Colin. 'Donegal, of course.'

But first we make a detour to the seaside at Strandhill, partly to put Pat off the scent in case she's following us. Pouring with rain, it doesn't look wildly inviting and I wonder for a moment if my memory isn't teasing me. But there it is, The Venue – or the Strandhill Bar as it was on the old days – where I'd witnessed one of the greatest gigs ever. Planxty had holed up here for a while and one night they played a gig for the locals. And what a night it turned out to be. The boys were in top form – that man Liam Og O'Flynn is indeed a god among pipers – and the audience went crazy and brought them back for about 300 encores. The whole place was in a frenzy, dancing on chairs, dancing on *each other*, screaming their heads off. And that was just the band. Eventually Planxty persuaded the audience to go home and flopped, exhausted, in the bar. And that's when the fun *really* started. So they tell me. Tunes, drinks, banter, drinks, tunes, banter, drinks, tunes, drinks, drinks, drinks. Is this what they call *the craic*?

En route to Donegal we make an unscheduled stop at Drumcliff. I was dying for the loo after a surfeit of Pat's a-pox-on-Donegal coffee and we pull into a car park with a large church in the background. The only other thing parked there is a big green bus emblazoned with an image of a leprechaun drinking Guinness and the words 'Join The Paddywagon'. A straggly bunch of young Americans slouch off the Paddywagon in baseball caps (the wrong way round, natch) and seem perplexed about what they're doing here.

'Come *on*!' shouts a purposeful team leader at the front, a nine-footer with an impossibly deep voice. 'Come on, we all studied Yeats at school, might as well pay our respects …'

Ah yes, of course, *Yeats*. William Butler, no less. He could write a bit that boy. Ireland has a proud and glorious history of literary greats and they don't come any greater than WB. So if this is where he's buried I'm anticipating a grave to die for. I see the giant American marching towards the church, looking confused and peering at the smattering of modest gravestones directly in front of the church. He visibly wilts. 'Is this *it*?' he mutters to himself in disappointment. 'Not much of a send-off for the guy …'

Indeed it's not. A D-list grave for an A-list celeb. I gaze at the modest Yeats gravestone and read the inscription. 'Cast a cold eye on life, on death. Horseman pass by …' What's that mean, then?

I'm still trying to fathom it out when I hear the chilling rasp of a growling voice that seems to boom from the bowels of the earth. 'So who's this *Irwin* character then?' I spin round in alarm, anticipating seeing a bloke in a dark robe and no face with a pitchfork over his shoulder and a badge saying G.REAPER.

In fact, it's the nine-foot American from The Paddywagon again, who's slipped away from Yeats' resting place in search of fresh meat. He's staring at another nearby grave which is significantly bigger, grander and generally more *happening* than the Yeats' one. I sidle nonchalantly across, still feeling a tad shaky after my close encounter with death, and stare at the grave of the mysterious Mr Irwin. 'He must have been a hell of a man, this Irwin guy,' the American is saying, 'I mean, just look at the size of his *grave* …' Oh my, I bet that's what all the girls say, arf arf. Closer inspection reveals that the graveyard is full of dead Irwins. Which is a sobering thought. I leave Drumcliff Church feeling seriously spooked.

We plough on to Donegal, stopping briefly when I realise we're in

Leitrim and a remnant of last night's conversation comes flying out of the ether. 'If you're going to Donegal, you have to stop at *my* county,' insisted my convivial new best friend. '*Your* county?' 'Yes. Leitrim,' she said. 'It's only tiny but it's beautiful, so it is. But it always gets missed. Nobody knows it's there. So promise me you'll stop at Leitrim. Promise? *Promise?*' I promised and asked her if she was related to Pat the landlady.

So we stop the car over the Leitrim border. Briefly. A quick, admiring glance at the Dartry Mountains shrouded in the mist and on we go to Donegal. But as we cross the Donegal border something very *X-Files* happens. I'm playing Dervish's *Live In Palma* album and they launch into a tune called 'Up With Leitrim', telling the story of the great Leitrim flute player John McKenna. Originally from the village of Tarmon, McKenna worked in the now defunct Arigna coal mines before joining the exodus to America in 1911. There he worked for the New York fire department and was billed at gigs as Fire Patrolman McKenna.

Regularly duetting with James Morrison, he had a vast fund of polkas and went on to make many recordings which, when they filtered home, did much to promote not only the flute, but the tunes of Leitrim too. There's a John McKenna memorial at Tarmon, and I hesitate about making another detour to pay my respects, but decide against it. I'll only get lost and end up in a traffic jam in Limerick. But as we cross into Donegal I shout 'Up with Leitrim' just for the hell of it. It feels good. Just don't tell Pat, the Sligo landlady.

Donegal was the last Irish frontier for me. Slavering Irish-ophile that I am, I'd been all over the country listening to people telling me that I *must* go to Donegal, I'd *adore* its wild beauty … so I deliberately didn't go there. Not that I didn't believe them. I just didn't want to ruin the glorious image they'd painted in my head and tarnish the dream with the reality.

Then Altan were signed by Virgin Records, bless them, who decided to organise a junket so that hacks could see and enjoy Altan in their own environment at home in Donegal. I couldn't say no to that one, now could I? It didn't go completely according to plan. The plane Virgin had chartered to take us to Donegal (International) Airport had a touch of gastro-enteritis on the runway at Heathrow and we sat there for a couple of hours while they called for some medicine.

Now then. Journos on a jolly. It's not pretty. You know those 18–30 revellers with donkeys under their arms leering at everything that moves in their silly straw hats? They've nothing on this lot. And those England fans drinking Scandinavian bars dry and terrorising the natives? A bunch of pansies compared to a group of hacks with the scent of a record company's free booze in their nostrils. So two hours sitting on a charter flight on a Heathrow runway without a drink doesn't go down desperately well with the assembled hacks. The thing is half of the assembled party from Her Majesty's press have no idea who Altan are ('What's the group called again?' a radio person asks me as we while away the long dry hours before take-off) and have little interest in finding out. That cliché about music journos writing their reviews nailed to the bar while the band are playing? It's doubly true at a launch party.

It turned out to be a strange trip. It was late and dark by the time we made it to Donegal and were whisked off to a packed pub round Bunbeg way. Altan played a lovely set and may have won over a few philistines but Paul Brady stole the show singing 'Homes Of Donegal', a song written by a St Johnston schoolteacher, Sean McBride, in 1955. Afterwards we were scooted back to the Ostan Gweedore Hotel where the fun began in earnest … until news filtered through that the IRA had broken its ceasefire with a bomb attack on London's Canary Wharf. A couple of English news hacks in the party were instantly grabbing phones, suitcases and their marbles, trying to find someone to interview and hire cars to get them to Belfast. I could imagine the conversation. 'Hmmm, a *car*, you say? We don't usually have much use for one of those round these parts … no I don't rightly know *where* you'd get one of those for hiring.'

The seaside town of Bundoran looms colourfully into view. It feels a bit like finding Margate stuck in the middle of the Lake District. We stayed here a couple of years ago and even in the middle of winter it was doing somersaults to try to turn itself into the holiday capital of the north-west. Big banners in the town were optimistically announcing the opening of a plush, ultra-modern six-screen cinema complex and we trotted off to witness the grand opening. When we got there it was still a building site.

The Bundoran bars were full of painfully trendy blond surfers, there were amusement arcades through every doorway, fast food joints, a funfair, aqua adventure park and family entertainment with a capital 'E' in the big hotels as Bundoran tried desperately to be all things to all people. In fairness we did find a pub by the bridge which provided some decent diddley-i music between stories of heroics on surfboards and there was an hilarious night with a hypnotist who had lads running round the room pretending they were David Beckham and then performed a full-blooded interpretation of *The Full Monty*.

This time round we reach Bundoran and, in the words of Hal David, walk on by. We give Ballyshannon a miss too, though this may be a mistake. 'But Ballyshannon is practically the oldest town in Ireland, how can you miss it?' says a disapproving Ballyshannon man later in the journey. I tell him that the golf put me off. '*Golf?*' he says, mystified, 'and what's wrong with golf, 'tis a great sport.' 'Ah,' I say, 'that's where you're wrong, it's not a *sport*.' And then I launch into my logical dissertation on the evils of golf ('Well, it's always played by fat bastards in stupid trousers for one thing') and my theory on why it can't possibly call itself a sport. 'The definition of sport,' I tell him authoritatively, 'is something that either has a winning line or is played in shorts.' He pauses for a moment to ponder this revelation. 'So cricket's not a sport then?' 'Apart from cricket obviously …'

Despite strenuous advice from Dervish to avoid it like the plague we decide to stop overnight in Donegal town. 'If you find yourself there, just keep moving,' said my friend from Leitrim. 'It really has nothing in common with the rest of Donegal. If you want to get to know Co. Donegal, don't go anywhere near Donegal town.' 'Don't they have music there?' 'Oh they have music … but nothing anybody in their right mind would want to hear.'

We arrive early evening and it doesn't look too bad. There's a lovely sunset over the bay, ducks glide around on the River Eske setting a tranquil scene and the ruins of the fifteenth-century castle gives the town a sombre, grown-up feel. We find a decent enough B&B on the edge of town and meet a super-fit ultra-trendy American girl called Marie who'd just run the Dublin marathon. How did it go, Marie? 'Ohmagoddd it *was awwwwww-some* …' 'Oh … *keeewwlllll*.'

And now time for the evening entertainment. Given Dervish's comments I wasn't holding my breath. I may have to settle for a few quiet pints and an early night here. As I conduct a preliminary reconnoitre in search of suitable recipients of my humble euros I see the Melody Maker music shop and realise I've been in this town before. I relax. We are old friends. No harm came to me before – I'm sure I'd remember if it did – and we will get on famously tonight.

I identify three likely venues advertising live music which, while hardly indicating that Tommy Peoples lurked within, seemed a pretty good bet. The Star Bar advertises Liam McLaughlin; The Voyage has a poster proclaiming a 'live band'; and, most intriguing of all, the Central Hotel has a sign boasting an appearance by Billy Furey.

The mind boggles. *Billy Furey*? Surely not THE Billy Furey? As it happens I'm a bit of a fan of the English rock star of the 1960s. He once owned a horse, Anselmo, which finished fourth in the Epsom Derby. Not many people know that. But he died years ago. Or *did* he? Has he been working in a supermarket all these years with Josef Locke? But I also know enough about him to note the subtle spelling change in his name. The name on the poster is BILLY FUREY. The old Billy Fury had no E in his surname. So, assuming this isn't merely a slip of the pen, it opens up other possibilities. Maybe he's a Billy Fury without-an-E tribute band like the Christy Moore one I'd seen in Tramore. Or … could Billy be a long-lost member of the famous Furey brothers of traditional music fame? Maybe Billy Furey is the eccentric cousin they've had locked up in the attic for the last twenty years and he's had nothing to do except practise uilleann pipes and is now the most thrilling piper who ever struck elbow on bellows.

There is another possibility … he could just be some bloke who happens to be called Billy Furey. But I don't like to consider that one at all.

So Donegal town, brace yourself, here I come …

8pm Central Hotel: Nothing happening here. It's a proper hotel and when I ask about Billy Furey they point me to the bar upstairs. It's vast and impersonal and, unless he's a buxom blonde, a bored barman or an annoying little kid rolling around the floor making irritating burping noises, there's no sign of Billy.

8.15pm The Voyage: A normal pub. A very *quiet* normal pub. A few scattered drinkers chat quietly in the corner, but no sign of music.

8.30pm Star Bar: A long thin bar that is promisingly full. I see the heads all pointing in one direction and hear the shouts and assume Liam McLaughlin is already in action pulling out a thunderous 'Fields Of Athenry'. But it's just the lads watching kick boxing on the telly.

8.45pm Central Hotel: A mic stand has appeared in the upstairs bar and lots more people have arrived. But they all seem like they're here for a wedding reception. The guys are at the bar getting pissed, the women are at the back getting bored. The only entertainment is supplied by the kids who all want to be Roy Keane when they grow up and race around the room trying to take chunks out of one another.

9pm The Voyage: It's filling up and it looks like some serious drinking is on the cards. A drum kit and other instruments of a musical persuasion have mysteriously appeared.

9.15pm Star Bar: The kick boxing is getting exciting, judging by the roars of the lads crowding round the telly. A man with silver hair and comedy moustache lurches through the door unsteadily clutching a huge amp and nearly decapitates the lot of them.

9.30pm Central Hotel: The blokes at the bar are starting to get raucous, telling dirty jokes about frocks and friars and totally ignoring a diminutive slightly harassed-looking chap trying to set up amps and mics around them.

9.45pm The Voyage: It's rammed. Can barely get in. Still no music though.

10pm Star Bar: The kick boxing is over and people are beginning to drift away … much to the chagrin of the guy still hauling in loads of equipment, which he adds to a stack that would already put Pink Floyd to shame.

10.15pm Central Hotel: The small, balding man perched behind a mic trying to peer above the backs of the heads of a meeting of The Tallest Blokes In Donegal Society is clearly not a Billy Fury without-an-E tribute band. Nor is he a member of the famous Furey clan. He is just a bloke called Billy Furey. But he knows how to give an audience what it wants. There it is, 'Fields Of Athenry'. Right off the bat, just like that. Straight for the throat, eh Billy? I like that in a vampire. Not that it makes much impact on the blokes at the bar, but it raises the spirits of their bored wives glugging gin at the back. 'Here's a little thing called … "Whiskey In The Jar",' says Billy, and then it's 'The Town I Loved So Well' and 'Dublin In The Rare Oul' Times'. I raise a glass to Pete St John, wink at Billy and move on.

10.40pm The Voyage: Saints preserve us. I get to the door but the sound of muddy electric guitars, snare drums and syrupy seventies west coast rock sends me fleeing back into the street.

10.45pm Star Bar: Liam McLaughlin is giving it his best shot though the audience is a difficult one. In truth the only people who seem to be listening are four Amazonian Americans of indeterminate sex swaying on their bar stools and giving him some grief. 'Say buster, I've been in Ireland 11 days and I haven't heard one Irish song yet!' complains one of them. 'Well, you sit tight now,' says Liam, twiddling with his Graeme Souness moustache, and goes into 'Needles & Pins'. 'That's not an Irish song!' says the American loudly to her friends all the way through it.

Every song Liam performs starts like 'Duelling Banjos', even Eric Clapton's 'Wonderful Tonight'. Ms/Mr America continues to complain that it's still not an Irish song and her cause is taken up by one of her colleagues. 'Say …' he calls to Liam, 'do you know a song called Rose of Charley.' Liam is baffled by this. He's clearly used to a variety of odd requests but 'Rose of Charley' isn't one of them. He does what anyone would do in the circumstances, he pretends he's from Barcelona. 'You *must* know it,' insists the man/woman, it goes like this … and she hums painfully and Liam looks confused. Yet in her discordant whining a vaguely familiar tune lurks. And then I twig what her 'Rose of Charley' really is and think of lovely Tamara Gervasoni in Kerry. She wants to hear 'Rose of Tralee'.

Liam still looks flummoxed and sings 'Danny Boy' instead. 'Oh that was lovely,' says a grateful Yank at the end of it. 'I just love that Rose of Charley.'

11.45pm Central Bar: Billy Furey is playing 'Hard Day's Night' and people are *doing the twist.*

I'm sorry, I can't take any more. Time for bed, says Zebedee.

We spend the next few days tootling round the wondrous nooks and crannies on the west coast of Donegal. We take tea in Ardara, paying respects to the birthplace of the legendary fiddle icon Johnny Doherty. We explore Dunkineely and Killybegs and Kilcar and – I'm not ashamed to admit it – we sup the odd pint. And we find ourselves in the tiny fishing village of Teelin, seeking out Cul A Duin, a pub now owned by Mairead Ni Mhaonaigh and her husband Dermot Byrne of Altan. A Gaeltacht area, this is serious traditional music country, and there are many tales of sizzling sessions at Cul A Duin. 'Oh yes, we have a bit of a craic at the pub all right,' says the elegant Mairead. And you'd better believe it.

The history of the traditional Irish music may be equally associated with house dances, crossroads dances and public ceilis – indeed not so long ago no publican would allow a traditional musician anywhere near the bar – but we now live in the era of the pub session. And while they may play huge concert halls all over the world, bands like Altan and Dervish recognise the spirit of the pub session got them where they are today … but will only keep them there for as long as they maintain those links. Which may explain why Altan and Dervish have their own pubs.

Altan's history is inextricably linked to pub sessions from the days Mairead and Frankie Kennedy first started playing fiddle and flute together when they were both training to be teachers. It was a great love story personally and musically as Mairead and Frankie married, continued to play in pubs, gathering other musicians around them along the way. They dipped their toes into the idea of a more formal band and, in 1987, formed Altan. In 1991, after four years of intensive gigging, building a devoted following which took them to the brink of crossover success, Frankie was diagnosed with bone cancer. I was in Dublin for the launch of their *Island Angel* album and was surprised Frankie was late for his own party and asked him why. 'I've been at the hospital,' he said matter-of-factly. 'Nothing serious, I hope,' I said. 'Oh, it's a long story …' he smiled, and changed the subject.

As far as he was concerned, though, it was business as usual. He made light of his illness and continued to play with Altan for as long as he could, before his death in September, 1994. 'Frankie wouldn't hear of us splitting,' says Mairead. 'It was what he always wanted for the band to be successful and in a sense it would have been a betrayal of everything we'd worked for together if we'd given up. It was hard, of course it was hard for all of us, but the music really did help us get through it. Now I still feel his presence with us. He's always there with us.'

Frankie Kennedy's death released a latent songwriting talent in Mairead. She wrote the poignant 'Time Has Passed' in Frankie's memory and the band drew strength from one another and prospered. With Cairan Tourish emerging as a strong focal point to present a fierce double-pronged fiddle attack with Mairead, Altan are now generally regarded as Ireland's top traditional band. A band which, despite all the tours, albums and acclaim, is still strongly flavoured by the countryside of Donegal. 'It's who we are and it's what we play, we can't change that and nor would we want to,' says Mairead. 'We could play Cajun or anything and we'd still play it in a Donegal way. That's just the way it is and we're happy about that.'

Mairead and the band's accordion player Dermot Byrne have subsequently married and Teelin is rocking to the sound of session music at Cul A Duin.

Not tonight though. Altan are away on tour in foreign climes and we move on. At Glencolumbkille we doff our caps to James Byrne, one of the great Donegal fiddler players of modern times, and grapple with the hairpin bends, tumbling mountains and gobsmacking views as we cross the deserted Glengesh Pass. It brings us to the town of Ardara, which seems wall to wall with knitting shops and is also the home of Packie Byrne, a whistle player, singer and raconteur who for many years lit up the British folk scene. Ardara is also the birthplace of the most legendary Donegal fiddler of them all, Johnny Doherty.

From a well-known family of travellers, Doherty and his flat cap were familiar around the county through the middle of the last century playing regularly at house dances, fairs and other events and his style became recognised as definitively Donegal. Yet what made his dynamic playing so special was the fact that he formulated a distinctive style that reflected not merely his own Ardara background, but the Scots Strathspey tradition and other regional eccentricities. The result was a sound that was uniquely, splendidly Doherty.

At Portnoo we gaze breathlessly at Gweebarra Bay looking for a friend of a friend's brother who has a restaurant here but find a dead seal on the beach instead. And at Dungloe we find ourselves negotiating a climb so steep and narrow even the sheep think we're mad for attempting. Right at the top there's a house with a big sign outside announcing: 'BEWARE: WAKE IN PROGRESS.' Already terrified by the hostile terrain, we couldn't really go any slower, but this unexpected new hazard is a puzzle. What exactly do we need to beware of?

A mad hearse driver? Drunken mourners? An invitation to join them? It's a worry.

And all the way we are accompanied by the reassuring sound of North West Radio. 'We've just had news in that a sheepdog is lost at Killybegs. He answers to the name of Archie so let us know if you have seen him … alert all farmers, we've just had a call from someone who's noticed a poorly cow in a field on the Ardara road just outside Glenties so will all farmers check their cows please …' That's the sort of stuff you want to hear, isn't it? No bloody Gareth Gates on North West Radio.

We go through the market town of Dungloe – trying to remember the words of 'Mary Of Dungloe' – pass the remote craggy headlands of The Rosses and decide to stay overnight in the seaside town of Bunbeg, where our chatty landlady provides tea, scones and an eloquent soliloquy on the delights of the area. 'Oh, 'tis a grand spot all right, it gets very busy in the summer but thank the Lord we need the business. 'Tis a lovely place to come for your holidays so it is and there's such a lot going on. Daniel holds a festival here every year, oh it's grand, so it is.'

Daniel? 'Yes, Daniel. He has done such a lot for this area, so he has, he's a grand man all right, God bless him …'

I stop her and buy one. Daniel? Daniel who? 'Y'know … *Daniel*!' I don't know Daniel and feel somehow deprived. 'I'm sorry, I don't know who you mean … lovely scones by the way …'

'Daniel *O'Donnell*.' The way she says it I feel we should all fall to our knees, raise our arms and chant 'We are not worthy'. So, erm, *Daniel* is from this part of the world, is he? 'Oh he is, yes, Daniel is from Kincasslagh, he's such a lovely man. Do you like Daniel?' I cannot tell a lie. So I feign a choking fit and flee outside. A few days later the *Donegal Democrat* breaks the shocking news that Daniel is to be betrothed. The lucky lady is Majella McClelland, a Tipperary businesswoman who met him in Tenerife and sweet, tiny, sleepy Kincasslagh is soon groaning with a mass influx of press, TV crews and well-wishers. Coach parties come in from all over Ireland and the UK when they tie the knot at St Mary's Church and Letterkenny grinds to a halt as the happy couple arrive for the reception and Donegal celebrates that its king has a queen.

We spend the evening chilling at Sean Og's pub in Bunbeg trying to get to put a finger on what exactly makes Donegal's music sound so rarefied. Traditional music varies enormously not only from county to county, but sometimes within counties. And nowhere is that demonstrated with more clarity than in Donegal. Fiddle player James Byrne says he could recognise which village somebody came from by the way they played the fiddle. Fiddle music, he said, would be played a lot faster in Teelin than it would be across the glen at Glencolumbkille. Other villages would have their own stylistic idiosyncrasies and while a lot of the tunes played in Donegal would be the same, the variations used in playing them varied enormously from place to place. They were differences accentuated by the best players, who'd try to put their own stamp on them. The criticism usually made of young players by the older ones is that they play too fast. Why do they play so fast? *Because they can.*

Donegal is one of the last outposts of Ireland's cultural individuality, a change reflected by the decline of the Irish language. Famine and emigration took their toll and there are lots of stories of children being beaten for speaking Gaelic after the language had been banned in schools by the British in the nineteenth century. Even Daniel O'Connell condemned the Irish language as 'backward' and said English was the language of the future.

Attitudes changed with the onset of the Irish Free State but critics feel its cultural aggression was a mistake and making the Irish language a compulsory part of the curriculum ultimately had a negative effect. There have been various initiatives since to raise the profile and increase the number of people speaking Gaelic with Irish language radio and television stations. But it doesn't seem to be working. In the 1920s the official figure of Irish speakers was 250,000; now it's under 30,000.

Portents for tonight's session at Sean Og's aren't good. The pub is showing *Coronation Street* and a group of Scots lads are holding a deadly serious pool tournament that threatens to explode into a major fist fight at any moment. A fiddle, guitar and flute player assemble almost apologetically at the next table and begin to play quietly among themselves, joined later by a boy with Downs Syndrome beautifully playing accordion. It's not the most thrilling session in the world and is hardly going to distract the Scots when it all kicks off on the pool table. Tomorrow night Sean Og's is having a ceili and there's a rock band the day after that, so you know there's nothing organic about it; this is scarcely the Altan/Dervish session school. Yet there's still something magical about having a quiet pint while a group play traditional music informally next to you. Well, there is in Donegal anyway.

Hang on, things are livening up. The pool players are stomping out and a giggling girl totters over to whisper earnestly in the flute player's ear. There follows a whispered consultation between the musicians and they launch into a jig. The girl kicks off her shoes, hitches up her jeans and I wonder for a minute if it's the flute player's birthday and he's about to get a lap dance. But no, the girl is off into an energetic if erratic step dance. Not quite Michael Flatley, she slips and slides around in her socked feet and the whole exercise loses its impact when you can't hear the beat of feet on the floor. It all ends in tears when she loses her footing completely, lurches backwards and lands in a heap on the flute player's lap clutching her back and groaning in pain. Those tonic waters are lethal in Bunbeg.

Next day we go see Leo. I mean, you can't stay in yodelling distance of Gweedore and not visit Leo's Tavern.

I'd interviewed Clannad on various occasions before and after they'd had hits with 'Harry's Game' and 'Robin The Hooded Man'. Virtually every chat with their singer Maire Brennan ended in warm, funny, touching anecdotes about her dad's pub in Gweedore. I'd heard so much about it that I felt a pilgrimage was essential. So at lunchtime on a winter's day in Gweedore a couple of years ago, we visited Leo's Tavern.

The long dark bar with the low ceilings and benches along the walls was empty and there was so little evidence of any craic that I wondered if we were talking about a different Leo's Tavern in a different Gweedore. But the gold discs of Clannad and Enya all over the walls were sufficient testament that Leo and Baba Brennan's offspring had done good and we were definitely in the right place.

There was bit of chit chat with the bar staff, we ordered another drink and then Leo Brennan appeared. Warm, flamboyant, gregarious and immaculately dressed with an unmistakeable twinkle in his eye, Leo was exactly how his daughter Maire had described him and within ten minutes we'd swapped life stories. Originally a Sligo man, Leo told me how he'd got the showbiz bug from travelling around with his own parents' showband. How they'd landed up in Gweedore and he'd go into the local pub to play accordion for the old fellers. How he fell in love with the local headmaster's daughter Baba and overcame her parents' initial suspicions of him and ended up marrying her. How he played sax and became leader of the family's Slieve Foy Dance Band and the adventures they had on the road in Scotland. How the rural dance scene went out of fashion and into free-fall and he knew the days of the Slieve Foy Dance Band were numbered. How he bought the derelict pub, knocked it down and rebuilt it from scratch. How he re-opened it as a music bar in 1968.

And he told me about his famous offspring. How Clannad and Enya had cut their teeth at Leo's Tavern before going off to conquer Ireland ... and the rest of the world. How the locals came out into the streets late at night to cheer Clannad home after their first appearance on *Top Of The Pops* singing 'Harry's Game' and they'd all ended up back at the pub for a session that went on forever. 'I still made them work, though,' he chortled. 'I told them I didn't care what number they were in the English charts they'd still have to serve behind the bar!'

And suddenly it was showtime. I was a bit nonplussed at first. We were the only two people in the bar, but the staff started running hither and thither laying tables, setting up amps and mics, adjusting the lighting, straightening pictures on the walls, putting on jackets, smartening their hair … The muzak was switched off and the sound of Enya cascaded all over the bar. And there was Leo, with a big beaming smile at the front door welcoming a coach party of pensioners.

Watching Leo was an education. He *was* Mr Entertainer. He flirted with the old ladies, had a wink and a laugh with the men, told a few jokes and tall stories, and found out where every single one of them was from and what fates had conspired to put them on the coach party from Ulster that brought them here. Sandwiches, beer, sherry, tea and coffee were brought and then he got up on the small stage at one end of the bar. 'I'll just play a few tunes on the accordion here,' he said. Leo was a revelation. He played tunes and sang ditties from specific areas where he knew the people were from … 'You're from Armagh aren't you, Ned. That's a lovely part of the world, sure it is, and you have some fine old songs down that way. Do you know this one, Ned?'

He recounted anecdotes about his own musical career, talked up Clannad and Enya's achievements and even introduced me to the pensioners as a special guest. 'Colm here used to interview Clannad when they appeared at the Royal Albert Hall in the city of London and all these places … tell 'em, Colm.' He had them laughing, crying, singing and, most disturbing of all, he had them dancing. You feared for their hearts, you really did. He got a few of them on the stage to do their own party pieces and various members of the bar staff got up to do a turn. The afternoon was positively surreal.

There was but one Brennan son left at home now to run the bar and, amid much goading from Leo and the pensioners, he too was prevailed on to take to the stage. If we wondered why he wasn't away making records and doing concert tours like all the others we soon found out. 'I'm afraid I don't have the music,' he said apologetically. 'Awww go on with you,' roared the pensioners. 'But I'll give it a go anyway!' The pensioners were on their chairs wolf-whistling. He sang 'Wild Rover'. Badly. But it didn't matter. The pensioners, all three sheets to the wind by now, drowned him out on the chorus, whooping and hollering and getting raucous enough to suggest there could be some sport in the back row of the coach on the way back across the border.

I expect more of the same as we pull into Leo's car park this time. Aye, aye, I'm thinking, something's up here, Leo's been splashing out. The whole place looks different. There's a big sign outside for one thing and a newly built stone wall with a nice car park. This has been refurbished with a vengeance. An extension has been built, the pub is now split by a large bar in the middle and staff run around in smart black t-shirts with Leo's name emblazoned over them. It's brightly lit and upbeat and the posters advertising quiz nights, parties and official functions leave no doubt Leo's has gone up-market. Last time we were here we had a bowl of soup and a toasted sandwich; now we are being offered a choice of steak, salmon, trout and various styles of chicken. Still, the gold discs are still on the wall and 'Harry's Game' reassuringly gets an airing before the night is through.

In the corner a family group seems to be holding an impromptu quiz. 'What is the process by which plants produce energy?' asks the mother of a child so small she barely reaches the table. 'What's the capital of Mongolia? What's the second largest river in the world? Name one of the enzymes involved in the digestion of food.' Phew. There really is no such thing as a free lunch. Or are they in training for *Who Wants To Be A Millionaire?*. Cough.

Leo's accordion is meaningfully perched on a stool, but there's no sign of Leo. I ask about him at the bar. 'No, he's not in tonight.' I ask about Leo's son, the one who can't sing. 'Sorry, he's not in tonight either.' I look distraught. 'But they should both be here tomorrow.' Any music on? 'No, not tonight … but there will definitely be music tomorrow.' Always *mañana,* eh?

Another day, another wild and majestic Donegal coast. We inch ever further north and look at Bloody Foreland, just because the name sounds good. And I remembered Leo Brennan saying something about the red streaks in the huge boulders there being the blood of giants who used to fight each other on the beaches. Then again I probably wouldn't buy a used car from Leo. When we get there I can't see any red bits in the boulders at all, but a passing English geologist assures me they are there … and you should see how they glow in the sunset. 'It's just like Amsterdam here at night time,' he says.

Across the cliffs you can see Inishbofin – which curiously means 'island of the white cow' – and, further on, Tory Island, which has its own king, although he has no power. A bit further north and we reach the town of Dunfanaghy. I've never been here before but I've been recommended a bar with no name – 'just ask for Molly's' – which I'm assured not only has some great music, but the best Guinness in the whole of Ireland. Why? 'Because the pumps are so close to the barrel.' No, I don't understand that either.

That night we find Molly's pub masquerading under the name of Michael's Bar. Inside it's quaintly tiny and as you sit on rows of stools facing the bar it feels like being on a bus. Not that I've been on a bus for 17 years and the driver certainly didn't serve the best pint of Guinness in Ireland but it has the same sort of symmetry. I make a mental note: if buses are like this nowadays get me a season ticket now.

Michael says this used to be a music pub in the old days and since he took it over 18 months or so ago he's been trying to revive the old values. 'Oh, it's a great craic!' he says. 'Sometimes we have eight or nine musicians in and there's a guitarist here you wouldn't *believe*.' So any music on tonight? 'Yes, there will be … we have it in the back room there.' That seems fairly unequivocal. None of this 'I wouldn't be at all surprised' or 'You never know' or 'I wouldn't rule it out'. I like this man. I ask him what time the music starts. 'Oh, about ten … it depends how thirsty the musicians are.'

That's a way off, but there's already a pretty good craic going on in this bar. There's no room to swing a cat but the stools behind me are rapidly filling and the whole area is so enclosed you become embroiled in a communal conversation whether you like it or not. And tonight's topic for debate is … *dogs*. A bloke at the end of the bar announces that he has a Rottweiler. Which produces a shocked gasp from me. Irish dogs are completely bonkers, right? And Rottweilers are meant to be a bit aggressive, whatever nationality they are. So an Irish Rottweiler … aren't you scared he might lock his jaws on your wrist and snap it right off? Cue a catalogue of dog horror stories. But the new pet owner is having none of it. 'He's a big puppy, I tell you … a gorgeous dog … *gorgeous* … course, it was a bit tricky at first. I'm his third owner in two years and when I got him home all he wanted to do was eat, fight and shag.'

For a minute I think the subject has changed to footie players but no, we are still on dogs and get into a fascinating discussion about dog training and the benefits of using a collar with a buzzer on it. 'See, what happens if the dog chases a sheep, you just press the buzzer and it gives him a little shock. After he's done it three times he doesn't do it any more.' I ask how you stop a dog chasing cars. 'Drive slow … real, real slow … that always confuses them.'

And then we chew the fat over the *chip wars*. It seems the whole of Dunfanaghy is gripped by the private feud between rival chip vans who ram each other at will and are constantly involved in unseemly shouting matches. Forgot Oz rules football, the regular head-to-heads between the rival chippers is the most popular sport around these parts. Forget Rangers v Celtic, Dunfanaghy is a divided town. Split by a chipper.

A loud, large, aggressive middle-aged Scotsman in a kilt arrives and suddenly the bar is getting very crowded. 'I like your kilt,' says my new best friend Frances. 'Are you taking the rise out of me,' says The Scotsman. 'Not at all, I think it looks very nice,' says Frances coolly, taking another gulp of a fierce-looking hot toddy. The Scotsman takes this as an invitation to get to know her a whole lot better, triggering a dodgy dialogue about what a Scotsman wears under his kilt.

Uh-oh, he's heard my accent. 'You English?' he says accusingly. 'Well, that's a good question ... ' I say, trying to buy time. 'Well?' 'It depends what you call English ...' 'I know what *I* call the English!' he responds wittily. 'Well, in a way, I suppose ... yes, I guess you could say I am English ... *sorta* ...' The Scotsman is looking angry now ...' but I have Scots ancestors.' I think this will get me off the hook but he's in on me like a shot. 'What CLAN?!' 'McDonalds.' Oh God, he's probably a Campbell. They massacred us at Glencoe, there's no knowing what they might do in Donegal. 'What's your tartan?' he's asking menacingly. Is this a trick question? *'What's your tartan?'* he demands again, his big round red face pressing closer to mine. 'Well,' I say nervously, 'it's a sort of a *check* design ... with greens ... and blue ... and, er, black ... oh and there's this little dab of red and the odd stripey bit and ... it's very nice actually ...'

Michael bales me out. 'I think they're starting the session now ...' I'm out of the door in a flash, into the courtyard, leapfrogging down the stairs, expecting to find a lively session. A couple of guys are making themselves comfy by a fire in front of a bright old Guinness ad – the one with the pelican flying over a city carrying a white bundle in its beak. One guy is wearing a garish sweater made of the wool left over when Joseph's mum made him the coat of many colours and the combination of sweater and Guinness ad is pure migraine material.

He then pulls out a long low whistle of unashamedly phallic proportions and I'm wondering how my mate in the kilt is getting on with Frances. Next to him there's a guy with a guitar ... and he knows how to use it. His hair – conducting a civil war of its own – could do with sorting out though. He plays with such a sure touch and instinctive rhythm that I know this is the guy Michael upstairs had promised I *wouldn't believe* when I heard him. He's outstanding ... but it's not the guitarist I don't believe, it's his mate's jumper.

The two musicians wisely ignore their audience – me and some bloke asleep on the sofa in the corner – and get on with it. They are excellent and gradually the room begins to fill. They open the barn bar and in no time at all the upstairs occupants descend in various states of merriment and the craic begins. I hide as I see the Scotsman in the kilt barge through the door, but now he has other things on his mind. In no time at all he's – unsteadily – on his feet singing 'Flower Of Scotland' at a terrifying volume. He sits down to raucous cheers from a suddenly full barn and ... we don't hear another peep out of him all night. The man has peaked too early and was last seen nodding off in the corner.

A big-breasted woman, meanwhile, has collared me and is re-writing my non-existent itinerary. 'Tomorrow,' she says urgently, 'you MUST go to Malin Head.' *Must* I? 'Yes, you MUST! It's the experience of a lifetime. I was up in the Big Sur in California and they said "This is the most beautiful place in the world" and I said "Ah, but you haven't been to Malin Head." It's an experience you'll never forget.'

Next morning we plan to travel south to Dublin. It's only the bloody capital, after all, and time is running out. But choking over a renegade chunk of black pudding at breakfast I pull out an old hankie to catch any stray innards and a grubby ball of paper falls out. I smooth it out, lay it on the table and read what it says. Two things: 'PERE LACHAISE CEMETERY, PARIS' and 'MUST GO TO MALIN HEAD.'

I ponder the Père Lachaise reference for several minutes. Something to do with Edith Piaf's grave? Jim Morrison? Georges Bizet? Frederic Chopin? Oscar Wilde? Is Tommy Peoples alive and well and living in Paris? Is that where we should be heading next? Oh sod it, let's got to Malin Head ...

Malin Head is the most northerly point in all Ireland. Even further north than anywhere in the official Northern Ireland. Which is all very *Irish*. We're already a long way into the north of Donegal and Malin Head looks a bit of a cakewalk on the map. Unfortunately, we don't notice the big wedge of Lough Swilly in the way. So south we come to Letterkenny – Donegal's biggest town with a decent session scene of its own – and start the long haul back up to the Inishowen Peninsula. It's a long road, but the further north you go the more intriguing it gets. The hills get steeper, the towns get smaller, the scenery more unruly, the roads narrower, the beaches more sandy, the waves more hostile and the pubs fewer and farther in between.

There is a real thrill about standing on the most northerly tip of Ireland, gazing in awe at the endless horizon over the 'EIRE' sign written in large boulders on the land in front of the cliff. There's not a soul to be seen, not a whiff of the heritage industry and scarcely a sound. Apart from the crashing waves. And the howling wind. And the squawking birds. And the goats balancing precariously on the rocks warning each other that an unidentified bodhran hunter could be on the premises. And Eileen Ivers and her flying blue fiddle belting out 'On Horseback' in my head. I have a flashback of the woman sinking a pint of Guinness without it even touching the sides last night and then telling me Malin Head is the most beautiful place on earth. And I think maybe she's not so mad after all.

I have one more pilgrimage to make while we're in Donegal. St Johnstone. This is the birthplace of Tommy Peoples and here there must surely be clues where to find the great man. Maybe he's even there now. People who travel a lot always like to go home in the end, don't they?

It's an unprepossessing drive down there as we cross the border into Northern Ireland, are caught in the traffic for Derry city centre, get completely lost trying to get out and eventually stuck between two huge lorries burying us in silt as we seek out the St Johnstone road. By the time we find it the skies are black, sleet is hurling from the skies and even the calming voice of Cara Dillon on the stereo fails to raise spirits. Still, a cup of coffee and a bun in a cosy little tea shop in St Johnstone while various members of the Peoples family join us to chat proudly of 'our Tommy' should sort us out.

We cross back across the border into Donegal and a sign informs us that St Johnstone is but a couple of miles west as we splash on through the farming country pursued by a vicious storm. We pass the St Johnstone sign and wait for the town to appear. There's a couple of shops and a housing estate with a bunch of kids shiftily prodding a smouldering bonfire with a stick. We slow and wait for more. But there is none. A group of elderly men are standing by the side of the road grinning. I note with alarm that one of them, who looks about 96, is wielding a rifle around his head and is laughing hysterically. I press the accelerator. St Johnstone looks like the sort of place most people just drive through. So we do.

Sorry Tommy. Dublin is calling.

Chapter eleven

DUBLIN: THE COBBLESTONE, MOLLY MALONE, BONO & BERTIE'S POLE

And so to dear dirty Dublin. Or dear, dirty, *dusty* Dublin. Yep, it looks like another 35 hotels will go up this weekend to play host to stag party revellers from Wigan and shrieking girls wearing angel wings and devil horns. The local pubs and hotels are supposed to be operating a ban on stag and hen parties these days (Barcelona is the preferred location for pre-nuptial mayhem in the brave new text-messaging world, apparently) but a brisk peek into Temple Bar swiftly reveals that nobody seems to have told the stag and hen parties. Unless, of course, the girl in full wedding regalia with an L-plate on her back doing 'Knees-up Mother Brown' and yelling 'I'm getting married in the morning' at 300 decibels is regulation behaviour for popping out for a quiet drink in Dublin these days. I ponder this possibility as a dozen females come hurtling along Grafton St in matching black T-shirts all bearing the slogan 'BABS WEDDING MARCH, DUBLIN'. A few yards further and a bunch of lads are having noisy piggyback fights, lurching waywardly across the street as they mount repeated medieval joust-style charges that cause even the stoical Hare Krishna Orchestra to flee for cover. Only the mad-eyed bagpiper in kilt and flowing red beard standing resolutely on the corner playing at a volume to waken the dead shall not be moved. The jousters suddenly get the full force of one of his blazing hornpipes and quietly dismount to disappear towards St Stephens Green to fill out their applications to join the Hare Krishna.

The first time I set foot in Dublin twenty-five years ago, I got off the airport bus and checked in at the first hotel that crossed my path. Wynns in Abbey Street. I've been back to Dublin on numerous occasions since and stayed at establishments of varying vintage, but had never been back to Wynns. The only thing I remembered about it was the beggar who hung around outside and collared me each day with convivial chit-chat. 'Tell me, sir, would you be English?' Having spent the previous evening accused of being an errant Dublin milkman, I freely admitted that yes, I was indeed English. 'Ah,' said my new chum, beaming fetchingly but swaying dangerously as he pushed his face close to mine, knocking me backwards with a pungent blast of something seriously toxic. 'Can I tell you something, sir?' I nod in the full knowledge that, whatever the answer, he'll tell me anyway. 'I've seen some things, sir …' That's nice. 'I've been all around the world, sir, I've met a lot of people.' You have? 'Oh, I have that, sir. I've met people from all over the world, sir and do you know something, sir?' I know nothing, I'm from Barcelona. 'I've met a lot of English people, sir …' Oh, here it comes … hundreds of years of oppression and persecution, bastard landlords, Irish jokes, 'coloureds and Irish need not apply' signs … I start to apologise for the sins of my nation but he's not listening. 'As God is my witness, this is the honest truth. No Englishman has ever let me down …'

I dug deep and gave him all my change.

I was in Dublin five days then and each morning that beggar was waiting outside Wynns to greet me and we went through the same ritual and it always ended up with him emptying my pockets. That first pilgrimage to Dublin had been a major culture shock. The tiny children begging on O'Connell Bridge; the drawn, grey faces of the old women; the overt fierce drinking going on at every street corner; the religious zealots shouting the odds wherever you looked; the dark, dingy pubs that, once entered, offered disarming conviviality and top grade intellectual debate. 'You wanna know the trouble with the Brits?' confided one bar-stool philosopher. 'The Brits are all bastards. But never mind that, what are you drinking?' And that's the crux of it. You can despise the race, but in Ireland it's never *ever* personal. I've met hard-line republicans whose hatred of the Brits knew no bounds – and they didn't care who knew it – yet on a one-to-one were always wonderfully warm, genuinely helpful and unerringly entertaining. For all the ills, Ireland can't help itself. It's an inveterately sociable nation and you are indeed welcome here, kind stranger.

In pursuit of symmetry, I decide to retrace my footsteps on that first visit to Dublin. Which means checking into Wynns. 'Wynns? Why are you staying in Wynns? We call it the *priests* hotel, it's full of priests and nuns,' says a Dublin friend who hasn't been to mass lately. 'Wynns looks exactly the way I left it a quarter of a century ago with its old-fashioned frontage and an oddly reassuring faded grandeur. Razed to the ground by fire during the 1916 Easter Uprising, Wynns was rebuilt a decade later and not a lot appears to have changed since.

'Priests, you say?' says the girl on reception, a trifle affronted, when I ask while they call it the priests hotel. 'I've never heard that one before but I've only worked here a few weeks and now you come to mention it we did have a father in for lunch yesterday ...'

A bus ride around town surrounded by American back-packers proves quite an education in the city's modern attraction. 'We might as well be in Pennsylvania,' says a well-scrubbed guy from Connecticut who's probably called Brad, gloomily surveying the building site that represents the outskirts of Dublin. Another guy in matching baseball cap steadfastly worn backwards, who's obviously called Curt, and swiftly informs the whole bus he works in a car factory in Germany, knows how to raise the spirits. 'I can't wait to get to the Guinness factory and *sample the goods*, hurr, hurr ... and you know what I want to see most of all? Bono! I wanna see Bono!' 'Hey, I think Bono has a pub in Dublin. Let's find his pub and have a drink with him,' says the third member of the party – let's call him Chuck – a voluble young man whose life story unfolds in a matter of seconds. Law school/rich daddy/parents living in Peru/year out travelling/flown in from Italy/girlfriend at home but likes to play away/a demon on the basketball court. 'I think,' corrects Brad, 'it's more a hotel than a pub, but we can still find it and see Bono, how cool is that?' And they burst into a cheery, but tuneless chorus of 'Sunday Bloody Sunday', which peters out after they've sung the title a couple of times and they realise they don't know any more words. It's probably not what U2 had in mind when they recorded it. But then they get into the real reason they're here. 'I'm gonna hit the first bar I come to and drink every beer they have in the place, and then I'm gonna check out all the *cute Irish chicks*,' says Chuck with a leer. 'Best pace ourselves,' cautions Brad sensibly. 'I hear that Guinness in this country is real strong.' Chuck gives him a sideways glance, disturbed to discover he's travelling with a complete wuss. Brad spots the look and tries to recover. 'I mean, I don't just wanna be drinking beer ... I wanna try *whiskey* ... I bet they have some real cool whiskies in Dublin.' He wins some points there all right, but ... 'and *Baileys*! Don't forget the Baileys!' Oh dear, he's blown it again. And then they start talking about ice hockey and I tune out.

First thing I see on setting foot in O'Connell Street this time round is a dirty great silver white pole in the middle of the street stretching into the sky as far as the eye can see. I stand there gazing at in dumbfounded shock for several moments with a group of equally bemused Japanese tourists all going 'What the feck!' I mean, it wasn't that long ago I was in Dublin and I don't remember this thing being there then. 'It's Bertie's pole!' says Joan McDermott, singer with the band Providence over a pint later. 'Bertie Ahern. We reckon it's his phallic symbol. See, he wanted to build some sort of sports stadium, Bertie's Bowl, ... but in the end they decided on a spire instead, so we call it Bertie's Pole.'

Fair play to the Dublin pirate radio station that offered a million euros to the first person who could successfully lasso the spike with a bicycle tyre. The last time Dublin built a monument as a 'symbol of the future' was in the 1950s, when a 'Bowl Of Light' was stuck on O'Connell Bridge. Essentially a pretend glowing fire encased in a giant goldfish bowl, it was there just two weeks before a bunch of students from Trinity College decided to liberate it at the dead of night as a rag-week jape and it was last seen doing the back stroke down the Liffey into Dublin Bay. Those responsible were apprehended and taken to court only to be praised by the judge and given the unofficial freedom of the city. Bertie's Pole – alternatively known as 'Stiffy On The Liffey' – represents a bigger challenge but come on, you Trinity College students, you know your duty ...

Dublin today is a very different beast from the one I first visited. Now it's one of Europe's most vibrant, thriving, cosmopolitan cities with a booming economy and is apparently in the rudest of health. The streets are jammed, the shops are full and the young people jabber constantly into their mobiles, planning the night's play in one of the myriad of night clubs and upmarket pubs. Yet you don't have to scratch far below the surface of internet cafes, stylish shops and open-topped tourist buses parading alongside the Liffey to find dear old dirty Dublin, present and incorrect, warts and all. And for all the excited, buzzy sense of fun and adventure tumbling over itself to shout 'PARTY! AFFLUENCE! PARTY! MODERN! EURO-PEAN! PARTY!' at you in full-lunged celebration of the twenty-first century, the underclass is still painfully evident. Late at night young guys looking like ghosts huddle, shivering under blankets, away from the glare of O'Connell Street on the Ha'penny Bridge. They can't all be remnants of a rugby club weekender from Cheshire. I try to talk to one but he just stares sullenly back, seemingly too wasted to string two words together. In any case, there are signs that the great boom bubble is bursting. 'We used to sit up here and look out of the window and laugh. One day we counted 18 cranes working on different building sites,' says RTE producer Harry Bradshaw at his studio in Merrion Square. 'Today I can only see four cranes ...' Actually, I can only see three, but he's probably right. 'The IT thing has collapsed,' he's saying. 'A couple of years ago people of 19 and 20 were earning £700 a day doing IT and they'd still be walking out after a week because they were being offered more money somewhere else. They'd have brand-new apartments in the city, a BMW, three holidays a year … and then suddenly the carpet was pulled from under them.'

Irish heritage, of course, has been a crucial factor in the rise of modern Dublin as one of Europe's primary tourist attractions. Trinity College housing the *Book Of Kells* and Ireland's oldest harp; the literary tradition of Wilde, Beckett, Yeats, Joyce, Behan, et al; a strong theatrical reputation; ancient churches; gorgeous Georgian buildings; Guinness and the whole culture of carousing. Oh, and traditional music. I was looking forward to visiting the Chief O'Neill Ceol Centre. This was – word had it – the ultimate attraction for anyone interested in Irish traditional music. A centre of excellence, involving a huge, ultra-modern multi-media interactive attraction providing detailed background, insights and samples of all facets of the history of the music to the modern day; as well as a hotel, an archive and a centre for live music. With *Riverdance* riding high, the whole world apparently in love with everything Celtic, tourists banging the doors down to get into Dublin and big money behind the project, it couldn't fail. As a testament to its authenticity it even took its name from one of the greatest heroes in the story of Irish music, Captain Francis O'Neill. Now here's a guy with an interesting story. Originally from Tralibane, near Bantry in Cork, he left home at 16 in 1865 to be a cabin boy on a ship. He ended up wandering around the States getting work wherever he could find it before marrying another Irish emigrant and settling down with her in Chicago. He joined the local police force, had a meteoric rise through the ranks and at the turn of the century wound up as chief of police. In the wake of the famine, a large Irish population had emigrated to Chicago and O'Neill, who himself played flute, fiddle and pipes, decided to collate the tunes the immigrants had brought from home. The project snowballed and in 1903 O'Neill published – and self-financed – *The Music Of Ireland*, containing 1,850 tunes. It was the first of several O'Neill collections and text books and is still recognised as the greatest reference work for Irish tunes.

So yeah, a trip to Chief O'Neill's in a must. And on a bright Sunday afternoon we stroll along the river, where one pub is called Inn On The Liffey and the next down the street is called *Out* On The Liffey. Only in Ireland, only in Ireland. There's a bloke wandering into the Voodoo Lounge with an acoustic guitar but he's dressed like a Goth, so we stroll on, past the Old Jameson Distillery into the square at Smithfield where U2 received the freedom of the city a couple of years ago. Smithfield's primary function for as long as anyone can remember has been as a market for horse sales and it's long been one of the city's less salubrious areas. It's still in part a building site, but it's obviously a rising area, with the plush O'Neill's clearly visible at one side of the square, a clear statement of intent. We wander across through a gaggle of children staring longingly up at the old Chimney Viewing Tower ('Flue With A View') and wondering how to rustle up the 5 euro required to climb it for a 'panoramic view of the city' and prepare to be dazzled by the techno wonders of the Chief O'Neill Ceol Centre. Except it's not a Ceol Centre any more. It's still called Chief O'Neill's, but now it's simply an upmarket hotel and apart from a few artefacts of musicians in the foyer, all clues to its recent past as a traditional music centre have been eradicated. Still, a woman emerges triumphantly from the hotel shop having bought a 66 euro bodhran and a green jacket with shamrocks all over it, so someone's happy.

I get the full story from Harry Bradshaw, the Irish music expert who'd been installed to run the Ceol Centre. With Celtic music on the crest of a wave, various businesses had come in to fund the project with a seemingly limitless budget. 'It was sensational,' he says. 'We had 13 galleries and we had an amazing concert hall with a six and a half thousand watt sound system and we made these incredible films. I told them Irish music was coloured by the topography of the country, so we had *sean-nos* singing from Connemara, fiddle music from Donegal and slides and polkas from Sliabh Luachra and hired a helicopter to film it all. We filmed 120 singers and it cost £750,000 to shoot! People were stunned. Academics came in from the States expecting to see something quaint and they couldn't believe it. We had all this technology and it worked!'

Sadly, though, the Ceol Centre didn't work. Harry says he knew there were problems when he realised that most of the people working at the centre hated traditional music. 'For them it was just about how many pints of Guinness they could sell, but traditional music has its own rule book and you have to play by it. They hated the musicians we brought in. One guy said "These musicians are so crap, they sit down when they play!" They thought traditional music should be about guys with beards and woolly jumpers shouting their heads off with these rabble-rousing songs, but that's not what traditional music is about at all.'

So the great Ceol Centre experiment was abandoned – coincidentally around the same time that the rock equivalent, the Hot Press Hall Of Fame, bit the dust too (so don't be fooled like me and go chasing after the signs that still direct you to it). At least Chief O'Neill's name lives on … and his spirit, too, in the pub across the road. The Cobblestone is perhaps Dublin's best session pub. I adjourn there for a quiet Sunday afternoon pint to overcome the Chief O'Neill disappointment and am immediately enraptured. The Cobblestone has its own CD, its own T-shirts, walls full of old photos and posters, wooden floors, a cheery countenance and sessions every night. Billy Connolly was even lured here to do some filming on his Irish tour. And this Sunday afternoon we are graced with the presence of not one, but two uillean pipers and a flute player. Top quality stuff it is, too. All three top-notch players. We sidle up to the front for a better view and are immediately beckoned to share the top table with the musicians. A rare honour. The musicians' table is sacrosanct and it's certainly not protocol to sit yourself down in front of them. It's embarrassing apart from anything else. For both parties. I mean, you are eyeball to eyeball with them when they are playing, what are you supposed to do? Stare into their eyes. Watch their fingers? Grin at your companions and nod approvingly? Pretend you haven't noticed them? And when they finish a set of tunes, what do you do then? Applaud? You can, but it's *really* embarrassing if it turns out you're the only one. Slap 'em round the back? Way too familiar. Ignore them? How *rude*. Make chit-chat? You feel like a groupie. Offer to buy them a pint? That's by far the best option if you ask any of the musicians, but on this occasion they happen to be a particularly sobrietous bunch drinking orange juice – very slowly – so the gesture's a bit empty. I go for the chit-chat option. 'Do you come here often?' The piper, a neat, tidy, soberly dressed man of no fixed age, has a right to look nervous. There's this guy who's been sitting opposite, not three foot from his nose, staring intently at him for the last hour and now he's trying to pick him up with a corny line. 'What I mean is will you be here next week? I mean … are you a regular, er, when did you start playing?'

Some more chit-chat down the road and I ask his name. 'It's Kevin,' he says pleasantly. 'Kevin Rowsome.' I choke on my Guinness. In uilleann piping circles there are few more legendary names than Rowsome. Samuel Rowsome from Ballintore, Co. Wexford, was one of the most acclaimed pipers and pipemakers of the nineteenth century, fulsomely praised in Chief O'Neill's dispatches. The Rowsomes have figured mightily in traditional circles ever since, most significantly Samuel's grandson Leo Rowsome. A mighty player, pipe-maker, repairer, broadcaster and teacher, he earned the title 'King Of The Pipers' and in the 1930s, revived the Dublin Pipers Club, where years later he taught and inspired many of the leading pipers of the modern age, Liam Og O'Flynn and Paddy Moloney included. He died suddenly at 67 in 1970, but his legacy remains huge and his name revered all over Ireland. I hold my breath. 'Are you related … to …

Leo Rowsome?' 'Yes,' he smiles, 'he was my grandfather.' The Guinness goes flying. 'Oh my God, what was he *like*?' 'Well, I was only seven when he died, but I'd say he was jovial. That'd be the word I'd use … *jovial*.' 'He was some piper, wasn't he?' 'Yes, he was, and he was also a great pipe *maker*. He made this set of pipes, actually.' I touch them adoringly. 'So I guess you had no choice,' I say, 'you know, being born into such a dynasty, you must have come out of the womb playing the pipes.' 'Actually no, it was my choice. It was never forced on me and I gave it up for a while. You know, in my teens, you get other interests. My friends weren't into it and it just wasn't fashionable to play then. But in time I came back to it and now it's *very* fashionable.' 'You don't play professionally?' 'No, I work in computers.' Oh. That's a conversation-stopper.

In The Cobblestone we also meet Kathleen, who's ranting about proposed new laws to ban smoking in pubs and restaurants. 'You come into the pub for a drink and a smoke, don't you?' Well, I don't smoke but … 'Where's the harm in it?' Well, I guess lung cancer is quite harmful … 'I mean, how are they going to enforce it? If you light up is the barman going to leap over the bar and tell you to put it out? You'd just tell him to feck off, wouldn't you? Or will they have gardai patrolling round to try and catch people smoking in pubs? *I don't think so*! I mean, restaurants already have no smoking areas but the smoke just drifts over to them anyway, so it's pointless, isn't it?' It's certainly a point of view, Kathleen. She tells us she now lives in Greystones, along the coast in Wicklow, where one of her neighbours is Ronnie Drew of The Dubliners, but she was raised in this Smithfield area of Dublin. 'In those days it was very poor and you had to move out of Dublin to better yourself. Now you move *in* to better yourself. But you're lucky if you can afford it now. The price of property in Dublin now! Unbelievable!' We talk about music in the area when she was growing up. 'Oh, there was loads of music in them days. They used to have all sorts of music in this pub. There'd be somebody on the piano and people would get up and do their party pieces. I went round all the pubs after Holy Communion, made loads of money!' Did you hear any traditional music? 'Oh, the main place for traditional music would have been Slattery's up the road. They'd have it upstairs. You wouldn't dare *breathe* in there, they took it very seriously, so they did.'

I pass Slattery's that night on what turns out to be a bit of a pub crawl. I'd bought *The Dubliner* magazine seeking inspiration from its 'DUBLIN'S 12 BEST BARS' front page strap and I'm wondering if there's time to fit in all of them when I come across a picture of Paddy Moloney with the Corr sisters. The heading says 'Local Man Paddy

Moloney Meets The Stars', but then goes on to describe Ireland's most famous uilleann piper as a fiddle player. If *The Dubliner* doesn't know what instrument Paddy Moloney plays by now then I'm certainly not going to trust its opinion about the best twelve bars in the city. I head back along a bustling O'Connell Street with its smell of burger bars and the hum of mobile phones and pause outside the luxurious Gresham Hotel. I've stayed here a couple of times, once on a junket to interview Joan Baez, and behaved rather badly. We were dining in the Gresham restaurant and I started abusing her hospitality, accusing her of selling out by staying in such a plush hotel and entertaining the press to lavish dinners when she was meant to be saving the world and bringing world peace. Which was a bit rich on reflection. 'If I am to perform to my best I need somewhere comfortable to relax and prepare properly,' she'd replied coolly. Which was fair enough really.

The Gresham was also the venue of the Mary Coughlan Incident. They don't come much more colourful than Mary. Raised in Galway, she suffered abuse and depression as a child and starting bunking off mass at 12 for a sneaky fag behind the bicycle sheds; she's been a rebel ever since. A feisty redhead, she shocked the good citizens of Limerick by posing nude at the local art college before moving to London, where she lived in a squat and embarked on a career as Ealing's first female roadsweeper. 'It was great,' she told me once, 'people used to invite me into their houses for crackers and a cold beer – it was thirsty work sweeping the roads.' In the end she went home to Ireland, married a teacher, had three kids in six years ... and that's when the fun really began. She met Dutch songwriter Erik Visser, who persuaded her to enter a talent contest singing his songs. She was so upset about being beaten by a girl who sang 'Silver Threads & Golden Needles' at the contest she threw the trophy at the judges and stomped out. By the age of 29 she was separated, but armed with Visser's songs, a smokily seductive voice and an obsessive passion for the music of Billie Holiday, she recorded her self-financed first album *Tired And Emotional*. It launched not only her career as a folk-blues-jazz-pop singer, but also her career as an establishment pain in the arse. She shocked middle Ireland by appearing on Gay Byrne's *Late Late Show* telly programme, advocating the decriminalisation of cannabis and campaigned noisily as a pro-divorce reformer. She was never shy of attacking the Catholic Church's attitude over birth control and abortion either.

She'd already gained quite a reputation as a carouser by the time I met her at the Gresham Hotel – she'd once famously thrown a pint of beer over the brilliant De Dannan fiddle player Frankie Gavin. On this occasion I was staying at the Gresham. Mary wasn't. Which was all well and good for a while. We sat in the hotel bar getting nicely tanked up and gossiping like a couple of old fishwives, getting the teeniest bit raucous as the bar gradually emptied until we were the last two left standing. It was an early hours job when Mary summoned the long-suffering young barman for another round. The barman, bless him, said he was perfectly happy to serve me – a resident of the hotel – but it would be more than his job's worth to serve my guest, a non-resident. Mary tried guile, charm, persuasion, bribes, threats … only stopping short of the 'Do you know who I am?' tactic. When he still refused to serve her she hit the roof. She let him have it with both barrels, a volley of oaths and obscenities delivered at full velocity that must have made the old Gresham think it was 1916 all over again. The young barman stood before her, unflinching as the insults and profanities kept on flying at him in a momentous tirade. When, finally, the eruption subsided, he merely smiled thinly, looked Mary in the eye and said, 'Ms Coughlan, I'm a very great admirer of your music, but not your manners. Would you be so kind as to leave the hotel now please?' She departed without a whimper.

That was also the night Mary revealed the secret of 'Ride On', one of Christy Moore's most popular songs and the first big song written by Jimmy MacCarthy. The horse metaphor is an obvious one for MacCarthy is a Cork man who, with a bit more luck, might have been a top jockey. He'd trained at the legendary Vincent O'Brien's stable in Tipperary, where he'd even got to work out on two of the greatest Derby winners of all time, Sir Ivor and Nijinsky. Instead, he turned to songwriting and 'Ride On' quickly took on a life of its own. The song's dark sub-text and haunting chorus has inspired a deep network of myth and mystery intensified by the refusal of Christy – or indeed Jimmy MacCarthy himself – to discuss its brooding meaning. When Christy Moore played a concert in London in 2002 one dipstick reviewer described the song as 'a simple elegy to a horse'. I mean, you don't get lines like 'When you ride into the night without a trace behind/Run the claw along my gut one last time' in simple elegies to horses. Reviewers, huh? In his own book *Ride On*, MacCarthy throws only partial light on it. 'It's a song about parting … the parting of lovers … emigrants … when illness or accident takes the life of a loved one …' But, admittedly in her cups, Mary Coughlan told me that night in the Gresham Hotel that she'd felt compelled to cover 'Ride On' when MacCarthy told her what had inspired him to write the song. And three sheets to the wind or no, I felt compelled to hear the story too. 'He was having a relationship with a woman and she became involved in a political party, which is the horse of eyes with flashing green, so that's obviously a nationalist party, possibly the IRA. He couldn't handle it so he told her to ride on.' I decide I want 'Ride On' played at my funeral. Straight after 'No Woman No Cry'.

Mary Coughlan spent most of her 30s in an alcoholic haze. She admits she was drinking two or three bottles of vodka or tequila a day and she hit rock bottom when her career began to falter, she went broke, lost her home, suffered a miscarriage and ended up in hospital fighting for her life. 'I felt lower than a sewer pipe. I hated myself and I hated everyone else,' she later told a BBC documentary on booze. In 1993 she went into rehab at Dublin's Rutland Centre and happily has managed to stay off the drink ever since and put her career back on track.

I end up evading the seething mass of Temple Bar and head through Grafton St towards St Stephens Green, with a fond glance sideways at the beautiful people filing into Lillie's Bordello. It's a swanky club clearly not designed for the likes of me, though they have foolishly allowed me in before. The band Altan had an album launch party there once, but kicked us out when it was time for the clubbers to come in and shake their tail feathers. Not that this diverted us from the serious business of the evening for long, oh no. In no time at all we'd reassembled at a pub on the quayside called the Fisherman's something or other that isn't there any more and the whole place was a swarm of sessions in all the endless nooks and crannies of the place. The doors were locked and Altan and their chums settled down for a long glorious night of music and drink. I was already feeling no pain well into the early hours when there was a bit of a kerfuffle at the front area. Bodhrans were put to rest, fiddles were laid in their cases, conversation ceased and something so profound occurred at the front door that even *drinks* were put down. 'It's the Peelers,' said the new best mate I'd never seen before or since. Sod's law, there's never a Venezuelan ambassador around when you need diplomatic immunity. 'Oh hang on,' he said, 'it's not the Peelers, it's … .' and he suddenly let out this extraordinary chasping noise (that's a cross between a choke and a gasp). At the front of a herd of people there was a grinning Paddy Moloney, shaking hands and hugging everyone in his path as he made his way to the bar. I could make out various other Chieftains with him, but who were those other guys with the long hair and the swagger? Only Mick, Sir Keef and Ronnie Wood. 'Jaysus, I must be pissed, I thought I saw the Rolling Stones there for a minute,' said my mate. 'No, you're all right,' I said, 'it *is* the Rolling Stones.' Paddy Moloney has long mixed with popes, presidents and princes (though I don't think he's ever met Prince) and on this occasion the Chieftains had been recording their uproarious version of *Rocky Road To Dublin* with the Stones for 'Long Black Veil', one of several albums with a glittering list of guest stars. We gawped for a minute or two, waved at them like eejits and returned to the pint in hand. 'I'm so happy it's them,' said my mate, 'I really thought they were Peelers.'

On an even hazier night at another time I was in this same place with Bono. I'd come to interview U2 on the eve of the release of their greatest album, *The Joshua Tree*. I found them in the studio playing, not one of their own songs, but 'Springhill Mining Disaster', a harrowing Peggy Seeger song detailing the horrors of a pit explosion in Nova Scotia in the 1950s. I wasn't sure why U2 were rehearsing it (they were later to perform it live) but Bono was giving it all the shapes and faces like he was back at Live Aid. There he was, throwing his head around, stomping his foot, waggling his arse. At one point I thought he was going to jump into the audience, which could have been a trifle embarrassing as the audience consisted of, well, just me actually. I mean, don't get me wrong, it's a rare and lovely thing all right, but it is a bit surreal to be standing there with Bono giving it the full 'Good evening, Colin, are you READY TO ROCK'n'ROLL?' I just pretended to be doing up my shoe-lace. Happily, he finished the song and said 'Fancy a drink?' and off we went. It turned into quite a session. 'Hello, Bono, you were shite on *Top Of The Pops* the other day,' said a docker as we elbowed our way to the bar. 'It certainly keeps you grounded, living in Dublin,' said Bono with a smile as we settled down to watch the boxing on telly and discuss the pressing matters of the day, such as how sexy female soldiers look in their uniforms in Nicaragua and the dangers of looking a complete arsehole on stage ('I do go a bit over the top sometimes, don't I? I just can't stop myself ...'). You have to respect U2. They weren't the first Irish band to become international stars, but they were the first who made a conscious decision to remain in Ireland when it was such a backwater of the music industry and that decision alone contributed significantly to a resurgent sense of cultural identity. We sank several pints that night and I must have been making no sense at all by the end of it, because Bono phoned me later at my hotel to make sure I'd made it back safely. I wonder if he does that when he goes out for a pint with all those presidents he harangues about the Third World Debt.

Paddy Moloney was indirectly responsible for my one other appearance at Lillie's Bordello. Another album, another junket, this time in 1999 for the launch of The Chieftains' *Tears Of Stone* album, which featured The Chieftains collaborating with different women artists. Among them were The Corrs, then at the peak of their initial rise to fame, who Paddy had wheeled in to perform the old warhorse 'I Know My Love'. 'It was very weird,' Andrea Corr told me, 'he sent us a tape of this funny old female voice singing this folk song and said "Do you think you can do it?" We listened to it and we couldn't stop laughing. We just looked at each other and said, What the hell is *that*?' It transpires the tape had been of Mary O'Hara, the Sligo harpist/singer, who became a teenage star, only to give it all up to join a convent for twelve years after the sudden death of her husband, the American poet Richard Selig, after just 15 months of marriage. While I was talking to Andrea I noticed her doodling on a bit of paper, which she shyly presented to me as I left. 'I drew a picture of you,' she said and signed it. It was rubbish. I stared at it for a while. 'Oh no,' she said, 'I hope I haven't offended you.' 'Of course not, I shall treasure it always,' I said. In fact that drawing served me well. It always broke the ice at dinner parties. 'Do you want to see Andrea Corr's portrait of me?' I'd say smugly. 'Wow, you met Andrea Corr? Is she as … *you know* … in the *flesh*?' 'Oh God yes,' I'd say knowingly. '*More*.' I really should have kept that drawing – I could have shown it to you here – but it disappeared down the back of the settee in a cloud of Bushmills one night and I haven't seen it since. That evening The Chieftains and The Corrs played a little showcase set together at Dublin Castle and we all adjourned to Lillie's Bordello after for a nightcap. Well, when I say *all* … it was just me and this other bloke and Jim Corr. 'Jim can buy the drinks, he's just sold five million albums,' said This Other Bloke, a tad unsubtly, I thought. 'Actually,' said Jim, passing his credit card to the barman, 'it's six million.'

It's late now, but I press on into the historic musical heartlands of Baggot St. If they're not roaring long into the night up here, my name is Jennifer. The Baggot Inn is closed, *writes Jennifer*. Refurbishment. The smoky Doheny & Nesbitts is seething but there's not a whiff of music. No worries, 'tis but a gentle canter to O'Donoghue's, perhaps Dublin's most famous traditional music pub of all. Last time I was here you couldn't even get into the pub it was so rammed, but we found a paving stone in the courtyard where a miked-up wannabe Christy Moore entertained us and a helpful barman ferried the drinks. There was a rugby scrum going on in the main bar, which had its own music. It was like a miniature Glastonbury in there that night.

It was at the turn of the 1960s that a motley collection of actors and cohorts from The Gate Theatre starting assembling for a jar and a few tunes in the back room of Paddy O'Donoghue's pub in Merrion Row. They started there because, well, it was the only place that would tolerate them. Ronnie Drew, who'd already been an electrician, a dishwasher and a telephone operator, had recently returned to Ireland after three years in Spain, where he'd taught English, learned flamenco guitar and become fluent in Spanish. The actor John Molloy had got him involved in productions at The Gate and after the shows Drew naturally felt the need for a jar and a sing. The sessions at O'Donoghue's gradually became quite an attraction, with Barney McKenna, already an inspirational banjo player accompanying Drew, along with Irish-speaking guitarist/singer/whistle player Cairan Bourke. Luke Kelly, a charismatic red-haired guitarist/banjo player and singer from the Dockside area, suggested they call themselves The Dubliners, after the James Joyce book. While Kelly was in and out of the band they recruited John Sheahan, a classically trained violinist who would initially just play a few tunes during their 'porter break'.

The rest is history. Sort of. They all had beards, drank copious amounts, knew a lot of ballads and how to give an audience a good time. Very loudly. The only thing they didn't have was Aran sweaters. Subtlety has never been their game and you can bet every song ever associated with folk music by the big mad world would have been sung at one point by The Dubliners. Very loudly. 'The Wild Rover', 'I'll Tell Me Ma', 'All For Me Grog', 'Rocky Road To Dublin', 'Whiskey In The Jar', 'Black Velvet Band', 'Irish Rover', 'Finnegan's Wake', 'Leaving Of Liverpool' and, of course, 'Seven Drunken Nights'. Very loudly. 'I had never seen such a collection of hairy people in my life,' said Billy Connolly famously of his first encounter with them in Glasgow. 'I'd never seen energy like Luke Kelly, I'd never heard a voice as extraordinary as Ronnie Drew's, I'd never heard banjo playing as amazing as Barney McKenna's and Cairan Bourke looked like a gypsy from one of his own songs who was quite likely to run off with your girlfriend if you didn't keep a close eye on him.' They were an antidote to the relatively sanitised balladeering of the Clancy Brothers and you could almost smell the O'Donoghue's sawdust on them when Ronnie Drew – with the fiercest Dublin accent in captivity and a throat that sounded like petrol and sandpaper – led the boys into one raucous, nerve-shattering bar-room chorus after another. Girlfriends were indeed kept under lock and key in 1967 when 'Seven Drunken Nights' mysteriously appeared in the British charts. It owed its success to the pirate station Radio Caroline, which happened to be run by an Irishman, Rohan O'Rahilly. Some real oddball tracks crept on the Caroline playlist between the otherwise uncompromising diet of poperama … the odd Neville Dicky piano tune; the unbearably sensitive 'Days Of Pearly Spencer' by singer-songwriter David McWilliams; some wretched piece of nonsense by Freddie 'Parrot Face' Davies … and 'Seven Drunken Nights'. A reflection of O'Rahilly's eccentric musical taste? Nah, more a reflection of cold, harsh economics. Caroline relied on advertising, hand-outs and sponsorship and one of its sponsors was Major Minor, the label that had signed The Dubliners following an introduction by Brendan Behan's brother Dominic. The result was wall-to-wall airplay for 'Seven Drunken Nights'. The other great wheeze Caroline introduced was its own chart based on … well, nothing at all, really. Just whatever they fancied sticking in it while they were washing their smalls out in the North Sea. So, suddenly The Dubliners were riding high in the Radio Caroline chart as well. Just as well, because nobody was playing their record on the mainland. It had been banned. RTE said the ideas nurtured in the song – blokes coming home so bladdered they didn't even realise their wives were playing ping pong under the sheets with other men – was not acceptable listening for the pure people of Ireland. Unlike the wife in the song, The Dubliners didn't take it lying down and even made an official appeal to the Taoiseach of the day, Jack Lynch, to intervene, denying (one thinks with tongue firmly in cheek) that the song was 'in any way suggestive'. They might also have added that they'd got the song from another O'Donoghue's regular of the time, the great Connemara *sean-nos* singer Joe Heaney, whose Irish-language version had been played on RTE with no questions asked. It cut no ice with Jack, though, who tossed their complaint straight in the bin. In fact, although the song is called '*Seven* Drunken Nights', you only ever hear The Dubliners sing about *five* of them. Imagine what might have befallen the puritan values of Ireland had they been exposed to the events of the missing two nights. Ban or no ban, Caroline had done its job and The Dubs were off marauding around Europe, terrorising Billy Connolly's girlfriends with their beards. Tales of their mad behaviour abound and there was the odd arrest too. Terry Woods tells the story of the time The Pogues and The Dubliners were together in Derry. After a not entirely sober night, Barney McKenna offered to do the driving. What he didn't realise was that he was driving an *automatic* car. Every time he put his foot on what he thought was the clutch the car screeched to a shuddering halt. They'd got 200 yards up the road (very slowly) when the RUC rounded them up and threw them all in the cells for the night to sleep it off. Ronnie Drew woke up in the night to take a leak, stumbled into the bucket in the corner and shook McKenna urgently. 'Jayzus, what sort of feckin' hotel have you booked us into now?'

Not that it's all been a barrel of laughs. Cairan Bourke and Luke Kelly both collapsed on stage with brain tumours and are no longer with us, and the personnel has changed along the way, with Ronnie Drew in and out of the band at various times. But after forty years they're still at it and worth a pint at O'Donoghue's.

I'm still across the road from O'Donoghue's when I hear the

singing from an upstairs bar. The courtyard is empty and there doesn't seem a whole lot going on downstairs either, but the singing is deafening as I climb the stairs and I look forward to flinging the door open to discover the latest stars of tomorrow or maybe even the ghosts of The Dubliners, circa 1962. I find neither. Just a bunch of pissed-up blokes in suits and ties having a crude sing-song. They sound awful, but they're big chaps too, so I avoid mentioning it when we fall into conversation. In fact, I avoid falling into conversation at all. They look like Peelers. Or rugby players. When they start grinding out 'Ole Man River' there's a huge rumble as Paul Robeson turns in his grave and I make my excuses and leave. Downstairs there's a quiet session going on and The Dubliners memorabilia on the walls keeps me amused for a bit, but it's been a long, hard day and I decide to retire to the tranquil sanctuary of my hotel fit for priests.

That's the plan anyway. A kerfuffle greets me at Wynns. There's a gardai car, a shattered glass window and a man with a pair of knickers on his head. A night porter is only too keen to explain what happened. An elderly guy turned up wearing a skirt, a bra and a pair of knickers on his head, announced he was Jesus and said he fancied a drink. When the staff denied him entry he punched a hole in the window. 'I dragged him off and he bit me!' said the porter, showing red teeth marks on his arm. 'Who was he?' I said. 'Well, he said he was Jesus ...' Hmmm, could he have been lying? 'Yeah, I heard he's actually a rich man who lives in a big house.' 'You want to get that bite looked at, he could have AIDS,' says Mrs Colin sensibly. Jesus in a skirt and bra at Wynns Hotel, whatever next? I guess we now know what attracts all the priests.

I'm still in a bit of a daze wandering around Dublin the next day. I always get goose pimples passing the Post Office, site of the 1916 Uprising and looking at the monument to Parnell above the proclamation 'No man has a right to fix the boundary to the march of a nation. No man has a right to say to his country Thus far shalt thou go and no further.' It inspires profound emotions ... so much history, so much bloodshed, so much pain, so much intolerance. And then I catch sight of Bertie's Pole and the spell is broken. Dublin's big on statues. They've even got one to Father Matthew, who apparently persuaded five million Irish people to take a pledge of teetotalism in the mid-nineteenth century. Just think of the legless stag parties dancing around the statue on a Saturday night as the revenge of the immoral majority, Father Matthew. Worst Statue Award, though, goes to the one of Molly Malone – 'tart with a cart' – in Grafton Street. It depicts her with saucy expression and suggestively low-cut dress, giving credence to the legend that while Molly sold cockles and mussels by day, she sold more intimate favours by night. I always thought the whole Molly Malone, cockles and mussels thing was a bit of a laugh. A ludicrously melodramatic song for schoolkids to sing and a story without basis in reality. A song also credited with having been written by James Yorkston, a Scotsman. But you can't keep the Irish away from a good legend and they take her tale seriously enough in this neck of the woods, claiming church records show the baptism of a Mary Malone on July 27, 1663, and a subsequent burial of the same person 36 years later are proof of her existence. Some academic even researched the story and reached the conclusion that the real Molly Malone was actually Peg Woffington, the mistress of King Charles II, and cockles and mussels were really metaphors for ladies' naughty bits. Don't go telling Sinead O'Connor it's all a load of rubbish either. She recorded a heartfelt version of the song on her *Sean-Nos Nua* album and talks passionately of evoking the ghost of the heroine while she was singing it. 'This is going to sound slightly bats,' Sinead tells me, 'but in the studio singing some of these songs is a bit like working as a medium. I move my personality aside and allow these people to come into me. I let the spirit use my body and do the talking.' You're right Sinead, it *does* sound bats. 'Well, since I was a child I've always been fascinated by the psychic world. I believe everyone has the ability to communicate with the spirit world and everyone is psychic, it's like a sense we can all develop. I lived in England for 15 years and trained on and off in psychic studies as a medium and got to under-stand a lot more about it. A lot of these songs are about the everlastingness of the soul.' Yeah, but 'Molly Malone', it's still cheesy, isn't it, Sinead? 'It might be cheesy if it weren't so chillingly *great*! It's just because of the way it's always been done, which is nothing to do with the song itself. When you get into the real character of Molly Malone and let the real spirit of the song speak then something very powerful happens. There's a person inside that song who will pull you in.' I gaze at Molly Malone's cockles and mussels for a few more seconds with renewed respect and move on.

The next day embraces a stroll around the beautiful Georgian buildings of Merrion Square and its surreal array of brightly coloured doors. The jaunty little statue of Oscar Wilde leaning provocatively against a rock at one corner of the park, plaques to the former homes of eminent residents, such as Daniel O'Connell, Austrian Nobel Prizewinner Erwin Schrödinger, painter George Russell and, two doors away from the current offices of the Football Association of Ireland, WB Yeats. Just a bit further along you find the splendid Irish Traditional Music Archive with its glorious library and a vast archive of mouthwatering recordings of many old legends of

Irish music that are seldom heard. I feel almost pious being in among all this literary and cultural splendour, but that's nothing to the feeling on a return to Merrion Square later on for the Dublin murder walk. Apart from the obvious trips to the Guinness factory and the open-topped bus around the city, any number of alternative walking tours await your attention. The literary pub crawl, the James Joyce pub crawl, the musical pub crawl, the pub crawl, the ghost tour … ultimately it really doesn't make much difference which one you choose, they all end up with you getting slaughtered in some bar at the end of it. In fact the murder walk doesn't seem desperately popular. There are just four of us on it. But that doesn't dampen the enthusiasm of the two acting students who lead us around St Stephen's Green and Merrion Square detailing ever more gruesome murders that occurred at different residences along the way. '36-year-old Geraldine Brady was walking along this very path on her way home at 11pm after an argument with her boyfriend, who she'd discovered had been sleeping with a younger woman …' says one of our students with cod drama. 'She was just walking past this point when she thought she heard something moving in the bushes …' Suddenly there's a bloodcurdling yell and his mate comes flying out of a tree and pretends to stab Mrs Colin. It gives her quite a turn, I can tell you. However, as the tour progresses and more and more bizarre tales of bloodcurdling murders unfold, we get wise to the idea that one of them suddenly sprinting ahead into the shadows could be the cue for an ever unlikelier re-enactment of some hideous slaying. It's hugely entertaining for all that and ends, as most things do in Dublin, in a hostelry. 'There seem to have been an awful lot of murders in this area of Dublin through the years,' I say innocently. 'Actually,' says one of them, without a trace of embarrassment, 'we made a lot of them up.'

There are always more pubs to explore in search of the craic. The Brazen Head looks promising. 'I haven't been in there in years, since they introduced pumps,' says my friend Tom. 'But they have music in there?' 'It used to be good but it's for the tourists now, don't go near it.' 'But it says it's the oldest pub in Ireland …' 'Oh jeez, there are 40 "oldest pubs in Ireland".You can't move for the feckers …' He points me instead at Hughes's bar which, with enormous difficulty, I eventually find in a back street behind the Four Courts. There's a gentle session going on in the main bar, but I'm distracted by the sound of 'The Mason's Apron' from behind the bar. I assume it's a cassette and ask the barman what it is. 'That? Oh, that's the lads …' 'Lads?' 'Yeah, the lads in the snug.' He directs me to the snug and I join them. It's very laid-back and informal, led by an accomplished fiddler, who's flanked by a girl on whistle, a bloke on mandola and the inevitable Japanese fiddle player. So many Japanese are in Ireland playing Irish music, I now have this vision of Tokyo as one big long St Patrick's Night hoolie. It's just me and three other people looking at the fiddle player telling jokes to his companions and I feel like a lemon until he suddenly launches into an impromptu pub quiz. 'Name the cowboy who rode Trigger?' he asks. Which totally stumps the Japanese fiddle player, obviously. And everyone else. 'Roy Rogers!' I yell from the back. 'YES!' says Chris Tarrant and suddenly I'm the toast of Hughes's snug. Drinks are bought, sandwiches are passed round, smiles are restored and conversations burst forth. We end up having a merry old time but when they invite me to sing I explain that I must urgently return to the priests' hotel because they're expecting an attack from an old man called Jesus wearing a skirt and bra with a pair of knickers on his head. They understand completely. They slap me on the back and send me on my way.

I spend several days in Dublin and the craic is indeed mighty. There's a memorable, if sauna-esque evening at Whelan's in Wexford Street where we go to see the Canadian girl band, the Be Good Tanyas. First shock of the night involves battling to the bar and finding myself squeezed behind a seven-foot guy in a strange raincoat and a hat straight out of a Buster Keaton movie draped inconveniently over the bar. 'Excuse me ...' I say ultra-politely, for we are talking gargantuan here. He doesn't move a muscle. I tap him lightly on the shoulder. No response whatsoever. 'EXCUSE ME!' I say in a tone that I think has just about the right undertone of menace and pat him on the shoulder. It feels oddly cold. With a raging thirst I decide this is no time for niceties and elbow him out of the way. Except he doesn't budge. Thankfully the guy to my left vacates the bar and I take his place, swiftly submitting my order before turning to give the big feller a glare he wouldn't forget in a hurry. I look him straight in the eye. Well, I would have done if he had any. Yep, another statue. Right there in the middle of the bar at Whelan's. I turn round to find the amused regulars bursting into a spontaneous bout of applause. Still, if you can't beat 'em ... I join them against the wall to snigger as another hapless victim begins to queue up behind the big feller. I find a square inch upstairs and am immediately engaged in a bout of life-swapping with the woman in the next square inch. 'They have some great things at Whelan's, you know ... you'll never guess who played a secret gig down here a couple of weeks ago ...' 'Er, Tommy Peoples?' 'Who?' 'Tommy Peop ... forget it, who was it?' 'Christy Moore! Totally unannounced. I was right down the front, it was fantastic.' 'A secret gig, you say?' 'Yep. Nobody knew about it at all.' 'So the place was empty then, was it?' 'No, it was rammed. You couldn't swing a cat.'

This night at Whelan's proves memorable in its own way too. You may be wondering how the Be Good Tanyas got their name. It transpires they took it from the title of a song written by a friend. A friend from California who now lives in Galway. And guess what? He's here tonight to play for you, because *this is your life*. The writer of 'Be Good Tanya' turns out to be a very peculiar specimen indeed called Obo Martin. He comes on stage in a green mask with bright orange hair held together in an oddball array of bunches, with matching orange shirt and beard, stripey kipper tie and mad green loon pants. He leaps around, hollers his head off and makes me laugh with his surreal songs which he tends to write – he tells us animatedly – on the roof of Jury's Hotel in Galway. The place is in uproar. I glance across and see the eyes of my friend the secret Christy Moore gig lover on stalks and that big feller at the back, I'm sure I saw him leaning against the bar a minute ago.

There's one more place we must visit before leaving Dublin – Na Píobairí Uilleann or, to put it another way, the Association of Uilleann Pipers. There was a time not too long ago that the complicated art of piping, and pipemaking, appeared to be gulping its sorry last breaths. Even as recently as 1968 the association had just fifty members. Now it has 2,300. So off we roam into one of the murkier corners of Dublin, where we suddenly stumble across the sedate oasis of Henrietta Street, home of Na Píobairí Uilleann. Except we walk past it three times. It looks just like one of those Georgian houses one of the actors would leap out from before unfolding some ludicrous tale of jealousy, death and intrigue on the murder walk. Only a modest plaque on the door gives any clue to the glories inside. We knock nervously, the door creaks open and a man sits inside taking money. 'Are y'here for the recital?' Oh yes, we are, and climb the stairs to the recital room to prove it. Tonight's recital features the fiddle player Kevin Glackin – younger brother of original Bothy Band fiddle player Paddy – and Sean Og Potts, son of the ex-Chieftains whistle player, also called Sean. The walls are full of lovely pictures of old pipers, they're serving coffee and biscuits in the kitchen and the music is unconditionally wonderful. 'My father used to spend all his time in the kitchen going through O'Neill's book,' says Glackin, 'he wasn't a man for the television.' Sean Potts' dad is here, gently wisecracking at the back and interspersing the music with cries of 'Good lad' and 'That's beautiful, Kevin' and is eventually invited on stage to join them. 'Oh!' says dad. 'I wasn't expecting to play ... that's why I brought my whistle with me.'

It transpires Sean Snr is president of Na Píobairí Uilleann and has played a major role in its resurrection as Ireland's piping centre. He left The Chieftains in 1979 and quite consciously resolved to dedicate the rest of his life to the pipes. 'We need a new roof here like, but it's all going grand,' he tells me. I'd first interviewed him on the phone several centuries earlier while he was working for the Post Office. 'So Sean, tell me how you started playing the tin whistle,' I'd asked. 'Right,' he said, 'it was like this … can you hang on there for a moment, I have a customer to serve.' There'd be a pause of several minutes and he'd return. 'Now what was I saying?' 'You were telling me how you got started on the tin whistle, Sean …' 'Oh that's right, I was, wasn't I? Well, it all began when …' pause ' … can you hold on there for a second, I'll just serve this gentleman …' And it went on like that for a couple of hours. After travelling round the world with The Chieftains and enjoying global adulation, the travelling took its toll and he decided to quit after one particularly terrifying plane journey in Nova Scotia and, unbelievably, went back to his old job in the Post Office. 'You must be proud of your son,' I say. 'Oh, I am and I don't mind telling you that he's a fine lad and a fine piper,' he says, as Sean Og cringes in the background. Sean also tells a good anecdote about Sean O'Riada, the godfather of modern Irish music with whom Sean played in Ceoltoiri Chualann. 'He didn't have a penny to his name in those days,' he says of O'Riada. 'He had no furniture or carpet on the floor – you were affluent then if you had a carpet. I was playing something that wasn't to his satisfaction and he'd be drawing diagrams and parallelograms on the floor to explain what he wanted me to do. I didn't know what he was talking about, so I just nodded and played it again and he'd go "That's very good, that's much better, Sean, you've really got it" and I'd be convinced I'd played exactly the same way as I'd played before.'

We finish our coffee and biscuits, shake hands with everyone in the room about fifteen times, stare at those glorious pictures on the walls a bit more, and start to leave, telling anyone who'll listen how much I adore the pipes. Then I hear a voice through the crowd. 'Are you going to the festival?' I swing round. 'Festival? What festival?' 'The Johnny Doran piping festival … it's up in the Wicklow Mountains at the weekend, are you coming?' Cancel that boat ticket, I'm on my way to Wicklow …

Chapter twelve

WICKLOW: PIPES, SEAMUS, SIOBHAN AND ... TOMMY PEOPLES, I PRESUME

One week left in Ireland. So much unseen. So much unsaid. There's still porter to be drunk. Songs to be sung. Tales to be told. Tommy Peoples to be found. And I still think the mother of all craics is sitting out there somewhere with my name on it. Let's go find it ...

SATURDAY/SUNDAY: *Glendalough, Wicklow Mountains, Co. Wicklow*
Johnny Doran was a travelling man from a travelling family. A colourful family, too, well-known all over Ireland for their larger-than-life personalities and a very special musical pedigree. Johnny's great grandfather was John Cash, a horse dealer from Wexford whose passionate uilleann piping and powerful character turned him into one of Ireland's great musical icons of the nineteenth century. Johnny's dad, also called John, was a respected piper too and the family moved around – living in England for some years – before moving to Dublin.

It was quite a legacy, then, that Johnny Doran inherited when he was born in Rathnew, in Wicklow, in 1908. Taught to play the pipes as a kid by his father and other members of the family, Johnny embraced the life of a travelling piper in his early 20s. Every spring he'd set off from Dublin with his horse-drawn caravan and head for Clare or Galway or Cavan or Longford or Monaghan or Donegal or wherever there was a fair or a race meeting or a hurling match. In fact, wherever a crowd gathered, Johnny Doran was likely to be there, playing his pipes in the fast, wild style with which he has become synonymous. They say he'd use the pipes to attract a crowd and once he'd got them in the palm of his hand he'd switch from piper to horse trader and flog them horses.

When times got tough – notably during the Second World War and the infamous winter of 1947 – Johnny found alternative ways of making ends meet, for a period working as a bricklayer's mate with his friend, the Roscommon piper Andy Conroy. But he was born to the road and seldom stayed in one place for long. Other musicians flocked to hear him. Many sessions were held in his caravan parked around the country and his highly individual, intense and emotional playing inspired a generation of pipers, notably the great Willie Clancy, who followed him from house dances to horse fairs.

Lots of legends followed him around too. They reckoned he was in the habit of sneaking out of his caravan at the dead of night to play in a field for 'the fairies'. Other times he would disappear into a tiny yellow tent. But he was highly acclaimed and often well-paid. It's said he could also make a lot of money busking. He had a highly unconventional style, standing up as he played, one foot resting on his pipe case. Followers said he was a revelation every time you saw him because he never played a tune the same way twice, constantly changing the rhythm patterns, using the regulators far more than anyone else.

Pat Mitchell, himself no mean piper, thinks Doran can be compared to innovative jazz greats like Charlie Parker and Dizzy Gillespie – 'people driven by the music to push the boundaries and pile variation on top of variation'.

And yet, for a subsequent generation, his fame was great but his music was largely inaccessible. Sean McBride, leader of the Clann na Poblachta political party, had seen Johnny playing in the streets of Dublin and invited him to perform at the party's big election rally at College Green. Johnny parked his caravan beside a high factory wall in Back Lane in the Christchurch area of Dublin prior to the rally. But on New Year's Day, 1948, Johnny was standing outside the van when the brick wall collapsed on top of him.

Johnny survived – *just* – but he was paralysed. They say his spine was irreparably damaged as rescuers desperately tried to pull him from the rubble. Propped up on cushions he could still play the pipes and attempted to resume his old life, but physically he couldn't cope any more. He died on January 19, 1950, at the age of 42 and was buried at Rathnew Cemetery.

For most people it seemed his music was lost too. Incredibly he only ever had one recording session – making nine acetates for the Irish Folklore Commission at their offices in Earlsfort Terrace in 1947. For many years those recordings were only available to a few, the legend all the greater for the inaccessibility of the music.

So when they told me in Dublin about the Johnny Doran Piping

Weekend in the Wicklow Mountains I knew I had to go. The fact that they were using the event to launch the first ever Doran CD was the icing on the cake.

Less than an hour's drive south of Dublin, the Wicklow Mountains are one of Ireland's many great wonders. The steeper you get the wilder and more evocative it all becomes. You can certainly imagine them being a haven for rebels and you can imagine, too, why in 1800 the British built the Military Road through the heart of the mountains to try and flush them out. Small wonder they shot much of the *Michael Collins* movie round these parts. That Military Road is still the primary access to the area leading you on an unpredictable twisting journey with an 'ooh aah' view around every corner. There are walking trails all over the place, a wilderness of moorland stretching as far as they eye can see, forests, waterfalls, loughs, the distinctly eerie Sally Gap pass and, yes, pubs too. This is serious fantasy land.

It's early evening when we finally scale the summit and arrive at Glendalough. The prospects of a B&B aren't looking good. 'No Vacancy' signs abound and when I do find a guesthouse with vacancies the door is opened just a few inches by a crabby-looking old woman. 'Do you have any vacancies for tonight?' 'Are y'with the festival?' she responds abruptly. 'Not exactly but ...' 'Are y'here for them pipers?' 'I suppose so ...' I stammer. She opens the door slightly wider and as I relax and prepare to step in, she snaps 'We're full!' and slams the door in my face.

We eventually find a guesthouse a couple of miles away. It's in a secluded lane by a babbling brook ... and boy, does this brook babble! I have bleeding ears after a short chat with the brook about life, the universe, everything. 'Wise brook,' I say, 'I come in search of Tommy Peoples.' 'Oh come on,' says the brook, 'does Tommy Peoples look the sort of guy who talks to babbling brooks?'

We find the large Glendalough Hotel, centre of proceedings for the Doran Piping Weekend and decide to test the water. It's virtually deserted and we order soup and Thai fish cakes and wonder if we have the right weekend. I'd been told that piping enthusiasts congregated here from various parts of the world, but the only thing international about it so far was the kid in the blue shirt of the French footie team with the name ZIDANE emblazoned on the back.

A wander past hotel reception offers a reassuring cameo, however, as a woman with a bevy of kids surrounding her is engaged in delicate negotiations with a woman behind the counter who is wishing she could press a button that would instantly sit her in front of the telly with her feet up on the sofa, fag in one hand, foaming pint in the other. She opens her eyes but the woman with the army of kids hanging from her arms, legs and pockets is still giving her a hard time. 'But you must be able to fit us in,' she's saying. 'I know for a fact that John Rooney isn't coming, we can have his room.' The reception looks warily at the children, who seem to be multiplying by the second. 'Yes, but it's only a single room ... it only has a single bed ... for one person,' she adds helpfully. 'So what?' says the woman, 'we'll manage.'

Another stroll, a pint, another conversation with my friend the brook and I return to the Glendalough Hotel. The transformation is astounding. The low roar of animated conversation and the hot swirl of pipes hits you from a distance. As you get closer and the sound of massed pipes gets louder and louder it feels like all the surrounding mountains have risen up as one and are dancing around their handbags. You can barely get into the bar itself. The seat in the corner where we'd leisurely had soup and Thai fish cakes a couple of hours earlier is awash with people of all ages, all playing uilleann pipes with touching fervour.

'The Doran festival is great,' Harry had said back in Dublin. 'You get all these pipers who come together and sit in the bar all day playing the same eight Doran tunes over and over again.' He was uncannily accurate. They're a motley bunch and they do keep playing the same tunes over and over in an erratic fashion, but it *is* great. There's kids of 11 or 12 there cockily swapping notes with the good ol' boys, who are lining up pints and chasers in front of them at a frantic rate. A teenage girl offers a lone fiddle in the middle of them all and stray partners and unemployed children perch on the edge of the action watching intently and busying themselves getting the drinks in and mopping brows. They look naked without an instrument. And the sound coming out of that bar ... well, if I was American I'd call it awesome. It's like that bit in *Riverdance* when hundreds of dancers tumble down from the wings and the rhythm of their feet lifts you high. Except here the volley of massed sounds comes from drones, regulator and chanter, not feet. Tonight at least in the Wicklow Mountains, the piper calls the tune.

Then there's a bit of a rumpus, the music slithers to a halt and a couple of people go round the bar flogging raffle tickets. I'm fascinated what the prizes will be. Some precious original Johnny Doran flat cap maybe? A set of pipes? A year's worth of lessons? A selection of pipe CDs? Then two grim-faced big men who look like they could be security arrive clutching big boxes and the excitement mounts. Everyone swivels round to watch intently as the prizes are placed on the table. A barbecue set. A clock radio. A bottle of whiskey. A box of chocolates. It's looking like the conveyor belt on *The Generation Game*. A spontaneous round of applause is accorded the arrival of the presents.

I fall into conversation with the guy next to me who, even in a bar dripping with pipers, is something special. From a travelling family in Limerick, his name is Mickey Dunne and he's tickled pink to be here. 'My father was friends with Johnny Doran, he played the fiddle with him,' he tells me. 'They used to travel together. Johnny would often pop over to the Dunnes' van and they'd often play together.'

So what was Johnny Doran like? 'Oh he was a *character*,' says Mickey, laughing. 'He was a great one for practical jokes all right. He'd get up to some things, he could be pretty wild.' Then he qualifies it. 'Well, he *had* to be. He couldn't have played like that otherwise.'

What made Johnny Doran so special? 'He took the pipes to places nobody thought they would ever go and no words can describe the gratitude we should have towards the Dorans,' he says. 'I regard it as a privilege to be asked to play at anything to do with the Dorans.'

Mickey turns up on stage with his daughter playing at the weekend's main showcase concert. It's all a bit surreal. We sit in rows gazing at a succession of pipers who all look a tad uncomfortable in such formal surroundings, one eye on getting back to the bar where they can play properly without all these people looking at them. Apart from the English guy in my right ear explaining how they *should* be doing it, the audience is polite and informed and – you sense – also longing to get back to the bar where they can hear this music properly.

The Doran family are here in force and when the formal proceedings flag there's plenty of comings and goings in their segment of the audience to keep the customer satisfied. Spread around Ireland and England, the family gather in force at this festival and, from the old guy who looks like Shane MacGowan to the women with hair piled high to the teenage girl spilling out of a red leather bodice and the shortest denim micro-skirt in the western world, they know how to enjoy themselves. They grin at each other when Peter Browne says 'I don't know where we'd be if it weren't for the Dorans' and they bow and wave and milk the applause when officially introduced from the stage.

There's an emotional highlight, too, when 13-year-old Mikey Doran gets on stage to play. Mikey is the grandson of Johnny Doran's younger brother Felix, himself widely celebrated as 'the last of the travelling pipers'. Aficionados will tell you he wasn't a patch on his brother, but, travelling around in his horse-drawn caravan and trading at the various fairs and race meetings, Felix was also adored by the traditional music community both as a piper and a storyteller. He wore a double-breasted suit and the badge of the Pioneer Total Abstinence Association. He must have lost it, though, because he also became known as a celebrated drinker.

Sean Reid, another great piper, from the Tulla Ceili Band, regularly met Felix on his visits to Clare and told affectionate stories, not only of his prowess as a piper, but his enterprise as a businessman. At one point he acquired a big, white Austin van and went around collecting car batteries and feather mattresses. When asked what he wanted them for, Felix said he was going to use them to manufacture his own pound notes. Ultimately he did become a successful businessman, ending up in Manchester with a thriving haulage contractor business and his own fleet of lorries. He did so well he commissioned Leo Rowsome to make him a 150 guineas set of personalised silver pipes with his name engraved on them.

When he died in 1972 he had one of the biggest funeral cortèges seen in Ireland. His son Michael played at his graveside and the pile of wreaths were estimated at nine feet long, six feet wide and four feet high.

Now Felix's grandson Mikey has picked up the baton and the emotions run high when he plays, both in the official concert and the bar afterwards. Born in England, Mikey hasn't been playing that long but already has an assured touch, which leaves you to question the old adage that it takes 21 years to be a proper piper – seven years of study, seven years of practising and seven years of playing. Mikey also seems to have embraced the family's legacy with some relish. 'My granddad was called The Last Of The Travelling Pipers, but obviously that's not true because I've just taken the business over.' And how did he start playing? 'Me grandfather learned me father and me father learned me. That's how I got me music.' And now there he is with a 'bling bling' bracelet on his wrist, a serious ring on his right hand and an aura of huge self-confidence playing a slow air that takes your feet from under you.

Apart from young Mikey Doran, there are still quite a few pipers around who maintain the wild style of the travelling pipers. Finbar Furey, for one. Themselves from a Dublin family of travellers, Finbar and his brother Eddie did a lot of pioneering work for Irish music in general and the pipes in particular as one of the few acts playing Irish music in England and Europe in the early days. Finbar always was a startling piper and with his shaggy dark hair, his huge frame and his gruff Dublin accent, he was also a charismatic if slightly scary character.

He turned the whistle tune 'The Lonesome Boatman' into an instrumental anthem of almost 'Fields Of Athenry' proportions, he belatedly turned himself into a singer and banjo player and – the most unlikely development of all – he became a pop star when the sentimental ol' goat resurrected a gushing romantic ballad from 1898 called 'When You Were Sweet Sixteen'. His dad Ted – himself something of a legend – would play the song and after he'd died, the brothers (Finbar and Eddie had by now been joined by more members of the family) decided to record it as a present for their mum. Not that it took very long. 'We started recording it at twelve and we were in the pub by one.'

Wandering around among new romantics, post-punk ironists and scantily clad dancers with Finbar when The Fureys performed 'Sweet Sixteen' on *Top Of The Pops* in 1981 was an education. 'Jay-zuss … *jay-zuss* … will y'take a look at that plunger,' chortled Finbar, pointing at a male dancer with white hair and turquoise mascara. 'What a roight fokkin' *queen*.' While awaiting their spot between Haircut 100 and Orchestral Manoeuvres In the Dark, the Fureys amused them-selves wandering around the studio pointing at the silly costumes, the mad hair and the bizarre make-up that was *de rigueur* in 1981 and shouting things like 'Jayzus, will y'take a look at that eejit' and 'Jayzus, they're all fokkin' queens.' Priceless, it was.

Finbar's influence – and Doran's spirit – is also evident in the playing of Dublin's Davy Spillane, perhaps the first to use pipes seri-ously in a rock setting with the band Moving Hearts. Davy didn't take up the pipes until he was 13 but a year later he'd left home and was out on the streets making his living as a busker. Pub sessions followed, then Moving Hearts, then his own band … and he has experimented with numerous different styles merging the pipes with bluegrass, jazz, rock, blues, new age and all manner of other stuff. Where his heart remains, however, was ably demonstrated on one particularly memo-rable track on his album *Atlantic Bridge*: 'Tribute To Johnny Doran'.

The man who best represents the Doran travelling tradition in the modern era, though, is Paddy Keenan. From a travelling family, Paddy was steeped in traditional music and a long line of pipers, but surely none of them had his level of rage and passion in their playing. Perhaps the most dramatic partnership of any band, anywhere, was Paddy Keenan and Tommy Peoples in the Bothy Band circa 1975. Peoples scraping away on the fiddle like a man possessed in that earthy Donegal style driving the dishevelled Keenan to ever more torrid outbursts of piping. Neither looked at the audience. Or each other. They never spoke either. They just looked at the floor as they played and that ground seemed to shake with the sheer emotional velocity of it all.

I once tried to interview Keenan when he was in the Bothies but it was the morning after the night before and it was nigh impossible. That floppy hair all over his face hiding tired red eyes, he greeted every question like an arrow through his heart and all I got on my tape was a succession of grunts. Apart from when I asked him what he thought about one herbert describing him as 'the Jimi Hendrix of the pipes'. His eyes narrowed as he looked at me and for a moment I thought he was going to grab a unicycle. Then with the merest trace of a glimmering smile, said: 'That was *you* that called me that.' It's a quote I still see used from time to time though, amusingly, it tends to be attributed to Donal Lunny. I, of course, will strenuously deny ever saying it.

The word in the bar is that Paddy Keenan will put in an appearance at the Doran festival this weekend. 'Paddy will come if he is able, of that I can assure you,' says a man nursing a chanter in one hand and several pints in the other. 'He usually comes to pay his respects to Johnny.' Sadly he doesn't make it. Maybe it's just as well. There's not a bed to be found in Glendalough for love or money.

Wicklow has plenty of other pleasures. 'You must go to Avoca,' says the cleaner at our B&B. 'Why's that then?' 'Fitzgerald's!' she answers in a tone that screams 'Give me strength, what a thicko ...'. I look totally blank. 'It's the pub in *Ballykissangel!*'

She steps back and awaits my excited reaction and the string of questions that invariably follow this revelation. 'Somebody in Wexford told me they filmed it there ...' Now she's all affronted. 'They were *lying*. It's here. Well, not *here*, but up the road.' So we forego the planned morning at the Doran lecture on making reeds for your pipes to go see the *Ballykissangel* pub. Our cleaner will be mortified but when we reach Avoca we completely forget to look out for Fitzgeralds. Which is a shame. Then again, *Ballykissangel* was crap. Instead we partake at Lynham's in Laragh, which has a picture on the wall of Paddy Moloney surrounded by a bevy of beauties. Right among all the Tour de France cuttings. Paddy lives around here somewhere.

I quite fancy spending more time here wandering round Wicklow's forests and loughs and pubs. Maybe we'll meet Paddy Moloney and his celebrity chums. Sadly, no can do. We have an urgent message from mission control and the summons is simple. Go north. *Now.*

MONDAY: *Craigavon, Co. Armagh, N. Ireland*
Everywhere I go one name seems to flash at me in neon lights: Seamus Tansey. It had started in Ring when they were talking about great sessions at Mooney's bar. 'That night we had Seamus Tansey here ... whooooooo!' they'd all said, digging each other slyly in the ribs and chortling heartily. And Donnchadh in Dungarvan had not only talked up the Tansey legend, he'd played me records of his glorious flute playing. 'Tansey,' he kept saying, laughing softly to himself. 'Tansey ... what a man ... what a *legend*.'

His name repeatedly crops up in the session pubs. 'Tansey ... one of the greats ...' they say. But then they always qualify it with a knowing laugh as if recalling a secret memory that cannot be divulged at any cost. I'd heard Tansey's flute playing on record – and indeed it is mighty – but you hear little of the iconic character they whispered about in such hushed reverential tones. In Sligo his name is everywhere. 'You *have* to meet Tansey,' said a Dervish. 'You can't write about Sligo music without meeting Tansey.' Oh, okay, I said, is he in Sligo? I'll go see him tomorrow. This fired another bundle of sniggers. 'He's not in Sligo. He, er, *left*.' So where is he now? 'He went to live in the north but you might have a hard job finding him.'

The intrigue intensified in Dublin and the more they laughed at their own memories the more imperative it seemed to find him. He'd written a book about Sligo musicians, *The Bardic Apostles Of Innisfree*, and Dublin was apparently still reeling from the launch party at the Cobblestone pub. 'You'll have trouble finding that book now,' says one eyewitness. 'It was a great night, but some of the things he wrote in the book upset a lot of people ... but Seamus doesn't mind upsetting people.'

After a series of false alarms, I get him on the phone. I nervously invite myself to visit. 'You should know,' he says abruptly, 'I am a man of opinions.'

News that we're going into the lion's den causes a great amount of merriment and banter among those I mention it to. 'Well, good luck ... as sure as hell you'll *need* it,' says the man in the garage selling petrol. 'Be careful, if you let him he'll eat you alive,' offers the guy in the paper shop. 'Wear a republican badge,' is the advice of the bag lady on the street corner. 'He may like you ...' says the guy at the traffic lights winding down his window. Then he adds ' ... but he probably won't' as he speeds off as the lights go green.

The workforce of a factory just outside Dublin gather to give the cut-throat sign as I drive past and a lone little old lady waiting for a bus sees me coming and laughs hysterically.

We break the journey at Dundalk, home of The Corrs. How, how, *how* did Dundalk produce The Corrs? You could imagine them being from Wicklow or Waterford or Kilkenny, but Dundalk? It's a mystery. Yet there's a moral in it for all of us. You can find beauty in even the ugliest places. We have a morale-boosting pot of coffee and ah, go on, one-of-those-nice-scones-can't-do-you-any-harm-now-can-it and plough further north.

Nerves are kicking in but there's no going back now. It's Tansey or bust. We cross the border into Armagh and attempt to follow the instructions to Craigavon. They'd sounded so simple on the phone but the roads always look different when you're on them. The phone line from Wicklow hadn't been that good and something clearly has been lost in the translation. Craigavon, Tullagally, Lurgan, Belfast ... we follow the signs as directed, we seem to be in the right ballpark, but can't nail that final step. I'd told Mr Tansey to expect us at 3pm and from what I've heard so far he wouldn't appear to be a man who suffers tardiness lightly.

I look at my watch – now beginning to acquire Gollumesque weight - and it's gone four o'clock. We investigate a succession of estates but Tansey's advice to "ask anyone - they all know me" yields no positive sightings. The mobile phone has died and this leads to an elongated detour in search of a public phone that works and then the small change to make the emergency call to Seamus for fresh directions. There follows 35 minutes of wrong numbers, which elicits one invitation to join a pub quiz team in Portadown and another to a church tea party in Dungannon, before realisation dawns that I've somehow written down the wrong number and in any case we are now in the north where the codes are entirely different. There follows a further quest for more change and in desperation I start keying in random numbers.

Completely unexpectedly I hit the target. 'Yes!' says a rasping voice at the end of the phone and I shout 'Seamus!' in joy and relief. 'You were meant to be here two hours ago,' he says with understandable impatience and I launch into a sorry saga of the dodgy phones and the roads with no names. He's particularly perturbed to hear that nobody I asked admitted knowing him. 'Liars! They're dirty fikkin' liars,' he's grumbling. 'They know me all right. They're just being awkward.'

'I've got things to do now, you're late, y'see,' he reminds me when I ask if I can call round now. Instead, he says he'll meet in Lurgan. Outside the Salvation Army place. By the taxi rank. In half an hour. The arrangement has some appeal. Even *I* should be able to find Lurgan. And the Salvation Army place.

Twenty minutes later I'm pacing up and down outside the very shut Salvation Army place looking for Seamus. In truth I'm not entirely sure what I'm looking for. I've seen photos of the great man but that was a while ago and I view every car, pedestrian, biker, unicyclist, juggler, pantomime horse, tug-of-war team that comes past the Salvation Army place as a potential Seamus. And then paranoia sets in. Did he really say the Salvation Army place? Is there more than one of them? Lurgan could be the Salvation Army capital of the entire world for all I know and the place could be swimming in them. Or maybe he meant to meet him outside the taxi rank. That's further along the road.

Just as I'm contemplating what I'll look like in a Salvation Army uniform and prepare to embark on the next lap of the taxi rank, there's the sound of cussing. I look across the road. There's a bulky character on a bicycle weighed down by a huge spray of bulrushes swearing and waving his fists at anybody and everybody in his path. Somehow I know I've found my prey.

I bound over, introduce myself, shake his hand vigorously and apologise again for missing him earlier. That's enough to trigger him into another tirade against his neighbours and those he's perceived as having deliberately led me astray from his door and put us all to a terrible inconvenience. 'We'll go back to the house now,' he says, 'you follow me in your car.'

It's not very far, but it's a tortuous journey. Uphill, rain spraying everywhere, he's not cycling fast and as I crawl behind all I can see are the bulrushes shaking on his bike. Behind me there are a long trail of cars which don't take kindly to being held up in a snail-pace procession. They start hooting and that instantly triggers another outburst from Seamus, his bike veering worryingly near the centre of the road as he swivels around to give every motorist in sight a volley of verbal abuse and two-fingered salutes. Will we ever get off this main road? Will we ever reach his house? And what are the bulrushes for?

Finally we make it to his home and yup, it is the very first place we'd come to hours earlier. We follow him into his front room and he's already halfway through a fresh set of profanities aimed at the locals he's convinced sent me off on a wild goose chase.

We adjourn to his study and, coat off, he's suddenly unexpectedly calm, charming even, as we pick our way through the bulrushes, which he's assembled to make into costumes for a local production aimed at re-igniting an old ritual. I tell him I've been to Sligo, to his home town of Gurteen. 'How is it?' he's asking. 'Did they tell you when they're going to make me Lord Mayor?' Oddly enough, they didn't, Seamus. 'Ah well,' he sighs. 'There was a bit of a flare-up in Gurteen about what I wrote in my book.' Were you nasty to them? 'No, I just wrote the truth. But in Ireland they don't like the truth.'

I'd tried to buy Tansey's book *The Bardic Apostles Of Innisfree* in Dublin but there was no a sign of it. Some even whispered it had caused such offence in traditional music quarters it wasn't welcome in Sligo or Dublin. 'All the people in the parish who aren't musicians love it but the musicians – or at least a *lot* of them – are *raging*. Well, not the musicians as much as their *families*. They don't like hearing the truth, that's all.'

Whatever else they think about him, people always acknowledge Seamus Tansey as one of Ireland's greatest flute players. He comes from a line of musicians and dancers from Coleman country. His

mother was a fiddle player and Seamus defied her wishes by abandoning the fiddle in favour of the flute simply because he didn't think
he'd ever be good enough on fiddle to match the greats.

His preference for the flute put a lot of noses out of joint. The flute
was always regarded as the poor man's instrument likely to give you
TB or some other nasty disease due to all the bugs. 'My mother told
me the flute would give me bulging eyes. She said "Play that thing
and you'll get red protruding eyeballs and a black protruding tongue
and you'll get a brain haemorrhage and faint and you'll get black-outs
and go mad and it'll move your brain around."'

His mother came round in the end and when he was 17 she
bought him a flute for £4/10s that he still has. He also played another
flute of less vintage sent to him by a cousin. One problem: it was
falling apart so they did what any sane person would do – they stuck
it up with glue. Which resulted in some entertaining gigs.

'When I started playing the flute, glue started oozing out of it. I was
playing away and I could smell this glue. So I was GLUE SNIFFING.'
He's laughing big time now. 'So back in the 1960s I was high on glue
before anyone had heard of it. I INVENTED glue sniffing!'

In those days pub sessions were few and far between ('publicans
thought it was very antiquated and there was no money in it') and
Seamus is proud to align himself with the ceili bands he believes kept
the music alive when nobody else wanted to know. 'We created the
cultural revolution,' he says. 'See, jazz was brought in during the 1920s
after the civil war when the country house dances were banned by
the clergy and they looked on these dances as rings of the IRA. They
threw the baby out with the bathwater, illegal assembly and all that,
and they herded the youth of that generation into halls and they were
met by jazz. It ruined the whole infra-structure of the country. Irish
traditional music was driven into the rafters and a whole generation
was given over to this whole fakkin' jazz thing. And after that it was
Glenn Miller.

'There was a small handful in the 1930s who kept it alive but they
had to emigrate and that was a big blow, but in the fifties and sixties
the ceilis started in the halls with the youth and a new generation
came up and the Irish music and dancing drove out the fakkin' jazz.
They looked on it as old-fashioned and put it back in the towns
where it belonged. There was an awful fight between the ceili bands
and the showbands and they threw everything bar the kitchen sink at
us. They made fun of us, told jokes about us ... and then when the
Clancys came it gave us a big boost.'

Sean O'Riada was the man credited as the godfather of modern
Irish folk music, with his visionary work with Ceoltoiri Chualann,

but he had harsh words for the ceili bands, with their rigid tempos. 'He drove a knife through the core of the cultural revolution of the time by criticising the ceili bands,' says Tansey. 'Irish music was fighting for its life and that was the wrong time to put the knife in. Yet he also presented us with a double-edged sword. At the time we were fighting with blunt instruments but then O'Riada came with Ceoltoiri Chualann, and between him and the ceili bands and the folk revival we had a sword.'

At a stroke Tansey then dismisses all the seventies bands that in essence got me into the music. He talks scornfully of the 'pot-smoking young pups' and 'long-haired lefties' that he believes ambushed Irish music and smote it a fatal blow with their cross-pollination. 'Suddenly it became in vogue to play Irish music. These people in the cities and the towns who'd spit on it before now wanted to get in on the act. Those in universities suddenly wanted to jump on the bandwagon.

'I began to see they were enemies of Irish traditional music. The real message of the music was being diluted to suit the pop-orientated people who wouldn't look at the side of the road we were playing on in the fifties. And it has got worse over the years. Even though there's never been as many young people playing Irish traditional music in Ireland as there are today to such a high technical standard, the whole bloody thing is at a crossroads. It is in more danger of dying out now than it was when it was banned from the country house dances. You get festivals and folk clubs but the people running them discriminate against the real traditional musicians. Classical, pop, blues, you name it, it's all being mixed up with the tradition, but the message of where it came from is being killed.

'You see them banging guitars and playing at 50mph and they haven't a clue what they're playing. That was all started by people like De Dannan and The Chieftains. See, Irish traditional music came from the very warbling of the birds and the sounds of the countryside, the bees or whatever and our forefathers harnessed that and put their own genius to it. It became the expression of their soul. And down through the years irrespective of any historical disasters that befell them, they held on to that music as their religion and every turn, every variation, every bit of vibrato had a meaning and expression.

'Then when this crowd came along with their jungle music mixed with this and that it killed all that. There can be no room for two cultures sitting side by side. In our music we should preserve a message that has come from the past and send it to future generations. That's the telepathic communication of all people, past, present and future, and that has been subverted by musical gigolos and prostitutes. They should get out of it and leave the music to purify itself.'

Leaving the Tansey home we search the map for a likely resting place for the night. We'd almost settled on Belfast – knowing we were bound to find some music there – when I see the name Carrickfergus. The song 'Carrickfergus' is one of my favourites. Sad, sentimental and not a little confusing. I saw Five Hand Reel play 'Carrickfergus' once and after a performance of tender, yearning beauty they announced that they'd been to Carrickfergus and it was a dump. But I'm on a high after Seamus Tansey's private tuition on the alternative history of Irish music and old flashbacks of Five Hand Reel won't divert me from Carrickfergus now.

It turns out not to be a dump at all. It turns out to be an attractive little town on the Antrim coast and an atmospheric little hotel right in front of the bay. I march in singing.

'I wish I was ... in Carrickfergus ...

Only for nights in Ballygrand ...'

The woman at reception stares at me in, well, *in horror* to be honest.

'But the sea is wide and I cannot cross over

And neither have I the wings to fly

I wish I could meet a handsome boatman

To ferry me over to my love and die.'

She looks deeply underwhelmed. It could be the red card here. 'Do you know that song?' I ask pleasantly. 'It's about here ...'

Disdain. It's disdain she's now using on me. 'Yes, I do know the song,' she says eventually, 'but I hate to tell you this, but it's not actually about *this* Carrickfergus.'

It isn't? 'No.' Are you sure? 'Yes.' Which Carrickfergus is it written about then?' 'There's a Carrickfergus in the south, it must be about that one. It's definitely not about this Carrickfergus.'

In that case, I say sternly, I don't want to stay here. Come on, Mrs Colin, let's go to the *other* Carrickfergus. The one the song's about.

Mrs Colin totally ignores me as per and we dine in the restaurant. It's a wet night and assured we won't find any sessions in town we have our own little sing-song in the bar.

'For I'm drunk today ... and I'm seldom sober

A handsome rover from town to town

Ah but I'm sick now, my days are numbered

Come all you young men and lay me down ...'

I collar the barmaid who's offering some neat harmonies on the chorus. So that song ... is it about *this* Carrickfergus? Oh, she says, of *course* it is. 'Some people say it is about another Carrickfergus in the south, but I like to think it is about this one.'

Contented she's supplied the right answer, I sleep a sleep of the just.

TUESDAY: *Westport, Co. Mayo*

At one point I was seriously contemplating calling this book *In Search Of Tommy Peoples*. Then again, various other alternative titles presented themselves along the way. *In Search Of My Braincells* for one. *The Difficult Third Chapter* for another. And let's not forget my mate Dave's original favourite: *Just What The World Needs, Another Bloody Book About Ireland*.

But Peoples loomed large on the journey. Seamus Tansey may very well disapprove of the Bothy Band, but listening to Tommy Peoples playing fiddle with raw aggression and emotional extremes on that classic first Bothies album, I fully understand Tansey's description of the finest Irish traditional music as an 'expression of the soul.' You hear Irish music played by many, many wonderful fiddle players from Kevin Burke to Martin Hayes to Liz Carroll to Eileen Ivers to Paddy Glackin to Frankie Gavin, but I never heard a fiddle played in quite the same earthy, explosive way as Tommy Peoples.

Born in Donegal, Peoples started playing fiddle when he was seven, moved to Dublin in his teens and became an acclaimed regular in the sessions at O'Donoghue's. He moved around a bit. Had a spell in the gardai, spent time with the Kilfenora Ceili Band after his marriage to Marie Linnane, daughter of the Kilfenoras' leader Kitty Linnane, and he lived in Clare, Dublin and Limerick. But it was in the Bothy Band in the mid-seventies that the bare-knuckled fury of his playing really took over. Equally trail-blazing henchmen like Paddy Keenan on pipes and Matt Molloy on flute added to a lethal concoction and for a short time there the Bothy Band were just brilliant. I was in the front row at Hammersmith Town Hall when the Bothies made their first ever appearance in the UK and I was shaking when I came out, so organically electrifying had the show been.

Nobody was too surprised when Tommy left the Bothy Band after one short, yet hugely influential year with them. Tales of his excesses were never far behind and the constrictions of a touring band and the disciplines necessary to keep a touring band afloat never rested easily on his big shoulders. One day Tommy Peoples was blazing away at the front of the Bothy Band, the next day he … he … *wasn't*.

It didn't seem to matter unduly. The Bothies replaced him with Kevin Burke and went on to many more adventures and we fondly imagined Peoples would be at the forefront of another exciting new product. A groundbreaking new band perhaps. Or a glittering solo career?

In fact Tommy Peoples just seemed to fade quietly away. In 1976 he did make a fine album, *The High Part Of The Road* with Paul Brady, and a year after that showed that the gobsmacking intensity of his playing remained undimmed on a mostly instrumental album with Brady and Matt Molloy. But he never much liked the record industry and while there were enough sightings and the odd solo tape or low-key self-made album, he was to all intents and purposes invisible.

The Rough Guide To Irish Music described Tommy as 'the most influential Irish fiddler of the last 50 years' but where was the man himself?

I heard many conflicting stories on my travels. He was in America/London/Australia/Albania/Papua New Guinea? In Wicklow I'd discussed the Tommy Peoples Mystery with someone convinced he was now living in Boston and he suddenly put the question: 'Why don't you look on his website?' 'Oh, don't be daft,' I say, 'Tommy doesn't have a website. *Does he?*'

In these scary modern times, when even places like Dingle and Lisdoonvarna have internet cafes, it's easy to check. And would you believe it? Yes, Tommy Peoples does have a website. Who'd have thought it?

But that's not all I found on the internet looking up Tommy Peoples. I found he was making an appearance. In London. I travel the length and breadth of Ireland looking for Tommy Peoples ... and he's playing in London. In the words of Alanis Morrissette, isn't it ironic? Except that Alanis's irony also involves that hideous nasally howl, obviously. And, as it turns out, my irony has a double twist.

Just a few days left in Ireland so we head south again. The idea is a gentle meander back towards Wexford and the boat in Rosslare. No dramas. No mad car drives. Simple. We make it to Monaghan. Another ex-member of the Bothy Band, Trioni Ni Dhomhnaill, is playing here tonight and we contemplate hanging around for her, but that's a whole afternoon away and an afternoon is a long time in Monaghan.

We make a momentous decision: we are going to go across country to Mayo. To Westport, in fact. To Matt Molloy's pub. So off we go across Monaghan and Cavan. One of Sharon Shannon's finest and most famous tunes is called 'Cavan Potholes', inspired by a particularly bumpy journey across the county. As my car starts doing a passable impersonation of a cat on a trampoline I realise she hadn't been exaggerating about the potholes in Cavan. They should open the Cavan potholes as a heritage sight.

As we plough on through Longford and Roscommon, Mrs Colin is attempting to book somewhere to stay in Westport. You'd think it would be easy. But she has the mobile phone in one hand, enough B&B and hotel guides to fill the British Library in the other, and the answer is always the same. Westport seems to be full. The only place with spaces available seems to be a hotel right in the centre of town. A very expensive hotel, as it happens. She tells them she will call back and goes through all the guide books again and repeats the ringing around. Each round of calls ends up back at the same hotel and each time she enquires the price has gone up another 10 euros. I have visions of the entire hotel staff draped over the reception desk taking bets on how long it will be before Mrs Colin calls again, when she will crack and what the final price will be. A couple of hours later, deciding that, inexplicably, Westport is indeed full, we crawl into the hotel, heads down and tails between legs.

We go for a wander around Westport, trying to fathom why it's so popular today and come across Matt Molloy's pub. It's a grand looking place all right and I'm standing outside admiring the original frontage that Matt insisted on keeping when he took it over when an oul' boy lurches into me. I stagger and trip on the loose shoelace I purposely maintain in a state of perfect undoneness for eccentric effect. I land in a heap and bang my head on Matt Molloy's window. I sit there trying to clear my head and I'm eyeball to eyeball with a poster in the window. It says: 'TONIGHT: TOMMY PEOPLES & ALPH DUGGAN.'

Clearly hallucinating, I shake my head to clear my senses and turn to Mrs Colin to tell her that I must have had quite a bang on the head, I imagined I'd seen a poster saying Tommy Peoples was playing here tonight. But she's not looking at me, she's staring at the poster too.

We bound inside Matt Molloy's pub. 'Tommy Peoples?' I say spluttering, 'is he playing here tonight.' 'Yip, he is,' replies the Australian barman. 'Definitely?' 'Yip.' 'Tonight?' 'Yip.' 'Here.' 'In the back room, yip.' I kiss him.

We have a couple of drinks in a pub up the road and chat to a couple of local musicians who are a bit sniffy about Matt Molloy's … primarily, it seems because Matt won't book them to play in his pub, preferring to bring in better-known musicians from other counties. 'Tommy Peoples is playing there tonight.' 'Oh, that's nice.' 'You won't be there to see him then?' 'Tommy Peoples? You kidding? Of course we'll be there.'

A couple of hours later we're back at Matt Molloy's pub. Through the bar decorated with wonderful old pictures and other memorabilia of Irish music, depicting the dazzling career of Matt Molloy through the Bothy Band, Planxty and The Chieftains. There's even the odd picture of Tommy Peoples, eyes blazing, bow raised as if he's about to go to war.

And, in a snug in a corner, there he is. He's changed, of course. That unruly black hair is now well groomed but flecked with grey and silver. He's not as bulky as he used to be either and there's none of the angry energy that seemed to cocoon him in the old days. There's a dignity about him now, a presence. He's changed all right, but I recognize him instantly. 'Tommy Peoples, I presume ...'

He's off the booze these days, but the caffeine keeps on coming as Tommy quietly brings me up to speed. He laughs when I tell him I've been searching all over Ireland for him and says he moved to the States – to Boston – a couple of years ago. Why? 'Oh, too many birthdays gone past,' he laughs. 'I went out there with Sean Tyrrell ... you know Sean? Yeah, well, I was playing out there with Sean and ... I dunno ... I just ended up staying. I thought why not?'

I tell him I hadn't heard him play for a long while, I'd wondered if he'd given up. 'No, never!' he says. 'It's a bug. I'll never ever get away from it. If I wasn't playing I'd be whistling.'

He admits, though, there have been times when he wanted to. 'There have been times when I've been disillusioned with my own playing. I could never fall out of love with the music, just my own attitudes to playing. I go through patches of doubt. Sometimes the concentration of a lifetime of playing seems out of focus. Sometimes there seems just too much focus on something that's not all that important.'

Happily, though, he seems at ease with himself and his fiddle playing. He keeps a low profile, he concedes, because he likes it that way, but he plays regularly on the Boston Irish circuit, playing for pub sessions, sitting in with the regular stream of traditional musicians passing through Boston, and doing a bit of fiddle teaching too.

'I'd never give up now,' he says, 'I've done it too long. I look back on the older generation who passed on the music through hard times economically or whatever and used the music as a way of getting together and celebrating even when things were bad. And what I like most about it now is the social side, seeing people I haven't met for about twenty years and knowing there is still a connection there.'

I ask him about the Bothy Band and that incredible spirit and understanding that seem to light bonfires wherever they played. They were such a thrilling band – 0 to 100mph in one swift stroke of Tommy's bow – and cut through all the usual crap about styles and musical genres. I don't care if you're a classical buff, a jazz head, a prog rocker, headbanger or opera connoisseur, the Bothies were one of the great bands of all time. But Tommy People quit after just a year when they seemed on the verge of an international breakthrough and indeed the band itself fell foul of the music industry and never achieved a speck of the acclaim due them.

'I have nothing but happy memories of the Bothy Band,' says Tommy quietly, 'just happy memories ...' But you often hear bad stories ... 'The bad memories I ignore,' he adds in a whisper.

You were a pretty wild bunch though, Tommy, from what I hear. Lots of carousing and partying. 'We had a lot of fun all right,' he grins. 'Why not? We were all of an age.' When I ask Matt Molloy the same question later his face creases in smiles. 'The Bothy Band,' he announces profoundly, 'were *unmanageable*, it's as simple as that.'

I know it's soppy but I have tears in my eyes when Tommy Peoples plays in the back room of Matt Molloy's pub in Westport. His style is very different now. Virtually unrecognisable from the flowing fury of his halcyon days, Tommy's playing is mellow. It's intricate, passionate and at times extremely beautiful and clearly he remains one of Ireland's most natural fiddle talents and I can't tell you what a joy it is to see him. He's accompanied by Alph Duggan on guitar and at the end of the night the gaffer, Matt Molloy, is coaxed up to join them on stage for a trip down memory lane.

I wasn't quite sure what to expect afterwards. Someone had told me the real sessions start behind closed doors after the punters have gone home and I know people who've emerged from a night at Matt Molloy's blinking in the unexpected morning light with tunes ringing in their ears and hammers slamming inside their heads.

But Tommy's teetotal now and with one last gulp of coffee he and his son Lochlane are swiftly away while Matt Molloy talks sorrowfully of the sudden recent death of The Chieftains' popular harp player Derek Bell. Instead, I fall into conversation with a couple of young Spaniards, who've driven from Dublin to see Tommy Peoples. 'Ever since I was leetle I want to hear ze Tommee play,' says Julio. 'Eee iz my 'ero.' 'At home we leesen to ze Bothy Band all ze time,' agrees Pablo. 'We work in ze hotel in Dublin. We came to leeve in Ireland because of ze Irish muzik.' 'Yess,' gushes Julio. 'So when we saw Tommee was playing in Westport we had to come and see him.'

Wow, I say, you came all the way from Dublin to see Tommy Peoples, what did you think? Pablo's face clouds over. 'I am so-so sorry,' he says, 'we meeesssed him.'

You missed him? What do you mean you missed him? 'Ze signs on ze roads are not good. We took wrong turn and got lost. We only just got here. Was he good?'

'Oh,' I say, 'he was the best …'

WEDNESDAY: *Ennis, Co. Clare*

Next morning it still all seems a dream. Tommy Peoples alive and well and playing in Westport. A morning coffee with Matt Molloy and we head south again. The vague plan is Cork by tea-time, unless we find something more interesting en route.

Immediately the plan is in trouble as we start wandering around the back roads of Mayo and Roscommon. We end up in the town of

Ballyhaumus. I decide we are going in completely the wrong direction and pull up a side road. It turns out to be a railway station and we pull up as passengers spill off the train. One bloke comes running after us banging on the window.

'Excuse me,' he says, 'I was wondering if you could give me a lift to Knock – I'll pay you handsomely.'

A look of horror crosses my face. If we're anywhere near Knock and all its shrines and holy experiences, we are in big trouble. I say sorry, we're going the other way. 'It's all right,' pleads the guy, 'I'm an atheist!'

We drive on through an area that seems unexpectedly politicised. A series of confrontational signs stand along the Tullam Rd. 'NO SLUDGE', 'NO CHICKEN LITTER', 'NO BELLYGRASS', 'NO WASTE PLANT!' And then BP Fallon comes on the radio talking about the Rolling Stones and revealing the rather shocking news that Ronnie Wood had once shagged the Canadian Prime Minister's wife Margaret Trudeau. One of the great figures in contemporary Irish culture without anyone really knowing exactly what he does, Fallon is in epic Beepspeak form quoting Wood's guide to life. 'You get to play music you love, you meet a lot of nice girls and some bad girls too and it's a fucking great life.' Oh, were it that simple for Tommy Peoples.

We roll on south without knowing exactly where we're going but when we see a sign for Ennis, we decided to have another crack. Ennis, the town that's permanently full. It has a mighty reputation as one of the most important towns for Irish music in the west, but they don't tell you how you get into it through the massive traffic jams and the barking priests. Still, one last time, we'll give it a go.

We drive straight into Ennis, no problem. Hardly any cars, B&Bs brimming with vacancies, it's a breeze. We find somewhere to stay – not your tip-top B&B but it'll do the job – at the top of the hill and wander into Ennis. No shortage of fun to be had here, I'll vouch. Custy's shop itself is a treasure chest of great old music and wonderful pictures and at every turn there's a pub offering traditional music.

We settle on Cruises and spend an hour looking at the pictures of traditional musicians on the wall. 'Any music tonight?' I ask the barman. He's affronted. 'I'll say so ... we have music every night here.' A group of musicians congregate at one end of the bar. We squeeze on to a table nearby and watch in wonder as the flutes and fiddles gather before our eyes. They start to play and the audience are immediately attentive and enthusiastic. Respect. Then an older guy marches purposefully through the throng, tramples over the Australians' backpacks piled on the floor and stands in front of the band. What's this? A pitch invasion?

A squeeze-box player is immediately on his feet passing chairs over people's heads, shifting everyone round to find a nice comfy spot in the middle of the semi-circle for the guy. But he has no instrument in his hand. What on earth is he going to play? You'd imagine he'd be a bodhran player but if he's got a bodhran in his pocket he's certainly not pleased to see us. We are taking bets on what he'll pull out of his pocket and my 5 euros on a tin whistle is looking good as he pulls out something thin and long. But it's not a tin whistle. It's a pair of drumsticks. And a piece of wood. There are no drums in sight, so what's he gonna do, play air drums?

But as the boys launch into the next set of tunes the guy arranges himself in front of the table, a glass here and there, takes aim, and starts beating out the rhythm on the wood. Good job it's not Frankie Gavin on the fiddle, mate, he'd have your guts for garters. But the spirit of Johnny Spoons lives on and the combination of the man beating the wood and the rest of the gang doing their diddley-diddley soon has Cruise's jumping. I could easily sit here and get pissed and possibly take the innovative drummer home with me, but you always wonder if there just might be another pub up the road where something even better is going on. And, you'll never guess what, but this one single time … *there is.*

We almost miss it. The Ennis pub crawl seems to have reached the end of the road as we stumble into that part of town where the awful seventies rock band is in overdrive and it's pouring now and we're tired and why did we stop at a B&B that you have to climb a hill to reach?

But Paddy Quinn's pub on the corner attracts my attention. It doesn't look much but the music sneaking out sounds good. One pint for the road? Just to get out of the rain, like? It's crowded … no, it's rammed. But we make it to the bar and as I order the musicians at the back start up. Through the noisy crowd, the fiddle cuts through and sends chills up and down my back.

There's something about that fiddle. The drive, the power, the passion, the intensity, the emotion. It almost reminds me of … well, I know it sounds silly, but Tommy Peoples. Balancing pints we shimmy through the crowd for a closer look. The nearer we get the exuberant depth of the playing seems to grow ever more gripping.

There's a girl with dark hair playing the fiddle in the corner. She's brilliant. And there's something about her that looks familiar. The unruly hair, the fire in her eyes, the daring belligerence of her playing. It couldn't possibly be … I get closer and apologetically spill some drink down the neck of the guy sitting directly in front of her. He makes his excuses and leaves and I sidle into his seat for the grandstand view. A theory has formulated in my hand. As she stops playing, I take a gamble and offer the theory. 'Siobhan?' 'Yes,' she says, taken aback. 'Siobhan Peoples?' 'Ah,' she says, 'now that would depend on who wants to know.'

I'd heard that Tommy Peoples' daughter Siobhan had inherited much of her old man's explosive style on the fiddle, but I'd never seen or heard her before. But here she was, playing Irish music as it was intended, with a pint in your hand and a mad grin on your face, and I suddenly felt very privileged to be here.

She looks about 21 and it's a bit of a shock to discover she's actually 31 and has two small kids at home. It's even more of a shock to discover that she's playing with a big handicap. 'You sound so much like your dad when he was your age,' I tell her. 'Actually,' she says, 'I used to sound a lot more like him until I started having trouble.' Trouble? 'Yeah, me fingers, two of them don't really work ...'

Not unnaturally Siobhan has been playing since she was very small. Her dad, after all, is Tommy Peoples and her grandmother Kitty Linnane was the pianist and leader of the Kilfenora Ceili Band for many years. Siobhan had a natural talent which people always wanted to hear. So she played non-stop throughout most of her childhood and teenage years. But when she was 16 she started to feel pains in two fingers of her left hand. Various specialists were consulted but no one ever came up with a solution. The general consensus was that too much playing had simply worn out her fingers and the only real advice they could give was that she simply stopped playing the fiddle.

This, she was not prepared to do. So she simply devised a new style of playing that didn't involve the use of those two fingers. 'They actually feel a bit better now,' she says, 'I can use them from time to time but I can't play the way I used to, I don't have the power in the fingers.'

She still sounds good, though. Frighteningly good. We sup more pints and talk a bit about her dad, about growing up in Toonagh and how her favourite sessions are the ones played in her kitchen with a couple of friends. Frank Custy, she says, essentially taught her to play, but her dad showed her a lot of things and was naturally a huge influence. 'He was always away somewhere playing but he would play around the house when he was home. I can also remember seeing the Bothy Band at Lisdoonvarna when I was four.'

Siobhan Peoples playing her heart out at a pub on a foul night in Ennis. It doesn't get any better than this. Except, the next night, it does ...

THURSDAY: *In the middle of nowhere, vaguely near Thurles, Co. Tipperary*
I can't remember who first mentioned there was a pub which had a
great session but which only opened on Thursday nights. It was probably my new best mate at the time at Mooney's pub in Ring. But at
various stages on the journey talking to people about pub music in
Ireland, the Thursday night pub in Tipperary kept getting mentioned.

As we set off from Ennis, Siobhan Peoples still ringing in my ears,
we debated long and hard where to head. Given that our ferry was
due to leave Rosslare at the crack of dawn on Saturday this would be
our last proper night in Ireland and it had to be a good one. I was still
feeling guilty having more or less forgotten about Cork on the way
up, so I did feel duty bound to make amends on the way back. But
random words and scattered recommendations kept flying round my
head. 'There's this fantastic pub in Tipperary, but it only opens on a
Thursday night …'

The notion of a pub that only opened on Thursdays appealed and
logic tells you that if it only opens once a week, it'll be good. So,
feeling lucky, we go in the direction of Tipperary. I have no information about it whatsoever. The only 'address' in my head is 'near Thurles
on the Newport road'. It's not much to go on, to be fair, and there's
probably a mighty session being cooked up in Cork or Bantry in our
honour as we speak, but the image in my head won't go away and we
drive to Thurles. And then we drive out of Thurles and along back
lanes to the village of Holy Cross.

In for a penny, we book in at the local B&B. There's a gorgeous-
looking pub over the road so if all else fails a night in there doesn't
look a bad alternative. The landlady, Anna, ushers us into a front room
full of hurling trophies, and brings us tea and biscuits and entertaining
chit chat about this, that and the other. I hesitate and then ask the
question. 'You wouldn't happen to know if there is a pub round this
way that only opens on a Thursday night, would you?'

Anna doesn't blink. 'Actually,' she says, 'I do.' And she's off telling us
stories about Jim O' The Mill. 'Oh, you'll have a grand night up there,
sure you will,' she's saying. 'I was up there a while back and my God,
I couldn't see anything the next day. You won't be expecting an early
night if you go up there.'

Jim, it seems, is a farmer. A farmer who loves music. He got a
license to sell drink on Thursday nights and every week opens his
farmhouse as a bar and invites local musicians to perform. 'There is
one problem though,' says Anna. 'What's that?' 'You'll never find it.
Not in a million years. I'll have to draw you a map.'

So she draws us a map. She tells us not to bother getting there until
10pm at the earliest so we go into Thurles for a Chinese supper in

readiness for the intrepid journey ahead. It's hard enough finding Holy Cross in the pitch black to start the journey, let alone the eight miles or so on further to find Jim O' The Mill. Finally, back at Holy Cross, we set off, through teeming rain, narrow bumpy twisty lanes and not a light for miles. It's an eerie journey and attempting to follow Anna's map proves increasingly difficult as little side roads we are directed to follow repeatedly turn out to be tracks up to farms and dead ends. We don't see a soul for miles until a car pulls up in front of us and a guy jumps out and says, 'Do you know a pub called Jim O' The Mill?'. He says he's been going up and down the road for hours and has seen no sign of a pub. According to my information, though, there is no pub sign. There is no name of any description. It's just a farmhouse in the wilds known locally as Jim O' The Mill.

'Follow me!' he says and screams off up the road. I've lost him in seconds, attempting to find landmarks in the darkness. 'We have to go over a bridge.' 'That was a bridge.' 'No, it wasn't, it was a bump in the road.' 'But I saw water.' 'That was a puddle.' We crawl on and, beginning to wonder if this all wasn't just a conspiracy by the Crackers Of The Craic Clan to have a laugh at our expense, we see a line of cars parked in the road outside a path leading to a large farmhouse in a dip. There's no sign, no sounds, nothing to indicate anything happening inside the farmhouse apart from Bovril and a suspense movie on the telly, but I know we have located Jim O' The Mill.

We walk to the house. It's 10.30pm and we can still hear nothing inside and the doors all appear to be locked. One of the doors is on a latch. I try to open it but it appears to be stuck. Then a red-faced guy puts his head round the door, opens it slightly and ushers us in. It's a house. But a house full of people. In the front room they are sitting on the floor, up the stairs, in the window facing a fire purring nicely while an old chap tells tall stories. In another room there's a group of them putting the world to rights while an old man plays the accordion. And in the kitchen they are packed around the bar as impromptu singing breaks out all around.

Back in the front room a mother and daughter sing a Breton song which has the place cooing, and various musicians and singers burst into action from different parts of the room without warning. I'm standing at the back talking to a local farmer who tells me he used to live in Bromley when he suddenly launches into a ballad. There's seemingly no-one in charge, no real order. Just an impromptu session with people singing or playing whatever they feel whenever they feel. Some have to be goaded. 'Give us a song John!' 'Oh all right then.' And the longer the night goes on the more impromptu performances seem to break out around the house.

A grinning man with grey curly hair makes his way into the front room with a coal bucket. 'Give us a song, Jim,' they shout, and I realize this is Jim … of Jim O' The Mill. He serves me a drink later and I shake his hand and tell him this is the best pub in Ireland. 'Oh, it's only a bit of fun,' he says, urging a young girl who's about to get married to sing a love song. 'I will not,' she says, 'but I'll buy you a drink.'

It's gone 3am before we leave and drinks are still being taken and songs are still being sung. This, in essence, is the crux of what this whole craic thing is all about. It's not for the tourists, though tourists seem to be very welcome. Any tourist hardy enough to find this place is certainly worth their place here and before the night's through I've been involved in numerous mad conversations about everything from Abba to mad George Bush to Dolores Keane to Cavan potholes to weddings to music hall to sunburn to farming to Bertie's Pole to the Celtic Tiger to B&Bs to the time of our ferry home.

We get invitations to visit new best friends up and down Tipperary and I know more about the perils of farming in the modern age when governments don't care and you have to fight for every penny than I could ever wish to know. I dance with a flame-haired woman called Joan, I am invited to a wedding and a wake in the space of five minutes, I get to slate the scumbag traitor Roy Keane with a man from Longford and I drink the health of the mighty man of honour Roy Keane with a man from Cork. I kiss a lady who's just sung a song about peace in our time and I laugh like a drain at a man who tells an impossibly long anecdote about tractor drivers in a bar which has a punchline I don't understand.

The old, the young, the infirm, all are welcome, all are present. They wear gumboots and anoraks and short skirts and overalls and bright jumpers and leather coats and bicycle clips and silly hats. Plates of bread and black pudding are handed round and we sit among the horse brasses and the hurling sticks and the medals and the farmyard pictures and the old clock and the little kittens quaffing and dancing and quaffing and singing and quaffing and listening and quaffing and talking bollocks. And then we quaff some more.

There's nobody famous here. Nobody who wants to be famous. Nobody who wants to do anything but have a good night out with some old mates and new mates and a bit of a song and a chat and a dance. Tomorrow they'll be back working the land or doing whatever else it is they do but they're not thinking about that now. Tonight is Thursday and if it's Thursday it's Jim O'The Mill. This is what life must have been like years ago when rural communities looked after one another, working together, letting their hair down together.

So what do you call it? A community get-together? A pub gathering? A session with a difference? 'I'd say it's a good craic,' says Michael, with his arm draped round me as he finishes 'The Parting Glass'. 'A right good craic this ...'

Michael knows what he's talking about.

FRIDAY: *Wexford, Co. Wexford*

That bar was round here somewhere, I know it was. Can't remember his name, but there were pictures of horses all over the walls. The bar had his name on it ... but I can't remember his name so that's not much help.

It's late, there's a crack-of-dawn ferry to catch at Rosslare and wandering round the back streets of Wexford probably isn't the best preparation for the long trek home. Okay, we'll just have one quick drink in this bar here and then it's back to the B&B, goodnight Ireland, put the kettle on, we're coming home.

We get to the bar and realize that YES, this is the place. Those racing pictures on the wall, the plaque commemorating a famous singing victory, the pervy old man trying to touch up a legless girl on the other side of the bar. It looks like the same barman too.

'Remember us?' I say pleasantly. 'Yes,' he says, lying. We drink to his health and talk about racing and Ireland and music. I remind him we've been going round bars in Ireland looking for traditional music. A light goes on in his head. 'Ah so it's the craic you're after is it?' 'Sure.' 'There's no craic, is there? See all that craic stuff is just for the tourists. Really, there's no such thing as the craic, is there?'

I think of Jim O' The Mill and the crowd thronging round his farmhouse, responding with a song and a tune and story and a welcome for the stranger in Tipperary. I think of Siobhan Peoples playing her fiddle as if the hounds of hell are on its tail at Paddy Quinn's bar in Ennis. And I think of Tommy People reuniting with Matt Molloy, rolling back the years and encapsulating the earthy heart and soul of Ireland in his fiddle playing in the back room of Matt's pub in Westport.

I think of Dervish buying their own bar in Sligo to follow their dream of a music pub where they and their friends can play every night of the week if they want to. I think of Altan's pub in Teelin and Leo Brennan and his Clannad theme pub in Gweedore. I think of the massed uilleann pipers squashed into the bar at Glendalough playing their hearts out for the memory of Johnny Doran. And I think of Doolin and Dingle and Dungarvan and Ring and Horse & Jockey and Clifden and Caherlistrane and Galway and Kinvara and Kenmare and Tralee and Killorglin and Dublin.

And I think of the vats of Guinness I've downed, the laughter I've had, the music I've heard, the race meetings that have gobbled up my money and the new best mates I've made.

And this bloke is trying to tell me there's no such thing as the craic. That it's all for the tourists. That nothing is real.

There, he's said it again. 'There's no such thing as the craic ...'

'Yes,' I say, *whatever* ...'

BIBLIOGRAPHY

Maire Brennan, *The Other Side Of The Rainbow* (Hodder & Stoughton)

Ciaran Carson, *Last Night's Fun* (Pimlico)

Liam Clancy, *Memoirs Of An Irish Troubadour* (Virgin)

Victoria Mary Clarke & Shane MacGowan, *A Drink With Shane MacGowan* (Sidgwick & Jackson)

Ronan Coghlan, *Pocket Dictionary Of Irish Myth & Legend* (Appletree Press)

PJ Curtis, *Notes From The Heart* (Torc)

John Fry & Eamonn O Cathain, *The Irish Folk Guide* (In Dublin)

RF Foster, *The Irish Story* (Penguin)

Geararoid O Hallmhurain, *A Pocket History Of Irish Traditional Music* (O'Brien)

Dave Hannigan, *The Big Fight: Muhammad Ali vs Al 'Blue' Lewis* (Yellow Jersey)

John B Keane, *The Bodhran Makers* (Roberts Rinehart)

Robert Kee, *Ireland, A History* (BCA)

Jimmy MacCarthy, *Ride On* (Town House)

Cian Molloy, *The Story Of The Irish Pub* (Liffey Press)

Christy Moore, *One Voice* (Hodder & Stoughton)

HV Morton, *The Magic Of Ireland* (Arrow)

Seamus Tansey, *The Bardic Apostles Of Innisfree* (Tanbar Publications)

William Trevor, *A Writer's Ireland* (Thames & Hudson)

Fintan Vallely, *The Companion To Irish Traditional Music* (Cork University Press)

Geoff Wallis & Sue Wilson, *The Rough Guide to Irish Music* (Rough Guides)

Eye Witness Travel Guide To Ireland (DK)

The Michelin Guide To Ireland

The Rough Guide To Dublin (Rough Guide)

Recommended Soundtrack Albums
Planxty, Planxty
1975, Bothy Band

The Master Pipers Vol. 1, Johnny Doran
The Best Of The Clancy Brothers & Tommy Makem, The Clancy Brothers
    & Tommy Makem
Long Black Veil, The Chieftains
Farewell To Ireland, Various Artists
Songs & Crazy Dreams, Paul Brady
Think Before You Think, Danu
Irish Dance Music, Various Artists
Her Mantle So Green, Margaret Barry & Michael Gorman
Lemonade & Buns, Kila
Live At Vicar St, Christy Moore
Best Of The Dubliners, Dubliners
Coumineol, Eoin Duignan
Irish Songs Of Rebellion, Resistance & Reconciliation, Ron Kavana
Past Masters Of Irish Fiddle Music, Various Artists
Harmony Hill, Dervish
Welcome Here Kind Stranger, Paul Brady
The Blue Idol, Altan
Along Blackwater's Banks, Sliabh Notes
Time On Our Hands, Siobhan Peoples & Murty Ryan
Moving Hearts, Moving Hearts
Harmony Hill, Dervish
Live In Seattle, Martin Hayes & Dennis Cahill
Heart's Desire, Niamh Parsons
The Star-Spangled Molly, De Dannan
Easter Snow, Seamus Tansey
From Galway To Dublin, Various Artists
Feadoga Stain, Mary Bergin
I'm Leaving Tipperary, Various Artists
Her Infinite Variety, Various Artists
A Woman's Heart, Various Artists